ADVANCE PRAISE FOR
My Father's List

"Brave, big-hearted, compulsively readable, *My Father's List* is a joyful affirmation of embracing life to its fullest after a terrible loss. Carney's energy to fulfill her father's dreams is infectious, and her refreshing vulnerability had me rooting for her on every page."

—**Katie Arnold**, author of *Running Home: A Memoir*

"Living out her father's bucket list was the vehicle through which Laura Carney would find herself and her freedom. *My Father's List* is a delightful book that reminds us of all the possibility that lies within each of us to do things we never dreamed possible. This book inspires and will touch you deeply."

—**Siri Lindley**, two-time triathlon world champion, Olympic coach, author of *Finding a Way: Taking the Impossible and Making It Possible*, speaker, survivor, and thriver

"In this call-to-action memoir, Carney pays homage to her deceased father, and in so doing, keeps him very much alive. It made me wonder what dreams felt complete to my own father at the time of his passing. And reinforced what Carney's father told her: 'You're the best thing I've ever done.' We are lucky to have a champion in a father, and I was moved to dream along with my own because of this book."

—**Laura Munson**, author of the *New York Times* best-selling memoir *This Is Not the Story You Think It Is: A Season of Unlikely Happiness* and the *USA Today* best-selling novel *Willa's Grove*; founder of the acclaimed Haven Writing Retreats in Montana

"With all the memoirs that have been written in recent years, you might think there was nothing new left to do with the form. Laura Carney's *My Father's List* would prove you wrong. This is an original, brave, and inspiring book that will make readers think about their own life goals—and maybe even their lives—in a whole new way."

—**Ben Yagoda**, author of *Memoir: A History* and *About Town: The New Yorker and the World It Made*

"I lost count of how many times I wiped away tears while reading *My Father's List*. What a gorgeous, exhilarating story of perseverance and the beauty we can make from grief."

—**James Tate Hill**, author of *Blind Man's Bluff: A Memoir*

"Real, honest, and hopeful, *My Father's List* is a story about what it really means to be brave and love without limits. It's about building a life after devastating loss and how the people we're sure we can't live without continue to shape and grow us after they're gone. It's a no platitudes story about how loss can transform, nudging us to become who we were meant to be all along. A wonderful, memorable read."

—**Janine Urbaniak Reid**, author of *The Opposite of Certainty: Fear, Faith, and Life In Between*

"Fulfilling her late father's bucket list required persistence and courage, as Laura Carney parachuted out of a plane, swam a river, rode a fast horse, and more. But the tougher challenge lay deeper, as she reckoned with her family's sometimes painful history and the hidden corners of her own heart. This is a profound story of faith, determination, and above all, love."

—**Dawn Raffel**, author of *Boundless As the Sky* and *The Strange Case of Dr. Couney: How a Mysterious European Showman Saved Thousands of American Babies*

"An expansive, illuminating memoir about Laura Carney's extraordinary undertaking of the seemingly impossible—a jolting, serendipitous journey sparked by pain and completed with enormous heart, intuition, wisdom, and spirituality. This luminous book is a thin place."

—**Ethel Rohan**, author of *In the Event of Contact*

"I had a chance encounter with Laura in Plains, Georgia, as she crossed off another item (meeting a president) on her father's list. The story of her and her journey inspired me inside and out, and I've followed her from afar ever since. Her remarkable story is now complete (or is it?) and *My Father's List* is her and her dad's gift to us all."

—**Arthur Milnes**, public historian, former memoirs assistant to the Right Honorable Brian Mulroney, former speechwriter for Prime Minister Stephen Harper, and author of *98 Reasons to Thank Jimmy Carter* and *Jimmy and Rosalynn Carter: A Canadian Tribute*

"This beautifully written memoir is an honest, deeply moving look at love, determination, and self-reflection. Anyone who has experienced the sudden loss of a loved one and worked to reconcile the past with the present will connect with Laura's incredible journey."

—**Karen Bischer**, author of *The Secret Recipe for Moving On*

"In *My Father's List*, writer and activist Laura Carney weaves the past and present together in exquisite detail and heartfelt prose. Her story of checking off items on her late father's bucket list is also a story of self-discovery, of that universal journey toward self-acceptance we're all on. Laura's powerful words show us that what we hold most dear—family and a father's love—transcends time, space, and even death."

—**Melissa Blake**, author of the soon-to-be released *Beautiful People: My 12 Truths About Disability*

"From beginning to end, *My Father's List* is a master class in storytelling. Carney beautifully and vulnerably shares the story of finishing her late father's bucket list while weaving in tales of life, loss, and learning to live authentically. Her poignant memoir reminds us that we are capable of more than we know and death is not the end."

—**Kiersten Parsons Hathcock**, author of *Little Voices: How Kids in Spirit Helped a Reluctant Medium Escape and Heal From Abuse* and cofounder of the National Institute for Law and Justice

"A beautiful reminder of the urgency to LIVE. In a tribute to her father, and even more so herself, Laura shows us what courage looks like in action. A moving, honest, and vulnerable account of finding out our truths and transforming the pain into something positive. Laura not only transforms her own but becomes an incredible inspiration for all of us to do the same. I read this in less than two days and I have already begun my own bucket list. A MUST READ, A MUST DO!"

—**Mary Latham**, founder of More Good Today

"An intertwined tale of loss and conquest, *My Father's List* is a meditation eager minds will devour."

—**Jim Freed**, author of *The Illiterate: A Novel*

"Honest, passionate, and brave define Laura Carney, who has not only honored her beautiful dad by completing his list, but also faced all of her fears in becoming her authentic self. This emotional journey will transform and challenge you to face all of your fears, believe in the goodness of people, and accept your path in life. Like a bottle of 1974 Mondavi, *My Father's List* is the finest memoir you will read. 'Well, history's about to change....'"

—**Shaun Zetlin**, author of *Emotional Fitness: Empower Yourself Emotionally Through Exercise* and *The Push-up Progression Series: A 24 Push-up Journey to Stabilization, Strength, and Power*

My Father's List

My Father's List

HOW LIVING MY DAD'S DREAMS SET ME FREE

LAURA CARNEY

Post Hill
PRESS

A POST HILL PRESS BOOK
ISBN: 978-1-63758-638-9
ISBN (eBook): 978-1-63758-639-6

My Father's List:
How Living My Dad's Dreams Set Me Free

Cover design by Jordan Wannemacher
Cover photo by Steven Seighman
Interior design and composition by Greg Johnson, Textbook Perfect

Post Hill Press
New York • Nashville
posthillpress.com

Published in the United States of America
1 2 3 4 5 6 7 8 9 10

For Steven

"When old age shall this generation waste,
Thou shalt remain, in midst of other woe
Than ours, a friend to man, to whom thou say'st,
'Beauty is truth, truth beauty—that is all
Ye know on earth, and all ye need to know.'"

—JOHN KEATS, "ODE ON A GRECIAN URN"

"Strange, isn't it? Each man's life touches so many other lives.
When he isn't around he leaves an awful hole, doesn't he?"

—*IT'S A WONDERFUL LIFE*

Contents

Foreword

"Miracle shall follow miracle, and wonders shall never cease."

—FLORENCE SCOVEL SHINN

It can take years to understand all that is lost when your loved one dies. As a mental health professional, a coauthor of a book about grief, and someone who has endured my own share of losses (including the loss of my father), I know that after the death of a loved one, the ground beneath feels uneven. And the suffering that follows is a silent cold because nothing is ever the same again. We're heartsick and long for that which no longer exists.

Many cope with their grief in a quiet, inner way because in the wake of loss often the intense pain that comes can be related to secrets and regrets. It takes a great deal of courage to move onward as Laura did.

In the process of living out her father's list, Laura's story intersects our own stories of loss and resilience. As humans we take comfort in knowing we are not alone with our fears, doubts, and sorrows. And yet, we as humans also have an uncanny ability to lose track of all the ways in which we are connected, leaving us feeling depleted and isolated. We each handle memories differently—some find hope in them and others decide to rearrange where they lie, no longer making them the center of one's mind.

There's a stillness that happens when grief sets in, and for some it can be paralyzing, but for Laura, it became the fulcrum at which new life grows.

Laura presents her story in unexpected ways and also with great wonder. Each time she does one of the items on the list, she puts us in touch with the part of ourselves from which love comes, so that the song Laura sings, or the miles she runs, or the letter she writes deepens our own understanding of what true love looks like.

At the end of the day, healing also comes from special and comforting things—a photograph, a conversation, a remembrance. When we can pair those things with bittersweet memories, we're able to hold onto our loved ones in a new and meaningful way.

Above all, in completing her father's list Laura invites us all to live with more truth, tenderness, compassion, and awe.

With heartfelt lament and bittersweet gratitude,

Kristin A. Meekhof, M.S.W.,
Coauthor of *A Widow's Guide to Healing*

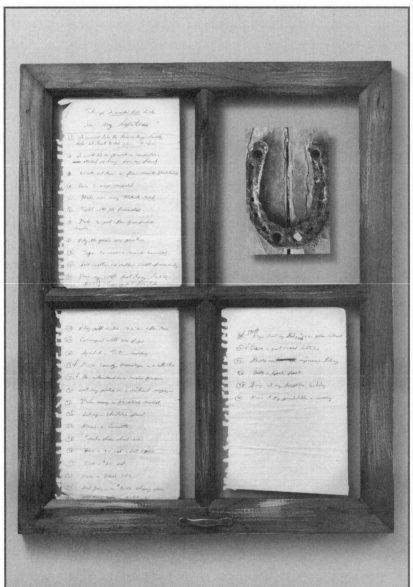

Prologue

We were visiting my brother in Salem, Massachusetts, when we found it.

As we gathered around Dave's granite-topped kitchen island, catching up on his wedding plans, my future sister-in-law, Jaime, went into their bedroom to retrieve something.

"Oh yeah," my brother said. "I wanted to show you this."

When she returned, her long blonde hair matching the walls of the rustic kitchen, she was holding a small brown suede pouch with a drawstring. She turned it upside down and out tumbled a silver ring and a driver's license, along with three pieces of folded notebook paper.

"We found it when we were unpacking," Dave said. "Do you know about this?"

I unfolded the papers and started reading. At the top of the first page was "Things I Would Like to Do in My Lifetime!" in my dad's handwriting.

He wrote the list when he was twenty-nine, covering both sides of each page. The first item said, "I would like to live a long, healthy life at least to the year 2020." The last said he hoped to dance at his grandchildren's weddings.

But both those goals were rendered impossible on August 8, 2003, the day he was killed by a distracted driver.

That summer I was twenty-five, pursuing my dream of becoming a writer in New York. My dad had encouraged this more than anyone, so

I knew I couldn't give up on it. He wasn't there when I accomplished my goal of working at a women's magazine eight years later. And he wasn't there five years after that, when I needed him to walk me down the aisle.

But on that afternoon in my brother's kitchen, I felt connected to him as we chuckled at his often indecipherable handwriting. I wondered aloud if he'd kept the list his whole life. He'd never told us about it. But then Dave remembered the World Series game he'd checked off.

"Look," he said. "He even wrote the score."

"As proof?" I asked.

Then something strange happened: we realized that many of his want-to-dos were things we'd already done. "I did that!" I cried about number thirty-one, "Get my picture in a national magazine." "And you did that!" I reminded my brother when we saw he'd wanted to record five songs (Dave recorded his with his a cappella group in college). All in all, there were thirteen items we'd accomplished. Not a small dent, considering he wrote down sixty.

But in my father's entire lifetime, he'd only checked off five.

Item number twelve said, "Give my children the most love, the best education, and best example I can give." He never checked that one off, but he should have. Because it's the reason I did this.

I decided to finish the list.

As soon as my husband, Steven, suggested it, I saw my dad in my mind's eye, smiling and nodding.

As the story goes, my mom found the list in a dresser in 1978, the year I was born, and read it in disbelief. She says they laughed over "have my own tennis court" and even harder at "correspond with the pope."

But at the time she was secretly concerned that the man she'd married had room in his head for much other than changing diapers.

I knew I was tempting fate by going after his ideas now on purpose.

* * *

THE LAST TIME I SAT DOWN alone with my dad was when I was twenty-five, a week before I moved away from home. It was my last "every Wednesday and Sunday." That's how often he said he'd see us when he left. And that's how often he did, for nineteen years, usually in restaurants, movie theaters, bowling alleys, roller rinks, sports arenas, swimming pools, malls, arcades, every park in Wilmington, Delaware, and in summers at the Jersey Shore.

My brother had moved to Arlington, Virginia, getting a job in accounting soon after college. I'd lingered in my mom and stepdad's house longer, which felt unnatural as I was two years older. As we talked over lunch, my dad knew I was embarrassed by this.

He told me he envied what I was about to do, try to find my way in New York as a writer, because it was something he'd wanted to do when he was my age. He told me that of all the talents my brother and I possessed, what made him the proudest of us was our kindness. He told me we were the best thing he'd ever done.

He said this all the time, "You're the best thing I've ever done," so that was nothing new. But I hadn't known it was our kind hearts that filled him the most with pride. He'd so often tried to predict our careers, athletic and otherwise, that somehow I'd missed it.

"You're audio," he'd say to Dave, "and you're visual," he'd say to me, acknowledging my brother's gift for singing, passed down from him, and mine for drawing. He'd say that someday we'd run our own business, with my brother as the accountant and me as the editor.

When it came to sports, you'd think we were forming a team he'd drafted. I had the excellent tennis backhand, but my brother had the "power forehand"—and later, in adolescence, the "power serve," backed by a muscular build I could no longer compete with. My tenacity on defense on the basketball court earned me the nickname "the female Bobby Jones" while my brother had "the second-fastest hands in the East"—"second" because my dad's were "first."

I didn't possess Dave's coachability; I was more flappable. So my dad taught me to take my time, to look squarely at the basket and visualize the ball swooshing through. To imagine success before it happened.

The day my brother finally beat me in a race was not a good one. At age eleven, my baby fat shed, I'd emerged a long-legged goose of sorts. "Look at those long strides," my dad said. "You're going to be a long-distance runner."

I was fed up. I didn't like being "the breaststroke champ" simply because I couldn't swim freestyle. I didn't like being applauded for treading water so furiously that I wouldn't go under simply because I was too afraid to dive. I didn't even particularly like playing goalie to Dave's swift soccer kicks or catcher to his pitches.

We were in our favorite park that day. And at eleven, with my feet in pink suede sneakers too big for my body, I ran off to put my long-distance-runner label to the test.

My father's cries of "Stop!" and "Where are you going?" were of little concern.

I'm doing this, right now, by myself, I thought.

I ran toward the park's mile-long track. After five minutes, I began to tire. But then I saw the first stop on the obstacle course that ran along its perimeter. Its familiarity comforted me.

In the summer my dad took us around the course on Wednesday nights. It was part of his exercise routine, and some stops were intolerably dull for children. But he'd pepper the course with jokes and trivia.

The first obstacle was the tire jump. The last was the balance beam. I had them committed to memory.

One by one they passed in my periphery. The yellow sand beneath me turned to clouds of dust. I began to lose my breath. I'd looked behind me a few times by then.

Why aren't they following me? I wondered. A moment of panic overtook me.

I'm really doing this alone, I thought. *It is completely up to me now.*

I slowed my pace to a power walk...and then to just a walk. And then I just wanted to make it to the balance beam.

Fully expecting him to be angry at the finish, I was surprised to find my father proud of me.

"I'm not a long-distance runner, Dad," I said, embarrassed to have walked most of it. I stepped onto the balance beam and started across it, one foot after the other. Slowly, surely...my preferred pace. It was my favorite of all the obstacles.

"Oh, but you are a long-distance runner," he said. "You are."

As I described my plans to him over lunch before my move to New York, my dad was the only person I knew who understood and approved of what I was doing. I was moving for an internship at an art magazine for only ten dollars a day. I was moving with only $1,000 in my bank account. I knew only one person, a cousin, who lived there already.

But something in me knew I could handle it.

And I think something in him did, too.

* * *

A MONTH AFTER FINDING my father's list, my brother's wedding was a snowy affair in New Hampshire—as cold and wet as my New Mexico wedding had been hot and dry. Dave and Jaime gave me the list framed as a wedding party gift, meaning anyone could now read it.

There were plenty of opinions to go around. My brother said he would help me with some of the items but not all.

A few weeks later, at Christmas, my mom and stepdad gave Steven and me a monetary wedding gift. It was meant to "invest in our future."

My mom hoped this would be a down payment on a house. She knew I might spend it on the list instead.

"That list was for a twenty-nine-year-old, not a thirty-eight-year-old," she said. She worried I'd go bankrupt pursuing this. Or even worse—jeopardize starting a family of my own.

I knew what I was doing seemed impossible.

But it was the main reason I had to try.

CHAPTER 1

Run Ten Miles Straight

The first time I reached the end of the Santa Monica Pier, I started crying.

A few days before, Steven and I had arrived in Los Angeles to visit my friend Kelly and her husband, John, who'd moved there from Delaware. I missed Kelly terribly and was excited. John, who's Mexican American, grew up in L.A., so for him, this was a return home.

Our first stop was the Getty Center. You can see panoramic views of all of L.A. from up there, from its white marble balconies. You can see all the way down to the beach. Even though it was the middle of October, it was warm and sunny, the way it feels on a fall day near sunset on the East Coast. As the wind picked up, John pointed out the blue of the ocean. Kelly laughed and made fun of his grand gesture.

At dusk, they took us to see the Hollywood sign from Griffith Park. While Kelly and John parked the car, Steven and I looked out at the small white faraway letters. Steven smiled at me, his blue eyes glistening behind his dark-rimmed glasses. He seemed happy. *Maybe he's jet-lagged*, I thought.

John's parents married in the oldest church in L.A., Our Lady Queen of Angels Catholic Church, on the oldest street in L.A., Olvera Street. So, the next morning, John and Kelly took us there.

We hopped on the train and got off at Union Station, with its warm wood and Art Deco tiles. Kelly led the way, pushing her sons, Kevin and Dominic, in their two-seated stroller, by the potted birds of paradise, through a courtyard of pink bougainvillea. After the Getty, I'd thought I'd never see bougainvillea again.

We spent three days with our friends and their toddler sons. Then John's father, Papa John, what they call him to differentiate the two, drove us to our hotel on the Sunset Strip, where we'd stay our last two days in L.A. We rarely rented cars then—we figured if we could get by without one in New York, we could get by without one anywhere, which almost never turned out to be true.

When we reached the Best Western, Steven flopped onto the bed and fell asleep. I Googled "history of Sunset Boulevard" and discovered the Garden of Allah.

If you've heard Joni Mitchell's song "Big Yellow Taxi," you know about it: Garden of Allah was paradise. Now it's a McDonald's.

It was built in 1913 by William Hay as a private residence. Six years later, he sold it to film and stage actress Alla Nazimova, who named the estate after herself. Seven years later, just before the stock market sank, Nazimova added twenty-five villas and turned it into a hotel. Guests like F. Scott Fitzgerald, Ernest Hemingway, Greta Garbo, Frank Sinatra, Ava Gardner, Errol Flynn, Lauren Bacall, and Humphrey Bogart all stayed there.

Like a lot of things in the 1920s, it became a freewheeling, debauched place—a constant party that sometimes devolved into orgies or nude swimming. And like a lot of things in the 1930s, as money got tighter, it fell into disrepair. Nazimova sold it and moved back to New York.

Artie Shaw once called it "one of the few places that was so absurd that people could be themselves."

Sitting in my hotel room cross-legged in a green maxi dress and learning about this place was the moment I fell in love with L.A.

Why haven't I ever heard of this? I wondered. *There's even a replica of it at Universal Studios!*

I hadn't heard of it for the same reason I hadn't heard of many historic artists' enclaves I've discovered since. These aren't the people any God-fearing educator wants a wholesome suburban American kid to become. They were bohemian, they flouted common decency, and they were oftentimes miserable.

But they were artists.

The next morning, we woke up early for what was supposed to be our beach day. As usually happens when we leave Kelly and John, we were bickering. We later learned to attribute this to being childless and being injected with an intense dose of kids for three days straight.

Our main argument was which beach we'd be going to, Venice or Santa Monica. I wanted Santa Monica because I'd heard it was cleaner. Steven wanted Venice because he wanted to see "weirdos" and didn't plan on spending much time lying down.

This was an ongoing fight we'd had for as long as we'd known each other. For me, "going to the beach" meant at least four hours on the sand. The long walks Steven generally associated with vacation were a shock to me.

When Steven didn't want to get off the bus, I gritted my teeth and stayed on a few more stops. Venice wasn't as bad as I'd feared, but it was the kitschiest place I'd ever seen—and I'd been to Dollywood.

Steven sat on the beach a few minutes, then left to get a sandwich. I agreed after he'd asked enough times to walk up to Santa Monica. "It's not that far," he said. It was two miles.

I was so grateful when we reached the pier that I ran to the end of it, like Tom Hanks does in *Forrest Gump*.

"I want to see the Ferris wheel!" I said.

But as soon as I got there, I started to cry.

I didn't know why I was crying. Maybe it was a release from the all-day fighting over stupid stuff, which in reality was about both of us wanting to soak up as much L.A. as we could on limited funds and not being able to agree on how to do that. Maybe it was sadness over the realization that my best friend now lived on the opposite coast, this was probably going to be permanent, and I didn't know what it might do to our friendship. But mostly it was because when I looked at the surprisingly calm body of water, the same one John had pointed to from the Getty five days earlier, it struck me that I was seeing something my father had never seen, would never get to see, and probably would have very much wanted to.

It wasn't until we found the list four years later that I knew this was true.

When Steven saw me crying, he said, "Aw," and hugged me.

I said, "My dad would have loved how beautiful this is."

I collected myself, and we started walking back.

"Do you think we should get married?" Steven asked, in a nervous, nonchalant voice.

The question was no different than if he'd said, "Do you think we should go see a movie?"

My heart sank. *"That's* how you're going to ask me?"

We'd been together nine years. I'd started asking about marriage five years in, when we moved into our first apartment—my high school best friend was getting married and I was her maid of honor, and she and her friends asked me often when Steven would propose, as though it was something I should be concerned about. He said at the time it didn't seem like a great plan financially, and it wasn't—I'd just been laid off from my first magazine job and was freelancing; he was working in his first job in his field, graphic design. Neither paid well (mine because I was spending all my money on my high school best friend's wedding). The fact that we managed to afford five days in L.A. four years later was nothing short of a miracle—or the result of extreme persistence.

Despite that, I internalized the pressure to be someone's wife, and I projected it onto him, most notably after family members' weddings. Once I got so angry that I slammed our bedroom door, and its full-length mirror came crashing to the ground. I'd become so obsessed with my public image that I'd shattered it.

Steven had his reasons to put off proposing, none of which had to do with how much he loved me. He was concerned he wasn't capable of being the provider he thought he should be.

So when he asked me on the pier, it felt like he was really saying, "Do you think I should finish my lima beans? Because they're good for me, right?"

And I didn't want to marry anyone who saw me as lima beans.

He got embarrassed and angry over my response. He said he was surprised. And then he said he really wasn't. "I have a ring back at the hotel," he mumbled, looking down at the water, "but you'd probably hate it."

"You have a ring here in L.A., but you just asked me this without having it on you?" I asked.

"Yes...well, you were crying about how beautiful the water was, and it seemed like a touching moment, so I went with it," he explained.

"But I wasn't crying because I was happy," I said. "I was crying because I was sad. Besides, we've been fighting all day—how could this possibly be the right moment?"

He later revealed that he'd wanted to ask at Griffith Park, but Kelly and John had ruined that when they took us there themselves. That's why he'd looked at me so wistfully that night.

We wandered our separate ways, but not too far apart, through the amusement park. I sat on the steps of a trailer, out of view of the crowd, and cried. Something in me felt eleven again. Something in me felt worthless. The feeling I'd had when my father left, when I was six, returned to my body in a way it never had.

It was sharp.

* * *

I STILL REMEMBER THE MOMENT he left, seeing his little gray Mazda back out of the driveway. I never remember his face when I think of this, just the car, which he often parked on the side of the drive, on the grass, which irritated my mother (because it "ruined the grass"), and the big mattress strapped to the top of it. I remember asking her where he was going, and her saying he'd be sleeping elsewhere for a while, and when I asked her why, her saying either because the bed hurt his back or because the bed was too small. Neither explanation made sense, especially given he was carrying the bed with him to wherever he'd end up, and these may just be the things I told myself to help my six-year-old brain process what was happening. My mother still says there's no way she would have said these things. It's more likely my father came up with that tale.

But either way, it was the first time I understood that there was something about our house, our family, that was causing him pain or not big enough.

Before their separation, my dad helped tuck us in at night and also woke us up. He sang lullabies, mostly "Too-Ra-Loo-Ra-Loo-Ral." Because his ancestors really *were* from Ireland, and because he often changed the lyrics to "Too-Ra-Laura-Laura," I thought he'd written it himself.

In the mornings, he told dumb jokes and sang made-up songs as he drove the kids in our carpool and me to school. After the kids got out, he'd hand me half a piece of Juicy Fruit, which went over better with my preschool teachers than with the Catholic kindergarten nuns.

I usually could tell he'd arrived home at night by the wet footprints on the primary bedroom's wooden floor, which my mother hated (because it "ruined the wood"), but which he always did anyway after taking a bath. Then he'd sit in his armchair in the living room and open the newspaper and give me the comics. Even before I could read, I knew this was an important thing, that this was something to be revered.

At the dinner table, he'd complain about his day, complete with impressions of every coworker. When my mom would try to finish the food on our plates, he'd do an impression of a T-Rex. After dinner, he'd make her Lipton tea, and sometimes he'd fill a demitasse with tea for me.

Our house wasn't quiet. Even if I couldn't remember this, I'd know from my father's tapes. He recorded himself singing, mostly at Christmas, and would record my brother and me, too.

My parents joked that he was the better-looking one—my mom thought he resembled a young Paul McCartney. I asked her once whom he thought she resembled, and she said a puppet from a 1950s TV show. She actually looks like Sally Field.

We lived in a two-bedroom red brick Colonial on a street called Sunset Drive, just off the Delaware River—they called it this because if you drove up the hill to our house, away from the river, you could watch the sun dip into it. They'd moved into the neighborhood because my dad's brother lived there.

My mom, Joan, grew up in an old Delaware family—her grandmother was a debutante, a college graduate, the secretary of a Civil War general, and a painter who studied under Howard Pyle. In my mom's family, the further back you go, the closer you get to aristocracy. My dad, Mick, grew up in a more urban part of Delaware. His Irish cop dad gave his sons a better education than he'd had. My dad called his grandfather a leprechaun (he was short) and joked he'd made a living back in Ireland carrying rocks.

In 1984, the spring he left, my mom had just separated my brother and me into two bedrooms. She'd spent hours visualizing this. The dormer-windowed upstairs of our house had only two rooms, so she moved my brother to the first floor, into the wood-paneled study. Shortly after this, my dad moved him back out. My dad would sleep in the study for six months, he said, and on his birthday, in April, he'd be gone.

When the divorce was finalized two years later, my mom converted the upstairs into a floor just for kids. I was moved into the primary bedroom and my brother into my old room. Like a king and queen on our thrones, we were separated by a small hall and a small bathroom. My mom would sleep downstairs in what had been the family room.

The only drawback to this arrangement was the French door on the western wall of my bedroom that led outside, onto the tar roof of the garage. Walking through it was always a special occasion. We almost never ventured it, and when we did, my mom quickly ushered us back in. She was certain we'd fall off and that letting us out there would only encourage us to try it when she wasn't home. She wasn't home every day after school for two hours, so I often broke this rule. I also often fantasized about sunbathing out there when I was older, or sneaking out when I was a teen to meet boys.

But at nine, I was less interested in sneaking out than I was in what might sneak in.

An anxiety began to emerge when my mom tucked us in—my brother and I were competitive even in this, keeping close track of how much time she spent with us and yelling across the hall if it seemed uneven. As though one was receiving more love than the other, as though her love was in short supply.

I did all I could to stretch out time, to avoid the moment my body hit the bed. Because once it did, I'd inevitably ask again why my father was gone and when/if he'd be coming back. My mom never had an answer other than "You're too little to understand. I'll tell you when you're older." My dad never had an answer when I asked him either, other than "Your mother and I still love each other very much."

My parents never had a fight, at least not one I'd seen. And so I mostly lay there, imagining myself at eighteen, picturing when I'd be "older."

When I couldn't attribute my anxiety to my dad's absence, I'd tell my mom worries left over from my day. She was a school guidance counselor, so she was equipped for this. Sometimes they were worries about the other kids at school. They were rarely limited to worries about me. But my compassion was born of a loneliness I couldn't name yet.

Once I found myself sitting on the floor alone in my bedroom, staring into a brand-new hand mirror, and singing "Edelweiss," from *The Sound of Music*, one of my dad's favorite songs, the song Captain von Trapp sings to his children when he regrets taking music from their lives. After a few lines, I began to cry and slammed the hand mirror facedown, accidentally breaking it. I picked it back up and saw my reflection, this time cracked and distorted.

I still cry whenever I hear "Edelweiss."

After my mom kissed my cheek and left my room, I'd debate which side to face, as I had a door on each. Then I'd say my prayer, the same one each night. I'd ask God to bless the same people, in the same order. I'd count as I bit down on different parts of my mouth. The molars were one. The front teeth were two. The molars again were three. The front teeth were four.

By the summer I was eleven, my rituals were no longer enough. My nighttime anxiety leaked into the daylight.

A house in our neighborhood had been burglarized. We had two insect infestations—moths who emerged from a box of cereal and beetles who crept in through the porch and found their way up the stairs. One night, we came home from a neighbor's house to find the front door ajar. We'd probably just forgotten to close it, but my mom thought someone had broken in. My dad drove over with a baseball bat.

I was becoming aware that there were dangers he could protect us from if he still slept under our roof. My nightly prayers expanded. *Please don't let anything bad or scary happen*, I'd ask over and over.

But it wasn't until he took us to Wildwood that summer that I knew something was terribly wrong.

My favorite boardwalk ride was the swings on Morey's Pier. It was a girly ride—my brother didn't care for it, and my dad couldn't fit into the seats. Knowing I'd be riding it alone, I loved climbing the stairs to the metal platform and choosing the best swing—one all the way on the outskirts, to get the most height once I was aloft. I'd smile and wave every time I passed my dad and brother below.

But this summer was different. I went through the motions. I asked if they wanted to ride with me, and they said no. I climbed the stairs and looked for a swing with trepidation. As the ride started and my swing took flight, I suddenly and for the very first time realized something: *This ride could kill me.*

The realization took hold of my body, and I froze. And I started crying. And I started yelling to the attendant to stop the ride every time my swing went by. I was embarrassed for my dad and brother to see me like this, but my fear of sudden death seemed more important.

After I got off, my dad tried to calm me down.

"I don't understand what happened," he said. "You usually love that ride!"

He led my brother and me to the Ferris wheel, his favorite ride on the pier. I steeled myself for a repeat performance.

As the wheel turned and our cart inched up, my dad pointed out the amazing view of the hotels and coastline. "You can't get a view like this from anywhere else," he said.

The ride stopped, and we were at the very top. And it got quiet. We were far enough from the clamor of the games and rides and barkers that it almost felt like we were in our own lofty tower. Even through the dark of night, I could see the waves crash along the Jersey Shore and felt strangely at peace.

In this one quiet space, I had nothing to worry about.

* * *

I REALLY AM WORTH NOTHING to anyone, I thought. *The man I love doesn't want to marry me.*

It was like the feeling I'd had on Morey's Pier, but painted in a much deeper hue. All I'd worked on for years, all of that was over now. This man, the one who supposedly unconditionally loved me, had ruined it. Because the truth was, he didn't want to be married. And he probably never would. My striving to fake normal would end in failure. Either that, or I'd have to leave him and be heartbroken forever.

We got the next bus back to the hotel. I sat in the seat behind him. We didn't look at each other. We didn't talk to each other. And Beverly Hills looked a lot less fun in the dark.

When we got off at UCLA to transfer, Steven sat on a bench. I stood by the trees, looking at the Mediterranean-roofed homes, wondering what it might be like to live in one, assuming all these bastards had perfect lives and a man who actually wanted to marry them.

"I want to see the ring," I said.

"No," he said.

I found out later that it was Lucite, purchased at the Museum of Modern Art for twenty dollars. It was unique and beautiful and the perfect gesture for us. But he didn't tell me any of that. Instead he said, "I only spent ten dollars on it anyway."

When we reached the hotel, I insisted we go out for dinner. It was late, but surely something would be open. I put on the printed maxi dress I'd planned for that night, and we ate a mostly silent Chinese dinner on Sunset Boulevard alfresco.

I can't remember how any of the food tasted. I just remember how sad he looked.

As we walked back, I said I needed to make a stop.

And I started walking toward paradise.

I strode into the McDonald's that had once been the Garden of Allah and used the restroom. Steven waited outside. I'd already excitedly told him all about it when he'd woken from his nap at the hotel. He'd taken a photo of me in my green maxi dress by the pool that night, in the bougainvillea-lined courtyard, and I'd had this feeling he was about to propose, but I always had that feeling then, and it always never happened.

"Was it worth it?" he asked when I came back.

"Yes," I said.

Back home in New Jersey, I decided I wasn't going to wait anymore. I found a diamond band my aunt had given me as a hand-me-down, and I asked him to marry me.

"No," he said. "You don't want it to happen like this."

"OK," I said, "then I'm proposing to myself."

I placed the ring on the middle finger of my right hand.

What I loved most about the Garden of Allah was the stories about the women who stayed there. They were liberated women in the 1920s. They had careers. They drank, they smoked. They didn't need to be tied down by anyone. The notion that they could find a spot where they were accepted, "one of the few places," Artie Shaw said, "that was so absurd that people could actually be themselves," was amazing to me.

It sent me on a mission to find places like it.

A few months after we returned from L.A., my brother's girlfriend at the time invited me to her running-themed birthday party. I wasn't a runner, I told her—I'd given up on sports at sixteen. But I was determined to do well, or at least mediocre, so I started going to the gym in my office twice a week. My first day there, the coworker nice enough to go with me watched me fall off the treadmill. I never went with her again.

At first the pain of running even a mile seemed unbearable, so I set up a system. While listening to music, I'd run on the treadmill until a song had ended—about three minutes. Then I'd walk until my heart rate had gone down to 162. And then I'd start again. As I ran, I counted the windows on the New York City skyscraper facing me. As my eyes drifted left to right, the miles ticked off more quickly.

I used this practice when I ran a 5K that Thanksgiving in Delaware. The next morning, my brother woke me up to tell me my picture was in the newspaper. "If that's what happens when I run, I'm never stopping," I joked.

But I never did.

That spring, when I learned my sister-in-law Kate was running a half marathon in Philadelphia, I decided to do that, too. I didn't believe I could run more than three miles. So I set up a schedule of gradually longer training.

The next year I ran the New York City Marathon. The training was the hardest yet because it meant sixteen-mile runs, a lot of time to be pushing myself to do something so strenuous. There was nobody there to encourage me when I got tired. It was often sheer will that kept me going. I managed it by sticking to one rule: *No matter how poorly I'm running, I have to finish the distance.*

After a while, I wanted to give up less and wasn't so worried I'd have to. I started to enjoy being alone—I realized how necessary it was. When I had that time set aside just for me, I was separated from the clamor of the world around me.

In this one quiet space, I had nothing to worry about.

When I ran the marathon, I was amazed by how a person could feel so alone yet so part of a tribe at the same time.

Our wedding was six months before the 2016 presidential election. The day after Hillary lost, I signed up to run the L.A. Marathon for a nonprofit that teaches running to preteen girls. I wanted to give them what I'd lost at their age.

We found my father's list eleven days later.

As we read the list in my brother's kitchen, my eyes hovered over item twenty-three, "run ten miles straight"—I realized I'd never truly done it. Sure, I'd run a whole marathon, but there had been a lot of walking involved.

"Maybe I could run the first ten miles of the L.A. Marathon," I said, "and then run/walk the remaining 16.2."

When I told my friend Kelly, in L.A., about this, she said I was out of my mind.

"You're going to be way too tired to finish those sixteen miles!" she said.

Kelly wasn't a runner. She'd just become a hiker. The year before, she'd bought a Fitbit and joined a walking group at work.

If running for charity, the L.A. Marathon lets people run relay-style, meaning the distance is split. I told Kelly this to reassure her. "I'm sure I can find a woman to partner with."

"No," she said, "I'll do it. I'll be your partner."

I think she surprised herself, too.

We decided Kelly should take the first half because she's a morning person. That left the second half to me.

The L.A. Marathon ends at the Ferris wheel on the Santa Monica Pier.

It was no Morey's Pier. But it would have to do.

By March, I'd surpassed my goal of raising $650 for my L.A. Marathon charity. In the week before the race, after one email to the staff of the magazine where I worked, *Good Housekeeping*, the editor in chief donated $200, and the two editors below her on the masthead donated similarly.

This mostly happened because I'd spent the winter writing an article for the magazine, which was strange because I wasn't a writer for them—I was a copy editor.

My job was to fix mistakes.

Back in 2015, when I finished the New York City Marathon, I raised money for a safe driving group. One advocate was so impressed that she recommended me to the National Safety Council, a group that supported families affected by accidental death. By spring, I was on a plane to Chicago to meet them. My wedding was in two months.

In Chicago, eleven of us sat in a circle in a hotel conference room while NSC researcher Deb Trombley showed us charts depicting levels of distracted driving. In a PowerPoint, Deb projected a study that showed where drivers' eyes had gone while on the phone. Even when they'd used the phone hands-free, their vision through the windshield had shrunk four times. They'd missed stop signs, billboards, traffic lights.

Traffic lights.

I called Steven that night from my hotel room, crying.

"That seventeen-year-old never had a chance to see that red light," I said, lying across the bed. "I forgave her today for killing my dad."

Two days later, when Steven picked me up at the airport in New Jersey, we almost hit a man in dark clothes staring at his phone in a crosswalk. I screamed.

"If I'd been on the phone with you just now, you would have hit him," I said.

We never talked on the phone hands-free while driving again.

That week I shared what I'd learned in Chicago with a *Good Housekeeping* editor. Carla pitched my story idea to her editor, Meaghan, who gave it a green light. And then a week before my wedding, the editor in chief, Jane, said she was in, too. The only caveat: I couldn't write the article. I was too close to the subject matter, they said.

I left for my wedding triumphant. I'd be walking down the aisle not as a bride to feel sorry for, but as a reporter who'd prevented a similar loss.

When we returned from our honeymoon, the National Safety Council announced a 10 percent jump in car fatalities. It was the biggest year-over-year increase since the 1960s. I piggybacked on the news and wrote an essay for the *Washington Post* about what it had been like marrying without my dad. Then I shared it on Facebook.

The response overwhelmed me. It seemed every person I'd ever known had read it. For thirteen years, I'd rarely talked about my father's death. Now I'd written about it in the second-largest newspaper in the country.

That night I hopped in the shower. I turned on the faucet, and a phrase popped into my head.

Changing history.

It wasn't a phrase I generally used.

The week before my brother's wedding, Carla read the *Washington Post* story. "I only wish you could have written it for us," she said.

She asked me to write a personal essay to accompany the *Good Housekeeping* article about distracted driving. After two failed attempts, I showed her the blog I'd just created for my father's list.

"That's it," she said. "That's the story."

She showed it to Meaghan, who'd just lost her dad. She cried.

A week later, Carla said, "Meaghan's making your essay the central focus of the piece."

I walked to Starbucks. As I waited for my coffee, I watched a man and his two young children at the counter and started to cry—it was a boy and a girl, about two years apart. Like my brother and me.

When I walked back into the office, my phone blinked red. The National Safety Council had called, asking me to speak at a press conference in Washington, D.C. When I called back, they told me the assignment was top secret—and it would be televised. But I had to tell my boss so I could get the day off.

Soon their PR person was recommending me to news outlets. The *Today* show wanted me on, she said. I reported this to Carla.

"Please don't," she said, understandably. "They'd be scooping *Good Housekeeping* if you did. But don't worry—we'll get you on the *Today* show ourselves."

I couldn't believe all that was happening.

I'd hesitated to become an advocate when I learned about it. "I don't want my dad to be a face on a milk carton," I'd said.

But my main problem had been me. *I* was afraid of being the face of tragedy.

I'd been hiding tragedy all my life.

As I worked with the editors on my *Good Housekeeping* article, they wanted to change parts of it. At first I resisted. Then one afternoon I heard the voice again.

Just play ball.

I knew the voice wasn't mine.

It's impossible to explain the anguish of talking with law enforcement and lawyers about the violent way my father died. During the weeks I worked with our research team and legal department at *Good Housekeeping*, I slept poorly.

One night I walked out to our cold, wrought iron kitchen table, sat under the moonlight, and cried. I wondered if my dad could see any of what I was doing. I rested my face in my folded arms and stretched my arm out in front of me, palm open.

I felt him holding my hand.

In the first week of March my office received its copies of the *Good Housekeeping* with my story in it. I brought the bright-pink issue to dinner with my cousin Jenn and her family that night in Times Square—they were visiting from Maryland. The issue would be on national newsstands in a week.

Jenn texted me the next morning to say she'd shared the story with her daughter: "Thanks so much for meeting with us! When we read your article to Tali, I explained to her who your dad was, that he'd shown me *Back to the Future*."

After my parents' divorce, my cousins on my mom's side rarely saw my father. Jenn was the only one old enough to remember him. And her main memory of him was that she'd seen *Back to the Future* at his apartment when we were nine.

The day the issue of *GH* hit newsstands, I sent Jenn a picture of it in the train station. She texted back, "Look what's on TV right now," then sent me a photo of Michael J. Fox in *Back to the Future*.

Back to the Future is on channels like TNT ad nauseam, so it wasn't that strange a find. But over the next month, I noticed a series of weird coincidences. I heard the *Back to the Future* theme song, "Power of Love," by Huey Lewis and the News, twice in the subway station, and its other theme song, "Back in Time," in a Whole Foods, and a third song from the films, "Papa Loves Mambo," in a restaurant with my brother. I heard "Mr. Sandman" while teenage girls walked into a Dunkin' Donuts. A few months earlier, I'd made eye contact with the actor Michael J. Fox in front of my office (he'd come for an interview). On a visit from my brother the summer before, we'd driven by a DeLorean. By the end of March, I was meeting a man blinded by a car crash who said his favorite movie was *Back to the Future*—it was playing in the hospital when he woke up.

I looked up the origins of the movie and found an interview with its screenwriter Bob Gale. He said he got the idea when he stumbled upon his dad's high school yearbook and learned he'd been president of his class, something he'd never told him. It was like his dad had led this other life he knew nothing about.

After my parents' divorce, my dad never remarried. We sometimes saw his brothers, at holidays, but for the most part our time with him was one-on-one. He was a large man, with a twinkle in his eye and warmth in his smile; he gave hugs like he meant them. He had a booming laugh. His voice had a cadence—like he enjoyed hearing himself talk. He'd slip into an accent or slap tables to make a point. He drove in a newsboy cap and walked with a shillelagh, an Irish walking stick, for fun (though it mostly lived in his back seat). He was a salesman. He was a singer. He was a poet. He was a character. But despite his big persona, Mick Carney was also a truth seeker. He knew if someone was hiding it. Maybe because he was so good at hiding his own.

I rewatched *Back to the Future*. In one of the opening scenes, Marty arrives late to school because Doc has set all his clocks back. Principal Strickland calls him a slacker and says his father, George, was also a slacker, that "no McFly has ever amounted to anything in the history of Hill Valley." Marty says, "Well, history's about to change."

It was the phrase I'd heard in the shower after my *Washington Post* story.

Later, when Marty time-travels to 1955, he learns his father was a writer. Young George tells Marty he doesn't share his stories because he can't handle the rejection.

My dad was a writer. The week he died, I found a rejection letter from a publishing house in New York. He'd submitted a book manuscript, a short story collection, a TV screenplay, and several poems. He'd never told me about any of it.

On the drive back from the beach once my dad and I talked about whether life was dictated by free will or fate. My brother was asleep, which was for the best—he hated when we got too philosophical. My dad said he thought life was both. I told him it couldn't be both. It had to be one or the other.

But now I think he was right. Certain things happen that must always happen. Just like George McFly is Lorraine Baines's destiny—they are fixtures on a timeline.

It's how we react to them that makes all the difference.

"You can do anything you set your mind to," Marty says to the younger version of his dad.

Suddenly, I knew the answer to my question that night at my kitchen table.

My dad *could* see what I was doing.

And he was cheering me on.

I'm a person who gets cold very easily. I have low blood pressure and thin skin and absorb the temperature of my surroundings (much to Steven's dismay at night when I hug him with my "dead hands"). This was what I endured while training for the L.A. Marathon. During those sleepless weeks in February when I was working on my *GH* article, I was also running outside in the brutal cold.

What generally happened was this: I'd get a text from my friend Kelly on a Sunday about her incredible run in California. She was exuberant—she'd gone farther than she thought she could. I'd watch her accolades roll in on Facebook and remind myself that no sane person would go running on a twenty-degree night on the East Coast. And then I'd do just that.

Most of running ten miles straight is a mind game, I learned. Whenever I reached half a mile in the park, the point where I'd usually let myself walk, I'd tell myself, *No, you're not tired. Keep going.* Instead of stopping, I'd slow down a little, which meant I had to be OK with a twelve-minute mile instead of my usual ten-. And my runner's high kicked in earlier and lasted longer.

A lot of people told me I was crazy to run at night, but I worked such long hours that it was often the only time I had. It was also the best time for me spiritually.

Since starting the list, I was beginning to sense my dad's spirit more often. It used to be only when a certain song played or a lucky number showed up. What was happening now was brand-new.

On one of my early training runs, I struggled to get started. I ran to the restroom by the park and broke down. The night before, we'd had dinner with Jacy Good, a national safe driving advocate. I'd felt stronger at my wedding because of Jacy—after losing both parents in a crash with a driver on his phone, Jacy had walked alone down her wedding aisle...after she'd relearned how to walk. I pondered what it might be like to have lost my mom, too.

Wiping my tears, I ran back to the park and turned my music back on. It was "Big Girls Don't Cry." I laughed.

The night I finished six miles straight—the farthest my brother told me he'd ever run without walking—I envisioned my dad jumping up and down at the finish.

On the night I reached eight miles, my "You're not tired. Keep going" inner monologue became *I can't do this by myself anymore. Someone help me.* In the last lap, I felt an arm link with mine, pulling me to the eight-mile mark.

The most I reached in training was nine miles straight. And I worried all week before the marathon that I'd pushed too hard even doing that—you're supposed to taper before a race, not increase. Then Steven got sick with a cold, so I slept on the couch.

When we landed in L.A. the day before the race, Kelly texted me to say she'd rather greet us the next morning—she'd be leaving at 3:30 a.m. to start her half. This meant Steven and I would have the whole day in Los Angeles to ourselves.

Picking up the rental car was easy. We stopped for sushi at my favorite place, then got my lucky carrot juice for free. Then we spotted a copy of the *Good Housekeeping* with my article in it on a newsstand. Our first day in L.A. felt charmed. The only bad part was when I got Steven's cold.

Kelly texted, "Be sure to hydrate!" So I drank hot tea and took a bath. The next morning, I chugged the Best Western's passion fruit juice. I chugged coffee, too.

At 7:00 a.m., Kelly started her run seven miles south of the Getty Center, where she and John had taken us on our first trip to L.A. After 2.5 miles, she reached Olvera Street. She hit mile eight on Hollywood Boulevard, ran by the celebrity handprints in front of the Chinese Theatre, and then hit mile twelve after turning by Charlie Chaplin's studios. Our hand-off point was in front of McDonald's—the Garden of Allah.

At 9:00 a.m., we met John there to watch her finish. Still worried about my cold, I grabbed a banana from the stands and a tangerine and bottled water. The three of us looked for a pink Girls on the Run shirt and dark red hair. I wondered if Kelly would be exhausted. It was her first time running this much. Instead, she was blissful.

She slowed down and hugged me, then whispered: "You got this, girl."

Fumbling with my earbuds, I turned on my playlist. Kelly's glow had rubbed off on me. I ran up Sunset toward Santa Monica. Being where people usually aren't, running roads made for cars, made me feel like I was flying.

As I started down Santa Monica, I'd made it past one mile, where my inner monologue had to kick in so I wouldn't start walking. I ran by the water stands and noticed they were missing something important: water. Volunteers were handing out Gatorade instead. They handed out orange slices, too, so I took a little of each.

Most of the songs on my playlist were about California and girl power. I'd almost put "Shake It Off," Steven's favorite Taylor Swift song, at mile two. And now I wished I had—because this was when the peeing started.

By "California Girls," my dad's favorite Beach Boys song, I was letting my urine out in small spurts. *Use it*, I thought, remembering advice my brother once gave me.

I approached Rodeo Drive with streams of yellow down my legs.

A lot of the runners were slowing down now...a lot of them were walking. I'd forgotten when I agreed to be the second runner that when I reached mile four, almost everyone else would be at mile seventeen. In marathon running, mile seventeen is called "the wall"—when the human body starts to shut down if it can't up its glucose. When I reached mile seventeen in the New York City Marathon, I mistook a boy who handed me a banana for an angel.

The problem with everyone being in temporary decline was that I wasn't. I had to make a choice: Either start walking, like everyone else, or dodge them like zombies, not caring if anyone saw the pee on my legs.

I chose the latter. And for the first time in my life, I knew what it was to be in the spotlight. I'd feared it since publishing my article in *Good Housekeeping*—when the light gets brighter, every piece of lint shows.

But you can't be heard if you refuse to be seen.

As I reached my fifth mile, Lady Gaga sang "Million Reasons" on my playlist, and I was giving myself a million reasons to stop this torture. But then "Daddy Lessons" came on, a song Kelly played for me on my wedding day, and I knew I was halfway done. She'd played it mid-climb on Santa Fe's Mount Atalaya. Kelly's dad, Kevin, died a year after mine—from a heart attack during surgery.

She pretended like she'd played the song by accident.

As Dolly Parton sang "9 to 5," my feet on the pavement synced with the typewriter. *OK, someone help me*, I thought. *I can't do this by myself anymore.*

When nobody did, I thought, *Why did I ever think I could do this? I'm going to humiliate myself—and my dad.*

And then I heard it.

Your life, your choices.

It was the voice again.

Your life, your choices. Your life, your choices.

It wasn't a phrase I'd ever used.

As Taylor Swift sang "22," I realized my mile nine was mile twenty-two for most other runners. I had to reach mile twenty-three to be done.

Kelly and I were strangers when we were roomed together in college. Twenty-two years later, we're still friends. I couldn't keep her next to me—she lives across the country now. But I feel like I'm still twenty-two when I'm with her. And I guess that's how it will always be.

So it was fitting that this came on when it did. Because we did it.

I reached mile twenty-three and checked off list item twenty-three at the same time because of my oldest friend—who believed in me and believed in my dad's dreams, but most importantly, believed in her own.

Finally, I walked—straight to a Porta-potty.

As I kept walking, I gave myself what my dad called the "atta girl award"—I patted myself on the back. I still had three miles to run/walk until the finish line. Nobody was there to witness me check this off.

But making myself proud of me was enough.

When my dad wrote the list, in 1978, female marathoners weren't a thing yet. The Boston Marathon, the oldest in the world (except for the ancient Greeks), had only admitted female entrants for six years. The change was thanks to Kathrine Switzer, who in 1967 signed up with her initials alone. About two miles in, the race director grabbed her bib and told her to get out of "his race." Her football player boyfriend tackled him to the ground. Switzer said, "I'm going to finish this race on my hands and knees if I have to, because nobody believes I can do this." When I learned this, I thought about a text from my sister-in-law Sydney. Her eight-year-old, Savannah, had joined Girls on the Run because she "wanted to be like Aunt Laura." When Kelly's little girl, Ava, saw her walk through the door wearing her medal, she grabbed it and placed it around her own neck.

After I finished running, Kelly found me sitting by the side of the road near the finish line, eating a banana and staring at the Ferris wheel.

"We did it!" she said, high-fiving me.

"We did!" I said, adding, "Hey, something unfortunate happened...."

"What?" she asked, sitting on the ground next to me. "Did you shart?"

When we got home from California, I learned my *Good Housekeeping* article had gone viral. For a month, I received emails and Facebook messages from strangers. "This article should be required reading in high schools," one said. The Association of Magazine Media tweeted a link to it. I received calls for interviews—first from *Inside Edition*, and then from Ernie Anastos on *Fox 5 New York News* and Montclair State University, both on the same day. I was interviewed on podcasts, blogs, websites, and radio shows. My story was featured in the *Daily Mail*. I represented AAA and was interviewed in the Good Housekeeping Institute by *CBS News*, which meant talking to a reporter in the GH living room, which had hosted celebrities for one hundred years. It meant putting on heels and a bright dress and doing my hair and makeup. It meant coordinating interviews with *Good Housekeeping*'s PR person.

Backstage in the green room before my *Fox 5 New York News* interview, Ernie Anastos sat with me to prepare, his face covered in thick, tan makeup, his hair gelled.

"Your dad must have been a real family man," he said.

"I guess so," I answered. "Why do you ask?"

"Because if he wrote the list the year you were born, he was thinking about how your presence had changed him. When my daughter was born, it made me aware of my mortality."

I'd always seen my dad as a man who ran away. But maybe I was wrong.

Maybe he'd been running toward us all along.

When I sat down at the news desk, before the cameras started rolling, I closed my eyes to pray. This was an eight-minute segment—and it was live. The voice emerged in my mind, the one I never recognized as my own.

Born for this.

CHAPTER 2

Swim the Width of a River

I am five years old. My parents have taken my brother and me to our first amusement park—not the one on the boardwalk by the beach or the one at church in the summer. It's the next-best thing to Disney World: Sesame Place.

My father beckons me to jump into the ball pit. Kids are tossing blue plastic balls at each other. My dad is smiling.

I take off my shoes and gingerly step in, then realize its depth; my dad is up to his chest. My stockinged feet slip on the balls beneath me and gradually my toes wedge between them, sliding toward the bottom. I'm up to my chin in sweat sock–scented plastic.

My dad realizes his error and scoops me up, wades us over to the ladder, and places me on it. My little arms hang onto the handles. My mom shows up to take our picture, but only my father is smiling. My face is pale and wet with sweat and tears.

* * *

When I read item twenty-four, "swim the width of a river," a thought that occurred to my dad after "run ten miles straight," I imagined he'd gotten the idea from Mark Twain, his favorite writer, or maybe Jules Verne.

For Twain, the Mississippi River meant freedom. He grew up in Missouri and dreamt of working on a steamboat (and did, briefly).

When he took his pen name in 1863, he took it from the river. "Two fathoms, 'mark twain,' is the point where dangerous water becomes safe or safe water becomes dangerous," explains Ron Powers in Ken Burns's *Mark Twain* documentary. "He was always on that margin. That's where he lived, on the edge, between the lightness and the dark."

Twain published *Adventures of Huckleberry Finn* in 1884, when he was almost fifty. The river is a character in it. When my dad was near Huck's age, he fell out of a tree, breaking both arms—he'd broken a leg the year before. Each time, he was bedridden. He told us that story when he warned us about tree climbing. But I think it was one of the best things to happen to him. The forced bed rest made him a reader, and later a writer. He might not have fallen in love with Mark Twain and Jules Verne otherwise.

It didn't surprise me to learn my dad's second-favorite author wrote a book called *Voyages Extraordinaires*. But "swim the width of a river"? I mean, it's not *Twenty Thousand Leagues Under the Sea* territory, but it's not exactly the Lazy River at the water park either.

We used to make fun of him at the water park because while my brother and I loved the slides, he just wanted to tube all day. Lots of our excursions culminated in his falling asleep. In movie theaters. At the beach. His favorite stroke was the backstroke. He tried to teach me but always failed because I didn't like the water seeping in my ears. "You need to fill up with air to stay afloat," he said. He had no problem doing this. He'd float along, singing "Old Man River," joking about the water's warm spots.

When we swam in our local pool, I only ever beat my brother in breaststroke. But in my father's eyes, this made me Queen of the Waves—a feat not possible without Gertrude Ederle, the first woman to swim the English Channel. Most people said a woman couldn't do it. Ederle's first attempt, in 1925, was a bust. Midway through, she started floating face-first, so her coach pulled her out. She claimed she "wasn't drowning, but resting." The weather over the channel was terrible on her second try, but the twenty-year-old still beat the best swimmer's record by two hours. Which meant she was two hours faster than any man.

Ederle taught swimming only a few blocks from my office, so I decided to train there. But then I learned the first three visits at the Y were free, so I trained there instead.

I walked up for my first practice swim one night after work. I'd already chosen my river, the polar opposite of the English Channel: the French Broad. It's only 500 feet wide. Located in North Carolina, it was where Steven and I were going on Mother's Day for my nephew's high school graduation anyway.

River swimming struck me as something that *should* be done in the South. I pictured a Norman Rockwell setting with a rope swing, a glassy water surface, maybe a lift a la *Dirty Dancing* (filmed not far from the French Broad!). And I liked the river's history—it's the third-oldest river in the world. Early settlers called it the French Broad because it drained into French territory. But the Cherokee had other names for it. One meant "racing waters." Another meant "chattering child."

If this doesn't sound like a calm river...well, it's not.

My mom called when I was a block away from the Y—I'd left her a voicemail that I had good news. When I picked up, I told her: the *Today* show had asked for an interview. She seemed let down.

"I thought you were going to say you were pregnant!"

Since my *Good Housekeeping* article had attracted so much attention, my mom's stance on my father's list had changed. She'd overcome natural fears for a mother. She believed in what I was trying to do. She wanted to do a list item now. When my dad wrote the list in 1978, she'd found it impractical. When I told her my plan to finish it six months earlier, she'd called it impossible.

I didn't know what to make of her change of heart.

I yanked my new rash guard over my torso in the women's locker room, where some girls felt just fine walking around naked. I'd been teaching myself the difference between a length and a lap. My knowledge was passable enough to figure out how far I had to swim to finish a mile.

I swam nearly half a mile, which took me half an hour. But I was proud of myself for swimming even that. It was different from how I felt after a run. I experienced what writer Wallace J. Nichols calls *blue mind*: "a mildly meditative state characterized by calm, peacefulness, unity, and a sense of general happiness with life in the moment."

But a week before our trip, I started worrying. "You have to think about the bacteria and organisms in the water," a friend at work said. So I found a website that measured the river's toxicity. I studied the river-paddling map provided by French Broad Outfitters, who were by now growing sick of me—I'd written them four times. I messaged them one last time:

> *Me: "Hi, had one more question for you—I was reading about wildlife in the river, and your website said there are venomous snakes. Is it safe to swim 500 feet across the width of the river, or am I just asking to be bitten? Thank you so much for all your help!"*

> *FBO: "You are all good."*

The day before we left, a man in a safe driving group on Facebook added me, and he just happened to live near the French Broad. The advocate, Dan Dry, told me I could call him, so I did, hoping I'd found a snake expert. By then, I'd also read about a rogue alligator.

"It's not the snakes you need to worry about," Dan said. "It's the cold."

He remembered going tubing with his late daughter, who was killed by a distracted driver in high school. She'd tease him about how cold he got.

I told him I was sorry for his loss.

We set off for North Carolina on a Friday at 3:00 a.m. Steven wanted to drive through the night—my nephew's graduation was that evening. Then we'd wake up the next morning and I'd jump in a river.

As we sailed through the Blue Ridge Mountains, we listened to NPR. It was the Friday after President Trump had fired the head of the FBI. We traveled through the purple hills and lost reception.

Steven was excited about more than just seeing my nephew graduate. We'd planned to spend a few nights in Asheville, a place he'd always wanted to see. We'd also booked one night at the Grove Park Inn, a popular place in Gertrude Ederle's day. F. Scott Fitzgerald stayed there, too, in the 1930s, so he could be near his wife, Zelda, who was in a mental institution. After a few depressing years, he moved to the Garden of Allah. He died three years later. But Fitzgerald shared an editor with the most famous writer to come out of Asheville, Thomas Wolfe, who also died young.

Wolfe's life was plagued by the backlash his first novel received from the town. He took issue with the greed and glitz that had led to places like the Grove Park. He once wrote his mother,

> When I was a child, I daydreamed about having five or ten million dollars and spending it on steam yachts, automobiles, great estates, and swank. Now I know that happiness is not to be got at in that way: the only way I know is to find the thing you want to do with all your heart, and to work like hell doing it.

About an hour from our hotel, the sky turned gray. Steven slowed the car. A tornado warning blared for the town we'd just left. Grateful to have missed it, we kept driving. But this didn't bode well for swimming conditions.

The next morning, our hotel served something I'd never tried for breakfast: biscuits and gravy. At 11:30 a.m., we drove to the dock.

Never had I smelled honeysuckles so pungent as the ones that lined the French Broad. The window open, I reveled in them, then braced myself by the sewage plant.

We parked at Walnut Island River Park, a small piece of land with picnic tables. I checked the riverkeeper's website—Walnut Island was a go. I pulled off my jeans and threw them in the back seat and put on my bathing cap, goggles, and towel. I wiped my legs with bug repellent as Steven walked ahead.

"That current looks swift!" he said, and then, "you have an audience." Canadian geese squawked on a sandbar.

I posed for a photo and kissed him. Then I was off.

The water was cold, but not so cold I couldn't stand it. It was a deep grayish green, so I couldn't see what I was stepping on. But it was mostly slippery rocks.

My orange water shoes now seemed the smartest purchase I'd ever made but also the dumbest, as one kept slipping off. The river was thigh-deep, so I immersed as much of myself as I could, but at times I stood up and walked.

I'm getting over there, one way or another, I thought.

The rocks were so unwieldy that if the current didn't knock me down, they did. Each time, I fell square on my knees, which I was sure were bloodied.

My mom couldn't believe I was attempting this. It was something she said she couldn't do.

In 1957, when she was ten, she went to summer camp. The counselors asked the campers to jump in a pool, so she jumped in the deep end, despite not knowing how to swim. They had to pull her out with a pole. By summer's end, she was proud of her new skills. My grandfather picked her up from camp and took her to the beach, where she showed off in the ocean. Then a massive wave swooped in and tossed her out. She never put her head under water again.

My mom always says, "There are two kinds of people in this world: those who can swim and those who can't." She made sure my brother and I were the former.

Which is why I made it across the French Broad. It was because of my mother.

The day before, I'd taken a call from *CBS Sunday Morning*. The producer said she wanted to do a segment on me checking off a list item. As more people got involved in this project, I found myself confused. So often excitement led to disappointment, like when the *Today* show canceled. Every time the French Broad knocked me down, it made me think of those disappointments. I pulled myself up and remembered: *I set a goal for myself, and I'm going to meet it. It doesn't matter who pays attention when I do.*

As I neared the other side, I was several feet upriver. I scanned the branches for snakes, then climbed out, threw my arms up, and yelled. "I did it!"

Steven couldn't hear me because he was 500 feet away.

Suddenly it dawned on me: I had to swim back. I'd suspected as much, as the side I was on was just grass and railroad tracks. But it felt different now that I was actually doing it. I jumped back in. "This is crazy, this is crazy…" I muttered.

"*Why* did you want to do this?!" I yelled.

My father wasn't afraid of nature. It was where he was the happiest.

A current knocked me off my feet and I clutched a rock with one hand. I let the water pass over me, let my body be pulled, like Lois Lane in Niagara Falls. Then something shifted, and I laughed.

I was having fun!

A year earlier, when Steven and I honeymooned in Arizona, the daily temperature was 120 degrees. We hiked the Red Rocks, then rode roughshod down a natural water slide *Goonies*-style. Well, actually, I did; Steven carried our clothes.

If there were a way to experience life as a leaf or a twig, this would be it. I giggled most of the way—it was all I could do, because while this rush of water carried me down, I was looking up, flat on my back, at these towering red rock formations. Steven laughed, too.

When I climbed out at the bottom, something in me had changed. I hugged a tree on my way out. Lying on my back, letting that slide take me where it wanted, had been my first successful back float.

I tried to channel it as I hung onto that rock in the French Broad.

After the current died down, I risked walking again. I was standing on the edge of what might be a waterfall, I wasn't sure. I stood still. I prayed.

39

Please calm these waters.

First I felt the sun, and then I saw it. As yellow blanketed the river around me, a butterfly flew by. I looked around. I was only one swimmer, one person, surrounded by mountains and sun. I was the only person experiencing this—well, except for Steven, and the family picnicking, who likely thought me a lunatic.

But they weren't in the water.

Each time I fell now, it hurt less. Whether the waters were actually calm didn't matter. What mattered was I believed they were.

When Gertrude Ederle finished her English Channel swim, the last leg was the hardest. She got through it by singing, the rhythm of her voice mirroring the rhythm of her strokes.

When my dad back-floated in the ocean, he sang. Whether "Old Man River" or "Moon River," or some other corny song.

Johnny Mercer wrote "Moon River" about the river he grew up on in Georgia, to emphasize Holly Golightly's modest upbringing. She made it to New York despite her origins. It was why I'd chosen it to play as I walked down the aisle. Because my father loved to sing it, because my husband and I are "after the same rainbow's end," because Steven's a "huckleberry friend," at least to me.

A "huckleberry friend" is someone you experience life with in an easy way. Someone with whom you can be your total self. Like Mark Twain's Huck and Jim. They find their true selves on that river. When I read it, I understood why my dad loved Twain.

As I reached the last few feet of river, I again scanned the branches for snakes, then climbed onto the bank. When Steven saw me, he laughed, relieved I was still alive. But I laughed, too—because I didn't want to get out.

I never would have made it across that river without my mother's influence, but I never could have made it back without my dad's.

My mom made sure I knew how to swim.

But my dad made sure I knew when to start singing.

CHAPTER 3

Skydive at Least Once

A year after my wedding, when I was invited to check off "skydive at least once," my husband was the first to object. Steven's afraid of heights.

My brother had already gone skydiving with friends, Steven reminded me. I didn't *have* to do this.

It was true: I'd suggested when we read the list in my brother's kitchen that whichever ones we'd done, I wouldn't do again. We'd each blog about them. But the list was beginning to feel more like my assignment, and his to support me doing it.

The idea emerged when the TV show *Chasing News* called. The producer said they wanted to help me check off a list item on-air. Skydiving was the only one I thought compelling enough. I suggested we do it at the Jersey Shore, so I could see my dad's Ferris wheel the way he now saw it. *Chasing News* would pay for everything but could only do it on a weekday. I was now using every vacation day I had for the list.

The night before my jump, I couldn't sleep, so I watched an interview Leonardo DiCaprio gave Oprah about getting injured while skydiving and how nobody should ever try it.

I woke up the next day at 7 a.m. It was cloudy and rainy, not good conditions. I reached for my phone on the nightstand—I'd missed a call from *Chasing News*. The voicemail was so garbled that I couldn't make it out. But as we drove to Skydive East Coast, I got another call: Skydiving was postponed.

"Well," I said to Steven, "I guess we're going to Storybook Land!"

Storybook Land, it turned out, was close to the airfield. When I'd discovered this, we'd planned on going after, as a reward. I hadn't been there in thirty-three years.

I'd forgotten how weird it was.

The park consisted of a dozen small houses connected by a path that ran through them a la Candyland. The princess houses still housed princesses, lying on a bed, waiting for their prince to come.

When my mom and dad took me there as a kid, the princesses terrified me. I thought they were real.

Even though I was old enough now to know better, I was still afraid. Not of the princesses being real, but of my having become one.

* * *

MY SUMMER OF ANXIETY at age eleven, when I feared I'd die on Morey's Pier, subsided by fall. My trouble sleeping did not.

I usually slept with my mom when it got bad enough. But then she met my stepdad.

My mom met Jim, a fellow guidance counselor, at a divorcées' retreat at my aunt's church. We'd switched to an Episcopal one after the divorce. She didn't want to be Catholic anymore, she said, because the Catholic Church wanted her to annul her marriage, and she "couldn't just pretend it never happened." So I had a First Communion *and* a First Confirmation, which seemed like overkill to me.

A requirement for a First Communion is a First Confession. But I couldn't think of any sins I'd committed. "Maybe you were mean to your brother," the priest said. But I wasn't. We were best friends.

That summer my mom bought Dave a portable black-and-white TV, so we stayed up watching *Saturday Night Live* when she went on dates. She also bought him twin beds, so I started sleeping in his room.

When I started missing the school bus and sleeping in on weekends, my mom took me to a specialist in Philadelphia, who diagnosed me with a delayed circadian rhythm—my quality of sleep was poor, he said. But he believed I'd grow out of it.

I was a happy kid. If I wasn't reading books for hours on the living room couch, I was singing into a hairbrush to Madonna in the basement. On weekends, when Jim's kids visited, we staged lip synch shows in that basement. It was like having a party twice a month.

But I was also kinder than most kids. And at a certain age, kindness makes you a target.

In seventh grade my school bus started picking up orphans, who lived in an orphanage a neighborhood over. I befriended one—Ginny, a girl with thick glasses and wavy, short hair. We mostly put on leftover makeup from my modeling course after school—my mom said the course was good for my shyness and the slouch I'd developed. It also meant I couldn't sleep in on Saturdays.

At Barbizon, we'd learned about makeup, table etiquette, filming a TV commercial, photo shoots, and how to walk a runway. By the end of seventh grade, I was modeling dresses in the fanciest hotel in Delaware. My dad arrived late. He found me hiding in the dressing room and told me I looked like Cheryl Tiegs.

In eighth grade Ginny slept over regularly. She started stealing my clothes. A shirt would go missing, and I'd later find it in my closet with her initials on it. That fall, we met a boy we both liked who liked me. Shaun called on the phone at night to talk to both of us. But one night he talked to me longer, which sent Ginny into a rage.

She rounded up a few girls to taunt me in class. Soon this was happening on weekends, too. They'd drink and prank-call my house.

At a Halloween party, we sat in a circle in a living room playing Truth or Dare. A girl challenged me. I said, "Truth." She asked if I'd gotten my first period. I had, that summer, when my mom was on her honeymoon. My mom cried when she found out, upset she'd missed it. Ginny knew this story, but the girl didn't. They both said I was lying. A few minutes later, a cold sensation hit my tailbone, through the back of my dress. I turned around to find them pouring fake blood on it.

I ran to the bathroom—the dress was my mom's. Washing out the blood was what I focused on to avoid the horror of what had just happened.

I called my mom and asked her to pick me up. At home she said the same thing she always said: "You have to ignore them." She was well-practiced by then at talking me out of anxiety.

When I took to my bed, nobody could get me out of it. The humiliation had been too much.

One night, a few days later, I considered walking downstairs, but stopped when I overheard my mom and Jim. "She's not as strong as you," he said. He could have been talking about somebody else, but I assumed he meant me.

My mom said I needed therapy.

After my dad left, my mom called the priest who'd married them, and he suggested a Jesuit monk for support. Brother David later referred her to a therapist.

Dr. Dutton recommended a local children's therapist. I started going once a week.

My grandmother typically drove me, often grumbling I had no business seeing a doctor because I was "already perfect." On the rare occasion my dad took me, he said he didn't believe in psychiatrists.

When my mom drove, she reminded me what I should talk about while there. Afterward, she'd ask what was said. Sometimes I'd forgotten to bring up something. Other times, she disagreed with what the doctor suggested.

We were so close now that I was beginning to feel that whatever happened to me also happened to her, in equal measure. So I had to be careful about what happened to me.

Dr. Jemail mainly taught me meditation and hypnosis. The next year, when I was still oversleeping, my mom took me to see someone else.

Since remarrying, five years after her divorce, my mom had considered selling our house. At first whenever she and Jim talked about it, I ran to my bedroom yelling, "You can't make me leave!" and slammed the door.

Atop a white bookshelf in my bedroom then sat an old coffee tin I'd decorated in kindergarten; it read MY FAMILY in big, black letters. Out of it sprouted pipe cleaners ending in green paper leaves, each inscribed with a different name: MOMMY, DADDY, DAVID, LAURA.

I'd sit on my bed and stare at it, wondering if it was still true.

But when the trouble with Ginny started, moving suddenly seemed a great idea.

We moved across town on a Friday. I picked a bedroom in the same spot where mine had been in the old house, the sunset spot. The room was a more normal size, which relieved me—and no balcony! The night we moved in, I stared through a bedroom window to the street below, thinking about how I'd have to pretend what happened with Ginny had never happened if I wanted to fit in at my new school. I'd have to pretend I was OK with my mom's remarrying, too. I'd have to adjust to this new life, pretend to fit in with rich kids, even though I didn't.

I felt cloaked in shame but decided this was how everyone felt, all the time, and I was only just now seeing it.

I started seeing Dr. Yanez in ninth grade. Most of my high school friends were being groomed for the Ivy League. I was voted treasurer of my class. I'd never before experienced popularity, and I couldn't say no to any of it. I'd spent most of my life sheltered in the gifted program. I took projects to a level of detail where they didn't need to go, even if it meant an all-nighter that left me so tired, I had to stay home the next day. I'd stay at my grandmother's house when this happened. But in high school, this didn't work anymore—if I got derailed, I couldn't catch up as quickly.

My mom decided whatever Dr. Yanez was doing wasn't working.

My junior year I joined marching band. At a night game, I met a cute senior who played saxophone, who drove me to the diner where the kids who smoked and wore flannels hung out. There was a division in 1994 in pop culture at our school. Half of us were in a John

Hughes fantasy of our older siblings' youth. Jason wanted to be in the other half. Over coffee he told me about his grunge band, who played Smashing Pumpkins covers. They hadn't come up with a name yet, but they were thinking of basing it on *Catcher in the Rye*.

My dad never met Jason. My mom and stepdad weren't fans. They hated that he kept me out late. They hated that I wore his Nirvana shirts. To be fair, nobody liked this. By November of junior year, I was doing poorly in every class.

Jason was my first everything, almost. When his grunge band attracted groupies, his self-image changed. He acted like such a jerk that a friend said, "Laura, you have to break up with him." So one Friday I called him, hoping he'd call my bluff.

Nobody was home but my stepdad when I did this. Tearfully I went downstairs and found him in the kitchen. I'd begun avoiding places Jim might be. He had a way of sharing space that made you feel he didn't want you in it.

I told him everything. He said, "This is just what men do."

I left fearing this would happen again, and probably many times, because men suddenly change for no reason and abandon you.

Just like my dad.

That winter, I asked my dad what he'd contribute to my college funds. He said he'd offer a few hundred a year, as his father had. I asked him this in a Burger King and was confused when his eyes misted over.

My mom later said she found his answer dubious. She revealed he hadn't ever paid child support. Those times I'd seen him slip money under a vase on the mantel, he was only leaving $100, "for groceries," he said. And those times hadn't happened much.

The spring of my junior year, my history teacher assigned me a paper on the women's movement. I was excited because I loved feminism. But once I started reading *The Feminine Mystique*, I couldn't understand how there was this group of women's libbers in the 1960s but also one in the late 1800s—those who got women the vote. I couldn't make sense of what had transpired in between. How had they lost so

SKYDIVE AT LEAST ONCE

much momentum? I felt compelled to read all of Betty Friedan's book, not just some of it. For the first time, I encountered a project too big to complete. Simultaneously, my brain, like a car a few miles from Empty, was ready to give out.

In the middle of *The Feminine Mystique*, my depression won.

It reminded me of when I was in elementary school, when my gym teacher set up an obstacle course. It was my favorite week in gym. Climbing the rope was the final stop, which intimidated me. But the obstacle I liked least was the tunnel. It was made of parachute material, held together by metal seams. It rocked side to side as I crawled through. I had to keep going until I reached the light.

My depression at sixteen was like that tunnel. Except I couldn't crawl out, and nobody else could crawl in. After a while, I gave up hope of ever joining anyone again. The people in my life, whom I normally enjoyed life with, were blissfully unaware that I was stuck. And if I tried to explain it to them, they didn't believe me.

That Sunday, I missed going out to lunch with my dad, which unlike school was something I never missed. I stayed in bed and asked my mom to say I was sick. She must have told him what kind of sick I was, because he came up to see me when he brought my brother back.

"Your mother's concerned," he said, sitting at the end of my bed.

I asked him why he hadn't saved anything for my education.

"Why are you so materialistic?" he snapped. "Don't you have everything provided for you here?"

Then he said we would "heal together." He created a scheme where every week he would take me to church. My mom explained that I needed more than that.

Later that week he called my mom in the middle of the night, crying.

"Don't give up on Laura," he said. "She's just like me."

A week later, my mom took me to see her former doctor. Dr. Dutton told me about anti-depressants and put me on a brand-new one, Zoloft. He said we'd know in a few weeks whether I had depression if it worked.

On Easter, I was sitting in the dining room at my grandmother's house, eating angel food cake, when suddenly I crawled out of the tunnel.

"Mom," I said, "I feel better."

I got my grades up by the end of the year, but they still weren't what they once were. My mom thought an evaluation at the local children's hospital might help.

I'd always taken a long time to finish tests. In fact, I almost never finished them. This, plus my trouble waking up, convinced the doctors I had Attention Deficit Hyperactivity Disorder.

They took me off Zoloft and put me on Effexor and Adderall and prescribed talk therapy. They made me remove things from my schedule, like A.P. English and marching band. Having to call the drum major, my friend, to tell him I was quitting was the hardest thing I'd ever done—mostly because it meant my classmates would now know there was something wrong with me.

By graduation, I was happy to attend college in another state.

Getting a diagnosis of ADHD means extra time on tests. But this doesn't translate when you're a Fine Arts major, where there are no tests, only assignments. By the end of my first semester at James Madison University, in Virginia, I faced a pile of undone art projects I'd been given extra time to do and only a week left to do them. I didn't go to bed at night but kept taking the Adderall as prescribed—every six hours (they'd meant in the daytime). By the end of the week, I'd slept three hours each night, and I still wasn't done. When I went back to school after Christmas, I took to my bed. My mom and stepdad drove five hours to campus to take me home. My dad had said at graduation that I wasn't ready to attend college so far away, but nobody listened—least of all me.

My mom convinced me to apply to University of Delaware, the state school. I'd take a few classes that summer, then move onto campus, she said.

But I'd have to switch to a new doctor, too. I couldn't get my prescriptions from the children's hospital anymore.

The first thing I noticed about Dr. MacIntosh, who resembled Barack Obama, was his paisley bowtie. His office was nicer than the ones I'd been in. He said I had "separation anxiety," common in children of divorce. He prescribed talk therapy with his colleague, Mr. Raymond, who practiced a treatment called EMDR. He took me off Effexor and Adderall and put me on Prozac.

My mom and stepdad paid for our education but suggested my brother and I earn spending money. So I found a job at a coffee shop. My coworkers had tattoos and dreadlocks. All were well-read and cultured and talked about visiting New York. One day my dad came in, holding a copy of the district award-winning poem I'd written in high school. "This is some sophisticated stuff," he said while ordering his tea. "I read it again last night. You're a natural."

I blushed. He was always doing things like this.

EMDR stands for Eye-Movement Desensitization and Reprocessing therapy. One day Mr. Raymond, who looked like Santa Claus, pulled out the light machine, a black horizontal box on a stand with a row of tiny, green LED lights, which flashed left to right. The lights help you cognitively reframe an event. It's a treatment commonly used for Post-Traumatic Stress Disorder.

My second or third time trying it, I felt hypnotized. As Mr. Raymond asked what I saw in my mind, I told him I could see a small girl, by herself, sitting on a bed in an empty room. I said it felt like she was sitting in my heart.

"She's lonely," I said, crying. "She feels like nobody listens to her."

I said, "I think maybe the little girl is me."

I said, "I think maybe I'm the one not listening."

At University of Delaware, I still got extra time on tests, but I took them separately in a center on campus. And extra time for art assignments wasn't allowed.

As I wrapped up my classes my first summer, I met a tall blond Italian boy at a condo party. Afterward, I drove my friend home, repeating, "He's so beautiful."

Chris called the next day. We went on a date that night. In a diner after the movie, he shared a poem he'd already written about me.

Chris was a journalism major. He didn't care that I was on Prozac or that I'd given up on JMU. When we made out in his red Toyota, he told me he was born the same day Elvis died—in the same hospital.

Chris helped me move into my new dorm at UD. My mom wasn't taking any chances this time, so she hired a time-management expert, who met with me once a week. She mostly taught me how to make and adhere to lists. By the end of the semester, I had my mom convinced I didn't need the expert anymore. Chris was a good influence. He was a star at the college paper—good enough to get a newspaper internship. He encouraged me to apply for the graphic design program at UD.

But by the next fall, my design professors were advising us to work in the art studio all night—and even steal each other's ideas. The program was competitive—after the first year, half my class would be cut. The amount of time I devoted to it impeded on my other classes.

Chris now managed the whole sports desk at the paper, so when we saw each other, we were both tired. By the end of the semester, I had Cs in my design classes and Ds in the others, so my mom made me quit the program, leave campus, and come home. Chris broke up with me.

"When I'm not with you, I worry about you more than I miss you," he said.

The month I turned twenty-one, both of my last living grandparents died. This was hard on my mom, who was close to my grandmother. My dad said his dad had been dead to him for years. It was strange seeing my parents together at the funerals. Chris came to my grandmother's funeral, even though we'd broken up.

I was heartbroken. But then one day, as I cried in my Honda in the mall parking lot, a calm came over me.

I'm responsible for my own happiness, I realized. *Not Chris, not my parents. Me.*

I'd spent most of my breaks at my job at the coffee shop reading magazines, which I'd done since I was thirteen. I realized I didn't have to be a graphic designer to work for one.

I could be a writer.

That summer, I switched my major from Fine Arts to English. After I got straight As, my mom let me live on campus again. I started seeing a new doctor, who specialized in young adults. Dr. Cohn put me on Wellbutrin, which affects norepinephrine and dopamine, blamed for causing ADHD. My new plan was to get a degree in journalism, get a job at a magazine in New York, and then get a master's degree in art.

I was appointed city news editor at the school newspaper. But I became so immersed that I started skipping classes. I didn't tell anyone for months.

When I slept through a weekly appointment at the police station, the newspaper fired me.

This time when I went home, my mom's patience had reached its limit.

My dad dropped me off in front of the house one Sunday and said, "You're driving your mother nuts."

"Until you contribute to my education, you don't get to have an opinion on that," I said angrily.

His eyes filled with tears and he drove away. A month later, I watched from my window as he put three books on writing in our mailbox.

By summer's end, my mom, stepdad, and I were in my mom's old therapist's office.

I was told we were going for family counseling, but in the middle of it, my stepdad said, "Laura has some issues of her own to deal with first."

I was commuting to campus by car and felt the worst about myself I'd ever felt. It was taking me seven years to finish college. I'd loved working at the newspaper. I couldn't believe I'd screwed that up, too.

Dr. Dutton, who'd put me on Zoloft in high school, and looked like Russell Crowe, said my poor time management came from a new diagnosis called bipolar II. He said its sufferers go through "hypomania," what he thought I'd experienced at the paper. He said the best way to determine if I had it was to add medications.

First, he put me on Parnate, a monoamine oxidase inhibitor, or MAOI, something most doctors won't prescribe anymore. A patient taking an MAOI has to avoid foods that contain tyramine—mostly wine and cheese—or they risk having a stroke. The doctor is legally required to prescribe an antidote to a blood pressure spike when they prescribe it. Dr. Dutton told me to keep this little gel cap in my pocket.

After a few weeks, the Parnate started working. I felt calmer.

It was cold in Dr. Dutton's office, so he'd often bring me a blanket and warm tea. One day he noticed I sat with my arms and legs crossed, because I was cold, and said, "Laura, you are allowed to take up space."

His office had a wall of books he said I could read whenever I wanted. But if it was a book about bipolar or depression, he said, even if I bought it at a bookstore, I needed his permission.

"Have you always been so thin?" he sometimes asked. I took it as a compliment—until he added an atypical antipsychotic to my regimen. He didn't tell me Zyprexa makes people gain sixty pounds in one year.

Soon I was hungry all the time. I got a Big Mac every Friday on my way home from campus. I was still taking classes and writing for the newspaper, and by November I was applying for internships. I was also on four more medicines: Topamax, an anticonvulsant; Synthroid, a hypothyroidism med (though my thyroxin levels were normal); a diuretic (for the bloat he'd observed during my period); and Ambien.

By January, I couldn't fit into my clothes. I complained to Dr. Dutton, who reluctantly took me off Zyprexa—but said he had to replace it with another drug.

The first week after New Year's, he put me on Seroquel, which made my face break out in large blemishes. It was the first week of my internship at *Delaware Today* magazine. My mom felt so sorry for me that she took me to the Estée Lauder counter and bought me whatever

I wanted. When I complained, Dr. Dutton took me off Seroquel and put me on Risperdal, which gave me little blemishes. The next week he took me off Risperdal and put me on Lamictal, which gave me a flat affect and a delay when I talked. So he took me off that and two weeks later put me on a newer antipsychotic, Geodon.

He said he was frustrated by my sensitivity to side effects.

By March I was on nine medications, and in the previous seven months, had been on thirteen. A strange odor surrounded me, particularly after I used the bathroom. My urine smelled like plastic.

I asked my mom if I could stop seeing Dr. Dutton, but she said she would stop funding my education if I did. She wanted to find an answer, she said.

I was forever on the lookout for a tyramine reaction. My mom made me a Lean Cuisine dinner one night, not realizing Parmesan was in it, and my blood pressure skyrocketed. After a few more ER visits that spring, always false alarms, the nurses recommended I buy a blood pressure monitor. On one ER visit, a doctor asked what medications I was on. He was concerned when I said I was taking both Wellbutrin and Parnate. He left to make a phone call and when he returned told us Dr. Dutton said he didn't have me on Wellbutrin, that I was lying.

Dr. Dutton had said for a while he wanted my dad to come in. This was difficult, since my dad didn't believe in psychiatrists, but eventually I convinced him. I'd forgotten to warn Dr. Dutton the night he came, and he made my dad sit in the waiting room—he wouldn't let him into his office. My mom came into the office with me, and Dr. Dutton said she'd reported that I wasn't taking my Ambien. He said he'd have to stop seeing me because I "wasn't a compliant patient."

"Laura," he said, "you're a failure at life."

When I walked out I considered stealing a magazine. In my mom's car in the parking lot, I stared at the floor from the passenger seat as she lectured me.

"Laura, stop playing games," my dad chimed in from the back seat.

I told him he didn't know what he was talking about.

A few days later, my mom got me started with a new doctor, Dr. Rowen, who said there was no reason for me to be on so many drugs. She set up a plan to wean me off. But I'd been on the regimen so long that the withdrawal was excruciating.

We had our first family meeting in the living room that month. Slouched sideways on the couch, I told my mom, stepdad, and brother that it would be so much easier for them if I didn't exist. I said I wished they had another daughter, another sister.

"But I don't want another sister," my brother said, "because she wouldn't be *you*."

Dr. Rowen checked me into a treatment center the week after college graduation because I couldn't get off the medicines on my own. It was Johns Hopkins Hospital, whose mental health researchers are the best in the field.

My graduation barely felt real. At my brother's and my graduation party, my dad entertained everyone with jokes and impressions. But every time someone congratulated my dad, he said the same thing: "I had nothing to do with it."

After my mom checked me into the hospital, a nurse asked if I'd ever tried to hurt myself. She seemed confused that I was there voluntarily. The nurse at the front desk took anything that could be a weapon, including my razor, and said there was a time limit on bathroom use and our bedroom doors couldn't be closed. They'd come by to check on us every hour of the night, she said.

My mom left the hospital crying. She hadn't known they would lock me in. She told the doctors the hospital was a mistake, that she was sorry she'd agreed with my new doctor, who'd given her a different impression. But they said it was too late.

She told me years later that this was the worst day of her life.

The first thing I did was get on the computer, to chat online. I was missing the graduation party for Kelly, whom I'd sworn to secrecy about where I was. The only others who knew were my mom, dad, stepdad, brother, ex-boyfriend Chris, and new boyfriend Frank. I sprayed lavender and rose oil around my bedroom, which felt like a dorm room but less pleasant. Through the window I saw the medical students walking several stories below.

A middle-aged woman with a gray bob came into my room with her husband and kids. Her face looked raw. She was my roommate. I drew with the kids, which was what I always did with kids, who are always fascinated to find a grown-up who can draw.

In the living room, which resembled a study lounge, I met the oldest mood disorder patient, Esther, a Black woman who shuffled when she walked. Bipolar patients who take Thorazine have a telltale gait. A few other patients had it, too.

There were only seven of us when I was admitted, and I was the youngest. Esther was the sweetest old lady I'd ever met. But she kept talking about how thirsty she was—another effect of her medications.

The structure of our days was simple: Wake at 8:00 a.m. for breakfast; go to the pharmacy closet to get meds (for me, the doses were decreasing); meet with whichever nurse was assigned to us. By day two, I was weary of being asked about hurting myself. I realized the only way I was getting out of there was if I acted as sane as possible.

In the afternoon, we had our group session, which meant sitting in a circle in a private room, talking about our pasts and what we'd do when we left. One of the younger patients asked how she should explain her hospital stay on a job interview.

"Oh, you should never tell anyone you were in here," the nurse said. Everyone nodded his or her head in agreement.

Art therapy was my favorite time of the week, but not because they let us draw. It was because they let us go outside. A rectangle of light sat in the corner of the art room. A door opened onto a courtyard, about ten square feet. We were allowed out there for ten minutes.

As the sun hit my face, I noticed a tree whose branches had grown outward, through the chain-link fence. Even the tree knew nothing could survive being locked up.

On my fourth day we got four new patients. One was a girl finally younger than me, a longhaired brunette named Cynthia. She told me later that night, as we watched *Saturday Night Live*, that her parents were doctors in the hospital who kept her there to keep an eye on her. She seemed amazed I'd never done any recreational drugs. She'd already been in rehab. She talked a lot about running away to New York, and I told her I wanted to live there. She gave me her AIM screenname so we could stay in touch.

Cynthia told me how annoyed she was already with the other patients on our floor, the ones who were mostly our age or younger but not part of the mood disorder ward: the eating disorder group. They were pretty. Most wore pajamas and pushed around IVs. Most were considerate and pepped up to write letters back home.

The second new patient was twenty-nine but looked seventeen. Her skin barely sheathed her bones. Her blonde hair, cut short and spiky, adorned a face of edges; her blue eyes sat in hollowed sockets. She hunched in a wheelchair in flared yoga pants, a baby tee, and a hooded sweatshirt. The eating disorder patients prided themselves on not being the ward's "crazy" inhabitants, but the new girl's bipolar made her an exception.

By this day, my withdrawal had reached a peak, and I spent more time in my bedroom. There was a lot of chattering going on with the girls and their stationery. When my withdrawal headache got too painful, I walked away. And then the yelling started.

"There's too much noise in here!" the blonde girl in the wheelchair screamed.

The shrill filled the living room and ran around its corners and down the halls. Everyone around her stopped and stared.

"There's too much noise!"

She'd only been in the ward one day. I couldn't imagine what they'd done to her in that time to make her as overwhelmed as I felt.

After three days, I'd had enough of watching that much pain. I wanted to scream for these people—I wanted to reach into their hearts and take out what others called illness. I wanted to make their pain real and separate, so they wouldn't embrace it anymore.

But I had no power to do that. It was hard enough to do it for myself.

So I hid.

"There's too much noise!" the girl yelled.

When two of the male nurses picked her up out of her chair, I ran back to my room. My back against the doorframe, I heard a high-pitched voice trailing down the hall, the slam of a heavy metal door, and a thud. And then silence. The patients told me later the nurses gave her electric shock therapy.

For the rest of the week I hid from the noise when I had to, but mostly out in the open with headphones. My Discman blocked it out, and if I closed my eyes, I could pretend I wasn't there. Almost.

The third new patient arrived at dinnertime, a heavy-set, bald British man in his forties, there for schizophrenia. He told me his name was Nathan Ulysses Thomas and he'd always found it funny that his initials spelled NUT.

"Oh! My initials spell LAC," I said.

"Well, then," he said, "what are you lacking, Laura?"

By eleven that night, Nathan got a roommate when the fourth new patient arrived. A swarthy, confused twenty-one-year-old slid into the living room as I typed to my boyfriend Frank on the computer. He wore sweatpants, a disheveled sweatshirt, and one sock—no shoes. I overheard the nurses say he'd arrived like that. He looked like a were-wolf post-transition. In the middle of the night, he accidentally walked into my bedroom. The nurses in the hallway directed him back to his. At breakfast, Cynthia told me she was in love.

On the fifth day, my mom and stepdad came to visit. I'd become attuned to the beeping of the elevators outside my door. Something about how casually staffers came in and out annoyed me. The medical students on the street, small as ants, had no idea how good they had it. I was still in the middle of my sane routine, but I enjoyed introducing my new friends to my mom, who seemed despondent.

That night, after they were gone, I got a terrible headache and bout of dizziness when they decreased my Topamax too fast. It was the only medication left that Dr. Rowen wanted me to get off of. The nurses didn't believe me that something felt wrong, so I went to the bathroom to cry.

I pulled the lid down on the toilet and sat on it, resting my face in my hands, wishing I could rip the pressure from my head. I'd found during withdrawal headaches that if I sobbed, the pain would go away. Sitting there, I thought about how nobody I knew had been through this. Nobody had ever witnessed what I'd witnessed that week.

Suddenly I saw myself as the little girl I'd once been, and wept for her. I felt I'd let her down. She'd been my responsibility, and I'd slipped up, and now here she was, crying on a toilet in a mental hospital.

I vowed I'd never abandon her again.

The next morning, when I met with the supervising doctor, he said I'd be released later that day. He said he wasn't convinced I had depression, but believed I had anxiety, which sometimes resulted in depression. He said he didn't think I had ADHD or bipolar II either. I tried convincing him otherwise.

I was happy to be free but sad to leave my friends. I'd let one of the eating disorder patients listen to my Discman. I'd been playing one song from the a cappella CD my brother's college group recorded on repeat: Sarah McLachlan's "Angel."

I left the CD with her.

When I saw Frank, I was relieved to tell him about my adventures in person. We'd dated off and on for two years. As we sat in the mall's food court, he said his parents had flipped through his high school yearbook, looking for a girl he could date instead of me.

"Why?" I asked.

"Because..." he said. "You were in a hospital."

I saw Dr. Rowen that week, and she put me on Depakote. When it started making my hair fall out, I said I was done. I weaned myself off my Wellbutrin alone and remained on a low dose of Parnate, which I planned to also one day get off of.

"And you did that all by yourself," she said. "You've got a good head on your shoulders, you know."

* * *

AFTER THE HOSPITAL, I hid that I'd been there. Like the nurses had recommended. I hid that I'd been like a sleeping princess: a girl who can't wake up.

Steven and I drove to the beach after our Storybook Land visit, the day skydiving was postponed, stopping on the way at Whole Foods. When he got back in the car, he said, "I changed my mind about skydiving. I was just thinking as I stood in line in the store of who my heroes are, and I realized you are one of them. You're my hero now. Not just because of what you've been through, but because of what you're doing with it."

Maybe I'm not a sleeping princess after all, I thought.

Maybe I'm the prince.

The night before my new skydiving date, I barely slept.

I woke up the next morning to a sunny, clear sky. The drive was an hour and a half. I rarely drove anywhere anymore, but Steven couldn't get off work. When I arrived at the airfield, I was relieved to learn that Rohan Mohanty, the reporter skydiving with me, was late, too.

The airfield was small and populated only by men. Rohan joined me at a picnic table to watch a training video, narrated by a man with a long, black beard. "What is this? *Duck Dynasty*?" he asked.

Rohan didn't seem like someone I'd befriend. He wore Ed Hardy shirts and lifted weights. He was the kind of handsome TV anchors are, with chiseled features and a broad, white smile, gleaming next to his brown Indian skin. He'd just jumped out of bed for this—his hair was a mess. He smoked. But as soon as he got his camera working, he went into a different mode.

Rohan said it was his shared birthday week with his toddler son and dad, whose recent death had compelled him to take the assignment. I told him I shared a birthday week with my dad, too.

Nuclear George, Rohan's tandem skydiver, showed us what to do when we stepped off the plane's wing. "You want to keep both hands on your shoulder straps," he said, "never on the tandem jumper's hand." He held his left fist out and slapped it with his right hand, yelling, "Don't...do...THIS!" The tandem jumper would hold a video camera, and he'd also use that hand to pull the ripcord. Next, we were to hold both arms out and smile.

When the parachute opened, we'd have five minutes before landing. Nuclear George said he didn't want anyone breaking bones. I couldn't tell if he was joking.

As we walked toward the plane, Rohan yelled into his chest-mounted camera, "We're doing this for all the dads out there! Happy Father's Day!"

I was chosen for the seat beneath the dashboard, which wasn't a seat at all. I felt like my cat whenever we take her to the vet. The pilot looked twelve. He was flying a plane with three whooping men and me. The door didn't close all the way; as we neared 10,000 feet, I could still see the ground growing smaller through the gap. I was seated too low, thank God, to look out windows.

As they laughed and hollered, I looked around and realized every man jumping was a dad. I closed my eyes and said a silent prayer. When I opened them, suddenly there were no longer three dads in the plane, but four—my dad was there, too.

Isn't it amazing, I heard him say, *that I didn't get to do this in my life, but you do?*

I had nothing to explain why he'd wanted to do this, except for a few lines he'd written in his book. Mick Carney wrote *The Why? Generation (in a Why-Not World.)* in 1976, the year he was married. He tried to have the book published the year I was born—the year he wrote the list—but ended up self-publishing and giving copies as Christmas presents. My mom bound them in her teachers' lounge at school. In one chapter he described parasailing on his honeymoon, simultaneously scolding himself for caring more about adventures than typical honeymoon activities.

He'd ascended 150 feet when he floated above the Bahamas. My plane had now reached 20,000.

When a tandem jumper straps you to his stomach, there's no going back. As I kneeled forward, my tandem jumper, a handsome Brazilian named Jones, aimed the camera at me and asked how I felt. "Great!" I lied, then whispered, "I love you, honey," in case it was the last time Steven saw me alive.

Every noise muted, and a voice in my head said something.

Let go.

Jones opened the door and jumped.

At first, I screamed. But then I was OK. Because I was flying.

I felt like Christopher Reeve on a green screen, except this scenery was all real. The bays and beaches and trees and highways and tiny little trucks moving along them were all real.

I focused on my instructions: hold onto my straps, then extend my arms and smile. The rest was up to God now.

Next thing I knew, Rohan and Nuclear George were twirling to the right of us, screaming all the way down.

Jones pulled the ripcord, and our bodies jolted. "Welcome to my office!" he yelled.

"I think I might puke," I yelled. "I'm so sorry!"

"It's very common!" he yelled back.

My vomit floated mid-air, then some fell on me. When I landed, that puke would be on TV. I suspected that somewhere my dad was laughing.

Our descent was soft and serene, like an invisible hand had caught us. Rohan was less lucky. George had steered them ahead so we wouldn't collide. Their landing was the most difficult he'd ever executed.

"It's OK," Rohan said. "I'm better at jumping than most."

He told me about the time his friends dared him to jump off a cliff. He'd nearly drowned. Rohan's mom, unlike my mom, hadn't given him swimming lessons.

"What did it feel like?" I asked.

"It felt like letting go."

Rohan pulled out his microphone, laughing about the puke. "What do you want to say to our audience about today?" he asked.

"I just want to say that as scary as this was, it wasn't nearly as scary as losing your dad because of a distracted driver," I said, looking at the camera. "I jumped out of an airplane today so that you will remember not to use your phone while driving."

Probably not what my dad had in mind when he wrote item twenty-eight.

"Speak to a TV audience."

"When you jump out of a plane with someone, you get to know them really fast," Rohan said in the TV segment. After our jump, we talked for two hours straight.

Rohan's dad, an immigration lawyer, had been in his late sixties when he died of a heart condition nobody knew about. One day he took a nap. Rohan couldn't wake him up.

I texted my mom to tell her I was OK and called Steven. He told me he'd been checking news reports all morning. "Why are you talking so fast?" he asked, laughing. Adrenaline had amped my energy, but I hadn't realized it because Rohan's energy matched mine.

After deciding our dads had arranged our meeting, we walked back to our cars. Rohan promised that one day I'd be the first guest on his talk show. This was his adrenaline talking, but some of it was his natural grandiosity. My dad had this, too. He always had a new idea, a new business, a new scheme. But I agreed to appear on Rohan's show, because unlike my reactions to my dad in later years, I believed he would have one.

I left the airfield and drove to Beach Haven—a day at the shore was my reward. Placing my towel on the sand, I pulled out a Joseph Campbell book and read:

There was an article in the New York papers a few months ago about a kid who dove into the Hudson River to save a drowning dog and then had to be saved himself. When asked why he'd dove in, he said, 'Because it was my dog.' Then there was the girl who went into a burning building—twice—to save her little brother and sister, and when she was asked why she'd done it, she said, 'Because I loved them.' Such a one is then acting, Schopenhauer answers, out of an instinctive recognition of the truth that he and that other in fact are one.

Tears streamed down my cheeks. I buried my face in my towel. I knew exactly why I'd done what I had that day.

I cleaned myself up and walked toward the ocean, thinking about the surfing list item. I stared into the murky water and said my thoughts out loud.

"You're next."

CHAPTER 4

Ride a Horse Fast

The day after skydiving, I told my husband in a Starbucks that I had nothing left to fear in life. Steven's fear of heights made this impossible to relate to.

"But at least this list item was free," he said.

Steven's money anxiety had complicated planning our wedding. It was part of why I'd come up with New Mexico—where we'd gone for our first dating anniversary, after our first year together in New York.

New Mexico was cheap.

* * *

THE YEAR AFTER THE HOSPITAL, I applied for every journalism job I could find. I also emailed and messaged whatever guy struck my fancy online, no matter where he lived. I wasn't long for Delaware, suspecting that any number of people knew about the hospital.

Telling each new guy about it was like a test. By my twenty-fifth birthday, after being dumped the fifth time, I lay on the couch at my dad's apartment, where we were celebrating our shared birthday week. He said I was like him, cranky when sleep-deprived. "What's up with you and these guys from another era?" he asked. Michael, who'd just broken up with me, wanted to live in the year 1939. Chris had loved Frank Sinatra so much that he'd worn a fedora.

I wrote to Steven that day. It was snowing, strange for late March. Unlike the others, I hadn't found Steven on a dating site. I'd found his LiveJournal, one of the earliest servers for blogs. I loved the writer Dave Eggers, who ran a popular literary journal. In 2002, Eggers guest-edited an anthology that included a story by a writer I looked up on LiveJournal, and listed in her group of friends was someone whose group of friends listed Steven.

When I read Steven's profile, I couldn't get over how many of his interests were like mine. He showed a vulnerability I'd never seen a man show in his writing.

When I saw that he lived in Seattle, I laughed. This could never work.

First, we chatted about writing. He told me he'd started a literary journal. Then one night he sent me two photos. His blue eyes seemed familiar and kind.

Finally, I summoned the courage to tell him about the hospital. At 2:00 a.m., I typed the whole story.

"I think you're an amazing woman," he said.

I cried.

When I heard him say "hello" on the phone the first time it was like when I saw his eyes in the photo—it was a voice I already knew.

I told him I wasn't moving to Seattle. That year I'd dated guys as far away as Utah. I couldn't keep chasing other people's lives.

Later that week I heard back about an internship at an art magazine. It only paid ten dollars a day. But it was a magazine. And it was in *New York*.

I took the train up from Delaware. The interview was across the street from the Empire State Building. I walked around it afterward, looking up at its granite façade, its steel, lit roof, its spire that made it taller than any other building at one time.

A week later I got a call from the art magazine's editorial assistant, who asked how soon I could start.

Steven suggested visiting me three times that summer. If things worked out, he'd move in with a friend in Queens by summer's end, he said.

He set me up with my own LiveJournal account, and we read each other's entries every day. The voices in the writing he accepted for his literary journal were sometimes absurd. I learned there was room for my voice, too.

My mom bought my Honda so I'd have money to move with. My cousin Jimmy had moved to New York for an internship and was now working at the *New York Times*, so I arranged to spend a weekend with him that spring to look for an apartment.

The sun was bright the day I set out. My first apartment meeting, set up on Craigslist, was in Astoria, a northern part of Queens. The second was in Jackson Heights, or Little India, which felt like a foreign country.

The streets of Little India were lined with grocers and fruit stands, with fruits unlike any I'd ever seen and smells unlike any I'd ever smelled. Most of the men wore turbans. White mannequins in vibrant saris stood in the windows of retail shops, their teals and violets making them all the more stark. Rows of yellow-gold bracelets lined jewelry store windows, gleaming in the sun. The homes were garden apartments, with small plots of red roses climbing.

The scent of curry wafted out of the large brown marble entrance of the co-op when I was buzzed in. I walked by a wall of tiny mail-boxes, which looked like a card catalog, into an elevator that barely held two people.

Cristina, a Mexican American flamenco dancer, answered the door. At the end of the hall behind her sat a brown wooden piano with incense on top. The walls were white stucco, except for in the living room, where they were deep fuchsia. The furniture was sparse, and every surface held tall candles decorated with religious icons. Madonnas and crucifixes hung close to the ceiling.

Cristina invited me into the long, tall, white kitchen, whose one window had a view of the Empire State Building. I imagined sitting at its round table each morning, looking out at the city before leaving to conquer it. The back bedroom would be mine, she said. Jenny, who owned the place, was a flamenco dancer, too. Cristina would be in

Europe for a year. Jenny was moving in with her boyfriend, who lived down the hall. I'd pay $600 a month for a bedroom, but since they'd both be gone, the whole apartment would be mine.

A week later, my mom rode up with me so I could sign the renter's agreement and give my security deposit. She was terrified for me. Three weeks later I moved in.

I'd unpacked poorly when I moved home from college. I did an even worse job moving to New York. The magazine internship would only last three months, so I'd need more than just a suitcase, but I couldn't wrap my head around how much. In the end, my mom and Jim drove me up with a dozen packed garbage bags.

The day I moved in, and my mom tearfully left, I closed the door to my new bedroom and called Steven. "I think I made a mistake," I said. "My landlady is having sex in the living room."

Steven told me how proud he was of me. He said my internship would be wonderful and everything would get easier each day. And that he'd be there soon. We'd planned for him to visit by the end of the month.

The next day I got off the subway in Times Square and walked out into the big, bright streets. I checked my paper map for the nearest Internet café. I signed into AOL Instant Messenger and told Steven about the city. I hadn't brought my computer to New York. It didn't fit in a garbage bag.

My internship reminded me of being back at my college newspaper. I couldn't believe my luck. Nights were spent talking with Steven on the phone and weekends exploring. I'd walk all over, having no idea where I was going, but that was half the fun.

On the train each day I read Rainer Maria Rilke's *Letters to a Young Poet*:

> *There is here no measuring with time, no year matters, and ten years are nothing. Being an artist means, not reckoning and counting, but ripening like the tree, which does not force its sap and stands confident*

in the storms of spring without the fear that after them may come no
summer. It does come. But it comes only to the patient, who are there as
though eternity lay before them, so unconcernedly still and wide.

My first month in NYC, in the summer of 2003, was the rainiest on record.

The week before Steven's visit, I met with my landlady, Jenny, at a Starbucks on the Lower East Side. Jenny was Filipino and had long black hair. She wore dark lipstick and a black leather jacket. Despite seeming tough, she couldn't suppress her fear over a strange man from Seattle sleeping in her apartment. She thought Steven might kill me.

Steven was set to arrive at 10:00 a.m. at JFK that Friday. I woke up early and put in a load of laundry, hoping it would make me seem casual. As I rode the elevator from the basement, Frank Sinatra sang over the speaker, "New York...New York!" It was the only two lines the radio station ever played.

Steven called to say he was there. When I opened the heavy gold front doors, he smiled at me and hugged me, burying his face into my right shoulder.

It didn't feel like we were meeting for the first time.

It felt like he was coming home.

He'd gotten his wavy dark hair cut professionally for the first time in years that week and even bought contact lenses. He regretted his choice to wear a sweater.

"How was your flight?" I asked.

"Ha!" he laughed. "Terrible."

When we reached the fifth floor, Jenny was there, holding a black parka for the rain. "I noticed you didn't pack one," she said. Satisfied Steven wasn't a killer, she left.

I showed Steven our view of the Empire State Building, and we sat down in the kitchen. I asked if he wanted to watch the *SNL* anniversary show I'd taped. After ten minutes in my bedroom, I asked for a shoulder massage, my latest ploy to get men to touch me. I said, "I'm surprised you haven't kissed me yet." And he finally did.

We ordered Chinese food and played cards on my white bedspread that night. Photos and postcards from Steven's care packages lined my window.

We listened to Jeff Buckley, whom Steven had discovered when he was nineteen. The beauty in Buckley's songs is ineffable, his guitar and voice like divinity in the dark. They are joy and sorrow at the same time.

The next day, we had our first date at a restaurant in Hell's Kitchen, then meandered through the Lower East Side, stopping to see Steven's friend, a bouncer at a dive bar. We stopped in a psychic's apartment. She looked at my heart line on my palm and then skeptically at me. She said I would have a few loves in my life and maybe more than one at a time. She said my life line was long and would include tragedy. She said she saw a lot of travel in my future. When it was Steven's turn, she made me wait outside. I put my ear up to the door. She told him exactly the same thing.

I laughed and called it a racket. Steven said he hoped we'd be doing all that travel together.

When we stopped in a pizza parlor on St. Mark's Place, I asked for a job application. Steven was paying for the weekend; I had barely enough money to cover my rent.

We waited for the train back at the bright red station at Lexington Avenue and 53rd Street. I rested my head on Steven's lap. "I love you," he said.

"I love you, too," I said without thinking.

We'd both almost said it over the phone.

The moon shined brighter when Steven was there. I fit in his arms in a way I'd never felt before. I'd never known this was what love was—this feeling that you are OK, that you are safe with this person.

Steven's second visit was the Fourth of July, which was filled with thunderstorms like most of June. This made Steven giddy. We stared at the Empire State Building, lit up red, white, and blue, from my kitchen in the dark.

"Why do you love storms so much?" I asked.

72

"When I was little, my mom said it was the angels bowling," he said. "I calmed down all my classmates in kindergarten by telling them the same thing."

It was harder to say goodbye the second time.

In late July, I finally found a paying job, as a hostess at Outback Steakhouse.

In August, Steven visited again. He walked me to my first magazine interview—at *BlackBook* for a copy editor position. I'd found a spelling error in a letter to subscribers at my internship, so the research editor set up the interview. On the way we saw a puddle shaped like a heart. Steven said it was a good sign.

The Friday of his visit, we boarded a Chinatown bus to meet my family in Delaware. We met my dad for lunch, and I was just as proud to show him my name on a masthead as I was to introduce him to the love of my life.

We told my dad about my spelling error catch, and he told Steven he wasn't surprised, as I was "a spelling bee champ" as a kid. I reminded him I'd only gotten fourth place. He said the same thing he'd said then. "You were robbed!"

He told us he'd been getting heart palpitations. Since his enlarged heart diagnosis, he'd been putting off surgery. He also told us he'd just broken up with his live-in girlfriend after catching her making out with someone under a table at a party. "I never want you or David to speak to her again," he said. He'd moved into a studio apartment across town but wanted this kept a secret.

I stopped in the bathroom as my dad paid the bill, leaving him alone with Steven by the doors. As I walked back out, I overheard them.

"Well, you seem like a nice young man...." my dad said.

"I try," Steven told him.

My dad had never said this about anyone.

On the sidewalk, my father grinned, held out both arms, and gave me a big hug.

Steven and I drove to a bookstore, and I cried in the parking lot.

"When will it ever end?" I asked. I meant my worrying about my father.

On the bus ride back to New York, I glanced at a billboard and gasped. Instead of reading what the billboard said, I'd seen something else.

"I just got a feeling that I saw my dad for the last time today," I told Steven.

"What do you mean?" Steven asked. "You're just worried about his heart condition. Don't worry, he'll be fine."

The next week, after Steven left, I was coming home from work at Outback Steakhouse one day when a Black man in a denim jumpsuit got on my train and sat next to me. He was a security guard at a veterans' hospital, he said, then showed me his ID. But there was something off about him. The veins in his arms pulsated like blood was flowing through them for the first time. His deep brown pupils seemed to vibrate.

He asked if I was alone in New York and told me to call my family. "Moms worry," he said. Then he told me about the veterans in the hospital where he worked. Some dismissed them as crazy, he said. "I know," I said. "But they have PTSD."

"Yes," he said. "Hmm...you seem to know something about this...."

Then, as gently as he'd glided on, when the subway doors opened he was gone.

When I got off in Jackson Heights, I couldn't shake the notion I'd met an angel.

I reached for my phone to call Steven and saw I'd missed a call from my brother.

"Call me as soon as you can," Dave said in his voicemail tearfully.

"I don't know how to tell you this," Dave said when I called back. "You need to come back to Delaware. How soon can you get here?"

"Why?" I asked. "Just tell me."

"Dad died yesterday. He was in a car accident."

"Oh my God," I said, crying. "I know."

I didn't know why I said that.

"What happened?" I asked, frozen in the sidewalk. "Was the driver drunk?"

"No," he said. "It was in the afternoon. A teenager crashed into him at an intersection."

I stood in front of the fruit stands, the street's busyness fading away. It was like I was surrounded by frosted glass. Dave explained that the police officer who'd tried to resuscitate our dad had searched through his wallet. When he found my brother's business card, he prayed it didn't belong to a son.

Dave said he couldn't reach our mom, who was in the Poconos with our stepdad.

"Let's get you on a train to Delaware," he said.

I walked down the sidewalk in a daze.

Every time I'd left my father, I'd leaned forward from the back seat of his car and kissed him goodbye on the cheek—I never knew if I did it more for him or for me, especially once I felt too old to keep doing it.

But I was suddenly glad I'd never stopped.

When I reached my apartment, I walked straight to my bookshelf.

My dad's book, *The Why? Generation (in a Why-Not World.)*, the one he wrote in 1976, compiled thirteen essays about how things had changed in the thirteen years since John F. Kennedy was killed. I'd brought it to New York, along with the legal pads and pencils he'd given me to "become a real writer." For most of my life, his book had lived in his back seat, next to the shillelagh. That summer, I'd finally started reading it.

I flipped through the back of the book and found what I was seeking:

When a person dies, his physical remains are buried or burned and returned to Mother Earth. This ash-to-ash concept of existence is not depressing when you look at the full scope of humanity. I can share in the greatest thoughts and inventions of the greatest people who walked the earth. Their spirit and influence will never die.

I called Steven. He booked a flight right away.

My brother picked me up at the train station in Delaware that night. We spent the next two days in the house alone, trying to reach my mom—the phone reception was still too bad. Finally, Dave got through. When they pulled into the driveway, I ran into her arms.

Though we all went to the funeral home together, my mom and uncle Jim, my dad's brother, took care of my dad's estate. My dad didn't have a will and owed money still for something—I didn't know what. He had a safe deposit box, but my uncle couldn't find the key.

For days I barely ate. Sleep was my only escape from the nightmare. But when I woke up, I had to remember it all over again.

Despite his forbidding, I had to tell my mom and brother where my dad's apartment was—to clean it. At the last minute I said I wasn't strong enough to help.

The coroner said my dad had died instantly, that his heart had stopped on impact, so there was no need for a closed casket. Still, by the time we got to the wake, he didn't look like himself.

His body looked peaceful and still. His face looked older, flatter. The strangest part was his hands—clasped gently on his stomach, a gesture I'd never seen him make.

My dad lived through his hands. They were always in motion.

My brother and I stood in front of the casket as everyone formed a line to greet us. It felt backward—two young adults, the only family to greet. Most of the people we'd never met. All of them seemed to know us.

When everyone left, we turned to pay our respects.

I stood between my mom and brother with an arm around each. But as they looked down at my father's body, I looked up.

Where are you?

My friend Kelly drove me from the wake to pick up Steven at the airport.

On our way back, we drove toward a large orange disk on the highway, a harvest moon. The biggest I'd ever seen. Steven said we were about to get a storm.

"Good," I said. "I hope it pours."

The next morning, I rode with my brother to the church. It was the church where our parents wed, the church where I was baptized, the church where our father went to school. It was where he'd once tossed his baseball cards in the air at recess and yelled "Finders, keepers!" He'd said he'd be a millionaire if he'd only kept those cards.

We opened the heavy doors and walked down the aisle. My brother had instructed the organist to play "Too-Ra-Loo-Ra-Loo-Ral." We would lay our father to rest with the song he'd sung to tuck us in.

Dave reached for my hand.

When it was time, I read my eulogy—an essay I'd written on Father's Day when I couldn't afford to send my dad a card. I'd been looking forward to hearing what he thought of it. I turned to find my brother in tears. "That was beautiful," he said. Then he read his.

On the way to the cemetery, the sky opened up.

"I just want to say..." I said to Dave as he drove.

But I didn't know what to say. Neither of us did.

My heart sat in my stomach as I watched my father's coffin lowered into the ground.

My oldest stepbrother, Scott, drove Steven and me to the reception at my uncle's house. Scott had met Steven that morning, as had most of my family. It was Scott's one-year wedding anniversary, and his wife didn't seem happy that this was how they were spending it.

"Ahh! My eyes!" she yelled as a bright bolt of lightning flashed across the sky.

At the reception, few people talked to me. It was like they were afraid. I sat in a corner with my plate, not eating, explaining to Steven who everyone was.

My cousin Jimmy, the only cousin who came, said he was lucky to find a train out of New York. Two days before, there'd been a blackout—even the Empire State Building went dark. I'd watched on TV the streets I walked every day, heard news anchors report that heat likely caused the outage. On the front page of *Time* magazine was a photo of hot, sweaty New Yorkers sitting on the steps of the library. One stood out from the rest, a girl in a white tank top and denim skirt. She surveyed her surroundings with a frustrated gaze. The caption read "Powerless."

I knew exactly how she felt.

After the funeral, we recapped the event at Howard Johnson's, a practice common with my family after weddings. Steven and I drove down to Baltimore's Inner Harbor, near the airport. Before he left, he reminded me that this would be our briefest time apart. In twelve days, I'd fly to Seattle, and then we'd drive back across the country so he could move to New York, just like we'd planned.

When I got back to New York, I asked for a month off at my magazine internship. I asked for two weeks off at Outback.

I tried to get to the airport on time that Friday but couldn't manage it. I was moving in slow motion. Steven had paid for my ticket, so he had to reschedule my flight, for later that night. I brought my Discman—music was helping me survive. As the plane flew up, out of JFK, and pushed its way through the clouds, we flew directly over the Empire State Building, upside down from above. My Discman played "The Only Living Boy in New York."

After five hours, my plane landed in Seattle. The air smelled like the ocean.

Steven had packed up his apartment except for his bed, which was a mattress and a box spring on the floor. He'd borrowed his friend's car to pick me up. We'd be renting an SUV in two days for our trip, despite my protests—an SUV had killed my dad.

The next day we toured Seattle. Steven kept saying our cross-country road trip would be duller than the route he'd taken with a friend when he moved there—they had crossed the Southwest. But I liked that the trip would be mostly fields and cows.

I met Steven's friends that night at a literary journal reading. I wished the person they were meeting was me.

The next morning, when it was time to pack the car, I couldn't. I froze. Steven forgave me. His neighbors helped.

As I got ready in the small bathroom, I noticed my eyes were puffy from crying, smeared with mascara from the night before. I put my hair in pigtails, which seemed like something an adventurous girl might do.

It didn't take long on the road for Steven to be pulled over. The cop let him off with a warning. As we drove through a large cement tunnel, I watched the girl in pigtails in the rearview mirror bob along.

We emerged into a wooded paradise. Tall pine trees lined the road to my right, yellow cliffs to my left. Steven pointed to a lake in the distance.

His plan was to clock eight-hour days of driving for an entire week. I soon saw what he'd meant about it being dull. This part of the United States is called Big Sky Country for a reason.

By evening we'd made it through Idaho and watched the stars come out, a sky more spectacular than any I'd ever seen. Mars was closer to Earth than it had been in 63,000 years. I told myself that was where my dad was, in that little red dot, guiding us.

That night we pulled into a Holiday Inn in Butte, Montana, which we called "Butt." It was my second time staying in a hotel with a man—the first had been the night after the funeral.

The next morning a police officer stopped Steven for speeding again. But when he saw it was Steven's birthday, he didn't ticket him.

I was under-caffeinated when I finally agreed to drive. I'd become car-phobic, to Steven's dismay, as we'd originally agreed to split the driving. "Is this the Rocky Mountains?" I asked. Steven unfolded his paper map and said yes.

* * *

MY DAD'S APARTMENT after the divorce was a two-minute drive from our house. On Sunday afternoons, we'd set out for the woods. Three walking sticks—one for each height—and we were off.

My brother often sped ahead, thrashing anything in his path. Our train's caboose, my dad would pound his walking stick and stick out his chest, proclaiming his new name: "Chief Big Bear." Dave was "Little Bear, our warrior," he'd say. He dubbed me "the navigator" of our tribe. I thought my title seemed less glamorous. I wanted to be a bear, too.

But when I complained, my dad explained that my role was the most important. I'd find our way into adventures, and I'd find our way back out.

At first, I was a terrible navigator. I daydreamed into groves of poison oak because I'd seen honeysuckles nearby. I stopped at every flower and butterfly. I'd spend a good ten minutes admiring the sound of rushing water or the shape moss formed on a craggy rock. But six-year-old boys get cranky when they've been climbing rocks all day. The same thing seemed to happen to forty-year-old men when they were ready for dinner.

And so, before the sun set, I'd find my focus. My dad would watch quietly as I guided us back home, despite the boisterous man he was.

Somehow, every time, I found the sun.

* * *

AS I CAREFULLY STEERED each curve of the Rocky Mountains, I was driving where Lewis and Clark had met Sacagawea. Our trip on Route 90 was their 1804 voyage in reverse. Sacagawea's husband had been chosen to be their navigator, but she ended up proving more suited. She had better language skills and more poise. Her mere presence confirmed that their mission was peaceful.

Sacagawea helped Lewis and Clark cross the Rockies on horseback and then led them to the Coast. My father loved Thomas Jefferson, and he loved Lewis and Clark. All that time, I'd considered being "the navigator" a slight...but he'd been comparing me to the most important woman in American history.

"My dad always said I was a great driver," I told Steven. We stopped in Bozeman, Montana, so Steven could take over. He didn't yet agree with my dad's assessment.

At sunset we reached Mount Rushmore. It looked smaller than I'd hoped.

We set out early the next day, one in which we'd cover five states. By nightfall we found a truck stop in Indiana and got the cheapest room yet. We had lunch the next day at a Chinese restaurant manned by an older white lady and her twelve-year-old granddaughter. We told her we were moving to New York, and she looked scared.

"Will you live near the World Trade Center?"

Signs for York, Pennsylvania, showed up at dusk, and Steven breathed a sigh of relief. He'd reach his parents' house just when he said he would.

I knew little about Steven's family except that his mom was recovering from an eye tumor and his father designed Stanley tools. I'd mostly heard about his redheaded nephew, who at age nine was too shy to look at me. His brother wasn't around when we arrived—but he rarely was.

The next day Steven and I sat in a diner for our first dinner as New Yorkers. And then he came back and slept at my place.

It took us eight months, but by our first dating anniversary, we'd saved up enough to go on vacation. Steven suggested we visit his favorite part of his first cross-country trip, the one he'd taken before meeting me: the Southwest.

New York had become like a security blanket. I hesitated to leave. But my favorite artist was Georgia O'Keeffe, who'd lived in New Mexico.

The first thing I noticed when we got off the plane was the cloudless blue skies. Despite how otherworldly it seemed, all mountains and sand, New Mexico felt like home.

Twelve years later we hoped our families would feel the same, when we got married there.

* * *

MY COUSIN EMILY GAVE BIRTH a week before our wedding, so she and her husband, Lee, had missed it. On our honeymoon, we planned to return to New Mexico a year later—and bring Emily and Lee with us.

The timing of the trip was convenient for my father's list: I needed to check off "ride a horse fast." Where better than in the Old West?

When we got off the plane in late June, the Southwest seemed just as we'd left it. We picked up Emily and Lee at the airport, then unpacked at the Inn of the Turquoise Bear, where we'd married. It was Emily and Lee's first time away from their kids.

The next day we drove north for a sunset ride at Georgia O'Keeffe's house.

The entrance to Ghost Ranch is marked by a cow's skull, one of O'Keeffe's favorite subjects to paint. A smoky-blue mesa rises like an altar in the distance. O'Keeffe called the mesa her "private mountain." She said God told her if she painted it enough, she could keep it. It's where her ashes are now.

I was surprised to be called up first with the horses. There were eight of us, and I would ride the alpha. They called my horse "Sancho," after the sidekick in *Don Quixote*. Emily saddled up behind me. Lee, who is six-foot-four, rode the tallest horse.

Sancho didn't gallop as much as he plodded. We made our way slowly under the orange-and-pink skies of Georgia O'Keeffe's backyard. It took me a few minutes to realize: Nothing about these horses was fast, except for how they pooped. Emily and I, in our crumpled cowboy hats, couldn't stop laughing.

Sancho nosed ahead, into the butt of the guide's horse. I felt bad subjecting him to this. Thinking of Steven, who hadn't joined us on principle, I whispered "please stop" when I pulled the reins and "please go" when I dug my heels in. I thanked Sancho.

The ride was only an hour. As the guide took us back to the stables, the horses sped up. It was suppertime. We passed a pattern on the ground I quickly recognized: horseshoes.

The horseshoe is a feminine symbol. Any symbol with an open end like that represents how life enters the world. When a horseshoe is hung with its opening pointed up, it's so one's luck won't run out. But when it's hung with the opening pointed down, it's so luck rains down upon you. The U-shaped position is more popular in the Western Hemisphere. But the arch position is traditional in the East.

When my father died, I feared losing anyone else. I believed the best way to avoid that was to live like the U-shaped horseshoe—to hold on tight. But I was beginning to understand that life wasn't like that.

Luck can only enter your life when you let go of it.

Love can only enter your heart when you give it away.

When we stumbled upon Steven, taking photos at the visitors' center, it was near dusk. The only restaurant still open in Santa Fe was an old-timey saloon. Steven managed to find something vegan. The rest of us laughed about our pooping horses.

The next morning, we hiked Mount Atalaya—the mountain where my friend Kelly played "Daddy Lessons" on my wedding day. Lee told me about his estranged dad. Emily talked about her family, too. We talked about our moms, who are sisters, and how they always tried to make the best of bad situations.

Emily was three years old the night my mom drove us to her house—away from my father. It was a few months before he moved out. I stayed in Em's trundle bed while my mom talked with her sister downstairs. I wasn't sure if it was because Emily was there that night, but I'd often envied her family's seeming normalcy. To learn that her family wasn't perfect—what family was?—and to hear Lee talk about his dad made me feel silly.

I told Emily I was thinking of writing a book, but I was afraid of telling the truth.

"I think you should follow your heart," she said.

When we reached the top, we were 9,000 feet above sea level. I'd climbed a mountain. On our descent, I picked up a piece of rose quartz—Mount Atalaya's made of it. It wasn't heart-shaped like the one Em bought for her daughter in town.

But it's still the stone of unconditional love.

Back in New Jersey, I wanted to know more about horses.

On our first visit to Ghost Ranch, on our honeymoon the year before, Steven and I had spotted a pen filled with mustangs. "I don't want to go over there," he said. "They might be abused." But when we did, one horse was friendly. He stuck his muzzle through the fence, into my belly.

"I hope you're getting a picture of this," I said.

I looked into the horse's eyes, feeling we were somehow the same. In Spanish, *mustang* means "stray."

When my dad wrote this list item, "ride a horse fast," he likely imagined himself the Lone Ranger, his favorite Western. Cowboy-and-Indian movies reached their peak of popularity in the 1950s, when my dad was a kid. But Hollywood softened how it actually was. Had the Spanish not brought mustangs with them to the new world in the 1600s, they couldn't have enslaved Native Americans, who'd never seen horses. And if Native Americans hadn't revolted, stealing mustangs and scattering them all over the West, cowboys couldn't have survived. There'd be no Lone Ranger. There'd be no America, too. Lewis and Clark crossed the Rocky Mountains only because Sacagawea found horses.

Thanks to the Bureau of Land Management, most mustangs are still wild. So I had been right on our honeymoon—the mustang who nudged my stomach *had* once been free.

I asked Steven to dig up the photo he took of me at Ghost Ranch that day. When I saw the horse's nose—the white polka dot above the white blaze—I gasped.

"It's Sancho," I said. "It's the same horse. I can't believe it."

"I can," Steven said, laughing.

CHAPTER 5

Talk with the President

I t started as a joke. When I filmed an interview for *Inside Edition*, the reporter asked which was the most impossible list item.

"Talk with the president," I said. The president I'd least like to speak with was in office.

But I really did think it was impossible.

When I was a teen, my mom sometimes called my dad grandiose. "He used to write these lists of the famous people he'd meet," she'd say. "Your father's not always living in reality."

My dad, an American Studies major, had written this goal after our most secretive presidency—the Nixon administration. There was a time when civilians could simply walk into the White House—a tradition started by my dad's favorite president, Thomas Jefferson. But after too many assassination attempts, that time had come and gone.

I received an email from a man in Alabama after my interview. "If any president will do," he said, "you should know that President Jimmy Carter still teaches Sunday school most weeks of the year, in Plains, Georgia."

My dad wrote the list in 1978, when Jimmy Carter was president.

I decided he qualified.

While anyone can do it, attending Carter's Sunday school is a highly regimented affair that provides no guarantee of actually talking with

87

him. I emailed Carter's press secretary and didn't hear back. Then in July, Carter passed out from dehydration at a Habitat for Humanity site in Canada. At ninety-two and ninety respectively, Jimmy and his wife, Rosalynn, still volunteered to build homes one week every year. I felt a new urgency.

I emailed Emily Staub, his health programs liaison, who responded to me the same day. She said she admired my persistence with the list.

In his youth, Jimmy Carter dreamt of traveling the world. He followed his uncle's footsteps into the Navy, manning nuclear submarines, but returned when his father was dying. His dad was revered in Plains, which inspired Carter to take over his peanut farm, run for governor, and eventually run for president. He forged peace in the Middle East. He won the Nobel Peace Prize.

The guy knows a little about persistence.

Emily suggested I take her tour of the Carter Center, then stay at the only inn in Plains, and the next morning sit in a reserved pew at Sunday school—guests at the inn get one. But when I called, the innkeeper said they were booked. Carter's crowds can reach 500—sometimes they have to watch on a TV in a separate building. I didn't want to fly down for nothing.

Then a woman in Atlanta who'd made texting while driving illegal told me her friend could reserve a pew. She tried to get me a few words with Carter, but learned he didn't talk to people after Sunday school.

I felt humbled so many people were trying to get me minutes with this man.

Sometime after 1974, when my parents met, my mom flew my dad down to show him her grad school, University of Georgia. She often talks about her time there like it was the most liberated of her life. The potential for seeing her old stomping grounds was almost enough to convince her to go on this trip, but at the last minute, she gave me an envelope of old photos and said, "You go with your husband instead."

I spent the next three weeks learning all I could about our thirty-ninth president.

We arrived in Atlanta by the grace of God—we'd nearly missed our flight. Then there was a problem with Steven's credit card for the car rental. So I thought, *What would Jimmy Carter do?* and showed mercy. This was probably why Steven agreed to climb Stone Mountain, though he said he was too tired. The photos my mom gave me were of her and my dad at the top.

After the Carter Center, I changed into hiking clothes in our rental car. Stone Mountain, said to be 280 million years old, is pure granite—and it's not an easy climb. We felt a sense of teamwork when we finished.

But because we climbed at sunset, we ended up at a Quality Inn in Plains at 11:00 p.m. We drove down narrow, dark roads in the middle of farmland, every once in a while spotting a Confederate flag. We were punch drunk by the time we got there.

And that's when we met the noisy Canadian.

I noticed his Jimmy Carter T-shirt at the hotel's front desk and asked where he'd bought it. We talked about our long drive from Stone Mountain and his long trip from Ontario. He'd been traveling since 3:00 a.m. He'd parked his rental SUV in front of the hotel, just behind ours, and as we walked back, we kept talking.

He was a graying bulldog of a man, the kind who talks the loudest at a party and the longest. He was shorter than me, smelled of cigarettes, and kept asking us to come to his room for wine. Pretty soon we'd been talking for three hours. We talked about news coverage of Donald Trump. We talked about the taking down of statues and how they'd handled that issue in Canada. We talked about President Carter, and he casually mentioned he'd written a book about him. He refused to tell us his name and insisted he didn't want to know ours, interrupting me every time I tried to tell him.

Steven and I left for our room. I belly-flopped on the bed.

"Who *was* that guy?" I said.

A speechwriter and historian, Art Milnes had mentioned his sister's last name and his first name briefly. He'd said he'd met Jimmy

Carter, George H.W. Bush, and Bill Clinton several times. I Googled him and found pictures of him with each man.

I thought about the questions he'd asked. "Don't you think Jimmy Carter already knows you're here? Don't you think he has your phone number? This town is only 600 people, he could easily get it from the hotel. I bet you'll receive a phone call from him within the week."

Steven was starving, so we climbed the grassy hill over to Waffle House for home fries. Vegan food is hard to find in Plains, Georgia.

The next morning, we parked on the main drag. Art pulled in after.

"Did I tell you, or what?" he yelled. He'd predicted he'd see us all weekend.

We stopped in a Carter souvenir shop, and Art asked, "Hey, if Jimmy Carter could sign anything for you, what would it be?" He pondered when in 1978 my dad had written his list. "I bet he wrote it after the Camp David Accords," he said. Art asked the clerk if he had a book about Camp David. He sold us a book about Carter's malaise speech instead.

Steven and I left for Carter's boyhood farm. It was hard to believe a president's only connection to the world had once been a telephone in an empty hall.

When we arrived at church Sunday morning, I gave the innkeeper I'd spoken with on the phone a code word my friend had shared with me, and she led us in like we were VIPs. I told her about my activism. "Well, you don't have to worry about President Carter texting and driving," she said. "He never drives!"

She seated us in the pew behind President Carter's.

As we sat through the emcee's instructions ("Don't talk to President Carter," "don't shake his hand," and so on), Art emerged from a back room—I could see Carter through the crack of the door. Art found his seat next to Carter's.

The president always starts the same way, by greeting the military. He said he'd been expecting Christina Aguilera, but her plane was canceled, so her fiancé was there in her place. He said he was happy to see Art Milnes. "He's written a book that's partly, a little bit, about me, and we're glad to have him."

Then the former president gave his lesson. This was my favorite part:

...each of us has a decision we can make when we're born, to shape our own lives. Our parents can't shape our lives for us—they might try, but they don't succeed often. Children can't shape their parents' lives. A wife can't shape her husband's life. A husband can't shape his wife's life. Every one of us has freedom and life and love from God. But every one of us also has the duty to shape our own lives. And that's the essence of faith.

We have constant access to our creator, in effect a father for us, or I like to look on God as a partner sometimes. And if I'm choosing a partner for my life, I'd like to have a partner who cared about me, wouldn't you? I'd like to have a partner who knows everything and can do anything! So, you've got a partner like that, every one of us has a partner like that. And we have constant access to God.

I stopped worrying about what anyone thought of my dad's list. God was my partner in this.

After the service, we lined up for photos. Being in a special pew, we went first. Art walked over.

"Good luck," he said. "I was once in your shoes. Your father is here with you today."

We waited while Carter posed with Pennsylvania Mennonites. I planned what I might say.

I jumped out of an airplane, I thought. *I can do this.*

The president apologized for keeping me waiting, which I took as an invitation to speak.

"Sir, my father wrote on his bucket list that he wanted to talk with you, and I'm checking that off for him today."

"Oh," Jimmy Carter responded. "Very good...!"

The emcee snapped photos on Steven's phone. As we turned to leave, Jimmy Carter reached out his hand to shake mine. His hand was large and soft.

"Come back down and see us again," he said.

"We will," I said. "Oh, and we met Art, and he's wonderful!"

As we walked out of the church, I clasped Steven's hand.

"I just checked off the most impossible list item," I said.

Or so I'd been told.

In the parking lot, Art pulled up in his SUV.

"How did it go!?" he asked.

We recapped the whole moment.

"So, who's Christina Aguilera?" he asked, smoking. "Is she some kind of bebop star?"

Art said he'd tried to arrange a lunch with President Carter after the church service but Aguilera had bumped us.

"But don't worry," he said, "I've made it my mission to tell him your story at lunch and convince him to have dinner with you. So, expect an invitation back down to Plains."

I looked for Art's email address for a week back home. I found columns he'd written for the *Ottawa Citizen*. One quoted his history teacher dad, who'd said, "Heaven is a mountain, and there are many paths to the top."

If we hadn't climbed Stone Mountain when we did, we wouldn't have met Art.

I felt uneasy climbing it. Stone Mountain is the king of Confederate statues. At the summit, I stuck my fist out, imitating my dad's pose in the pictures.

Later, I asked my mom which path they'd taken.

"We took the skyride, of course!" she said. "Can't you see we're wearing nice clothes?"

I read my dad's book, *The Why? Generation*, cover to cover that week, searching for Jimmy Carter. I found him in a chapter called

"Politics and Government." But what I liked most was in my dad's chapter on faith:

> *Lord, I ask Your help to make me a better person every day and beseech Thee for moral strength to search for the truth regardless of the odds of finding it. The answer to my questions is found in my soul. The task of my life must be to find this inner essence and manifest it for the rest of mankind. Actions must overcome wasteful words. For surely actions tell me that my prayers are heard.*

I had to laugh that in my quest to meet a U.S. president, I'd met a man of God. And a Canadian.

But that Canadian was right in the church that day. My father was there.

I just hoped he knew God heard his prayers.

A few weeks later, I signed up for surfing lessons at the Jersey Shore. The list item said "surf in the Pacific." But I needed practice.

At 10:00 a.m. on a Saturday we met my stepbrother Drew and his family on the boardwalk. I was surprised he'd agreed to join us—Drew and I rarely socialized apart from our siblings.

My dad loved surf music, so I guessed that was what this list item was about. We sang "Surfer Girl" and "Under the Boardwalk" on the way to the beach each summer. He'd change the lyrics of "In My Room" to "In My Bathroom" and make farting noises with his mouth. We never surfed, though—we only bodysurfed. Once my dad nearly fell asleep in low tide while watching us, and a stranger yelled, "Get a life, buddy!" My dad loved this so much that it became a private joke—a line he repeated for years. "Why is it the biggest women wear the smallest bikinis?" he'd often ask. A strange question from an overweight man. Our first night in Wildwood, we'd pick up ice cream cones while my brother watched TV—always banana for him, always peach for me. On the last day of the trip, he'd take a photo of me in front of Laura's Fudge—always from below, always making me seem like a giant.

We loved going to the beach with my mom, too, but her water phobia meant we couldn't swim far. Once she met my stepdad, I was relieved of having to watch my brother. But I also felt alone—in my stepbrothers, Dave had three new best friends.

Which is probably why I never took to surfing. My brother and three stepbrothers' favorite movie was *Point Break*, which they quoted from ad nauseam.

Steven and Drew carried their surfboards easily to the sand while I dragged mine. Our instructors showed us on dry land how to paddle and pop up. One said popping up was hard, glancing at me while he said it.

"What are you looking at *me* for?" I joked.

But after my twelfth unsuccessful try in the water, I gave up. I had worked until 10:00 p.m. every night that week and was recovering from the flu, I explained to my instructor.

Drew's son—my eight-year-old nephew Chase—had been watching from the beach. "I just made a fool of myself," I said as I waded back in my wetsuit. "You can't do any worse!"

Chase popped up on his first try.

Steven and Drew kept their surfboards another hour while I rested on the beach with my sister-in-law Kate. She told me she had struggled when she learned how to surf. "It's harder for women," she said.

"You *surf*?" I asked. It had never occurred to me to ask her to join us.

Steven and Drew quoted *Point Break* all day. On our way home, Steven said he couldn't believe I'd never seen it. So I subjected myself to the film. And it turned out to be the perfect movie—and directed by a woman! Keanu Reeves, "an F-B-I agent," goes undercover to break up a ring of bank robbers, who are surfers but also anarchists. After hearing their hakuna matata ideas, he becomes confused about his life choices.

"It's not tragic if you die doing what you love," Patrick Swayze tells him.

As the weeks went by, I grew fearful of checking off "surf in the Pacific." I'd reserved a lesson in December because it's when the waves in Los Angeles get the biggest.

Work was more hectic. Hearst had added *Redbook*, *Woman's Day*, and *Dr. Oz* to our monthly lineup, so copyediting, what had always felt like an artisan's craft, now felt like factory work. What was worse: when Hearst combined the magazine staffs, they laid many people off. But they put my department in a windowless closet. My bamboo plant couldn't live without light, so how could I?

Despite my busyness, or maybe to escape it, I agreed to complete a fifty-four-mile bike race in Arizona for a friend—Brendan Lyons, a cyclist nearly killed by a distracted driver. Like Jacy Good, he'd learned to walk again. By November I'd raised $350 for his nonprofit.

Steven couldn't understand why I was doing this. "It's too expensive," he complained. "We are traveling too much."

I told him my gut said I needed to.

Cycling wasn't a list item, so I told Steven I'd make it one. It was how I'd lose four inches from my waist (my dad had wanted to "have a thirty-four-inch waist again"—my goal would be a twenty-seven-inch waist).

When we arrived in Tucson, we stopped at the convention center to greet Brendan and pick up my bike. Our hotel was a few minutes' drive from my starting line.

After Steven dropped me off the next morning, I couldn't believe how many people stood before me—thousands of cyclists. Unlike running, this sport wasn't solitary. On the hills, any time I had to hop off and push, at least three cyclists stopped to ask if I was OK. One told me he liked my kit. Another offered a gear tip. Every aid station was like a party.

After four hours of cycling, I reached my last rest stop. The sun sat low on the horizon. My hands hurt, my arms hurt, my butt hurt.

Everything hurt. I started down the steepest hill, and took in the vista, the desert and the saguaro cacti.

Once when we were out for breakfast, my dad said he'd had a spiritual experience in the diner where we sat. As he ate pancakes at the counter, "What a Wonderful World" played. He watched people walk in, and the lyrics came to life, he said.

As I rode to the finish line, I heard this song in the back of my mind, reflecting on the kindness I'd experienced that day. But then I thought maybe I was hallucinating.

Because I heard it in my father's voice.

Thanksgiving at my mom's house in Connecticut was the best I'd had in recent memory. I usually went home wondering how my accomplishments would measure up to my brothers' or cousins'. But this year, I'd met a president.

I'd also signed with a literary agent. During Thanksgiving dinner, my cousin Jimmy said he thought I'd get a $250,000 book deal.

In the following weeks, the agent rushed together a proposal and failed to convince a publisher to buy our book idea, because it was only that—an idea. At Christmas he instructed me to write a hundred pages, so he'd have content to sell.

My sudden failure made Christmas harder.

Luckily my nephew Andrew, from North Carolina, had visited New York that week for school and met with Steven and me, so this became a topic of conversation.

My brother, Dave, and sister-in-law, Jaime, former actors themselves, said my nephew had hope for success in the theatre if he was cast in his school's shows.

"He should focus on teaching," my stepdad said. As a former high school guidance counselor, Jim often acted like a talent scout.

"Andrew's an honest, good person," I said. "He's passionate about what he does, and he's kind. No matter what he chooses, that will take him far."

"Hey, I could be wrong," my stepdad said, pointing at me. "When you moved to New York, I didn't think you had a chance in hell! Not a chance in hell!"

"I'm sure your inability to believe in me played a big part in my success," I said.

The next night, as I washed dishes at home, Steven mentioned he'd have to dip into our savings for our surfing trip—the savings my mom had given us for our wedding gift.

I thought of my dad. I had to tell Steven the truth.

"The money is almost gone," I said to him tearfully.

"Why are you crying?" Steven asked, smiling.

"Because I'm embarrassed. I spent it all on the list, and my mom said that money was for our future!"

"But you *did* spend it on our future," Steven said.

We arrived in Los Angeles two days before New Year's. Marilyn Monroe once lived in our hotel. Everything was white and smelled of powdery melon. A figure-eight shaped pool graced the atrium.

The surfing school was humble compared to the hotel: a turquoise van with wetsuits hanging from it. Steven was dubious.

We repeated the paddling practices I'd learned in New Jersey, and learned popping up. This time I balanced myself on one knee before standing.

"Is it OK if I do 'stomach, knees, feet'?" I asked.

"Whatever's clever!" Chuck, my instructor, said.

Chuck spoke like a valley boy but resembled a lion, though he was only twenty-two. Grinning goofily, he guided us into the Pacific. The blond fraternal twins in my class—sister and brother—had to be twenty-two, too, because they mastered the pop-up readily. But they were also Australian.

A few times I got up on my knees.

"You'd be a great kneeboarder!" Chuck laughed.

Kneeboarding took off in the 1970s. I doubted this was what my dad had meant.

In Ocean City, they'd taught us to cover our heads if a wave knocked us under. But when my fifteenth wave did this in the Pacific, I forgot.

My body turned upside down and into a 360-degree flip, pulling each limb in four directions, knocking my head onto the ocean floor in the process.

"Are you OK?" Steven yelled when I came up for air. He was surfing on his own, with no instructor.

"Yes!" I said. "That was incredible!"

I went out a little deeper, where it was quiet. Not far ahead, a fat seagull floated.

"This is it!" Chuck yelled.

I paddled. I propped myself onto my knees—and then onto my feet.

I stood for all of two seconds on that board.

"I had both feet on it!" I yelled, resting in the low tide.

"You sure did," Chuck said, walking by. "Check that one off the list."

In Hawaii, where surfing was invented hundreds of years ago, every member of society surfed. Kids, men, women, kings, peasants, priests... it didn't matter who you were. Hawaiians scatter the ashes of their dead in the sea, so they associate water with love. It was how I'd felt on that wave, how I'd felt riding that bike in the desert. Like I was one with nature—I needed only to surrender to it.

In these moments, my father's spirit was all around me.

I didn't have to be afraid.

"You did it!" Steven yelled, high-fiving me. He took a photo of me with my board. After lunch, I lay belly-first on the beach and texted my brother and stepbrothers.

"*Vaya con dios*," Dave said.

"What?" I wrote back. He sent me a GIF from *Point Break* of Keanu Reeves saying this to Patrick Swayze, just before he rides a wave likely to kill him. "I thought you watched it?" Dave said.

I looked up the phrase.

It means "go with God."

CHAPTER 6

Go to the Rose Bowl

I told Steven I didn't care what we did the rest of the trip, as long as we went to the Rose Bowl. It was my last list item of 2017. And I still knew little about the game.

The Rose Parade I knew about—it was on New Year's Day. But Steven chafes in crowds. The game itself was already asking a lot. The stadium holds 104,000 people.

We woke up the day after surfing sore. Our all-white linens and Marilyn Monroe hotel made me feel like a movie star. As we drove away, I rolled down my window and felt the sun. We were stopping in Pasadena on our way to Kelly's house, where we'd sleep the next two nights.

When I saw the Rose Bowl in the distance, I gasped. Workers were setting up for the parade. We didn't get close—just close enough to see its white façade and red rose.

At Kelly's house, the kids opened our Christmas gifts.

The next day at the skate park, I watched as my godson Kevin's red Mohawk helmet bobbed along below the rim of a cement rink, barely visible. Kevin was six, yet he refused to accept that he was too small to ride his scooter with the skateboarding teens.

"Don't you want to play with Uncle Steven and your brother?" I asked.

He flared his nostrils and pushed off with his foot. A large mass of long hair, sweatshirt, and baggy pants zoomed behind, nearly colliding with him.

Steven convinced Kelly we should have a vegan New Year's Eve, so we picked up takeout. The kids loved it. When John got home, he and I stayed up to watch the ball drop after Steven fell asleep. We talked about my dad's list. John and I rarely had deep talks.

John's dad, Papa John, had volunteered to drive us to the stadium the next day. As I riffled through my suitcase, I asked Dominic, Kelly's older son, who was playing in the corner, what I should wear.

"Oh...just wear what your dad would have worn," he said.

My dad played football, baseball, and basketball through high school, and he became captain of his basketball team. He watched the first nationally televised Rose Bowl games and the first Super Bowl, in 1967. And he always watched Monday Night Football.

But I couldn't figure out why he'd wanted to see this place.

The Rose Bowl traffic was lighter than expected. Papa John reminisced about playing at the Rose Bowl in high school. I didn't understand what an honor this must have been until he dropped us off and we walked through Gate N.

I caught my breath. This was why my dad had wanted to see this.

I'd never been in a venue so large.

I understood the basics of football, enough to know what was happening. As soon as we were old enough to walk, we were posed for photos with my dad's football in piles of leaves in the backyard. We played one-on-one, with my dad alternating as quarterback. He'd convince me to pull the ball out from under Dave, sing-songing, "Sorry, Charlie Brown."

"Whom should we root for?" I asked Steven. Georgia was playing Oklahoma, but both wore red. I chose Georgia because it was where my mom had gone to school and where we'd met Jimmy Carter. The T-shirts made the stadium look like a rose.

I texted my brother and stepbrothers to tell them where we were sitting. "Look for us on the teeveeee," I wrote. When Georgia ran out, every player kneeled to pray.

I had bought seats behind the Oklahoma end zone, which meant we were also behind the Oklahoma band, who played victory songs every time Oklahoma scored. And they scored a lot. By halftime, it was 31-17, Oklahoma.

Reporters on the sidelines asked the coaches what they'd tell the young men. Georgia Coach Kirby Smart said, "I'll tell them to relax."

At halftime, I began to wonder why I was there. I had no interest in football. And Steven was barely watching.

"Is there some reason you're in a bad mood?" I said. "You never clap, you never stand up. You're not taking pictures, which was the one thing you said you wanted to do."

"Football just isn't my thing," Steven responded.

"Well, it's not mine either," I said. "But we're here. I'm going to enjoy it. This was expensive."

Steven left to find something to eat. He returned with French fries before the start of the second half.

Within the first few minutes, Georgia running back Nick Chubb ran a fifty-yard touchdown, making the score 31–23, Oklahoma. Then, during Oklahoma's possession, Georgia's defense sacked their quarterback. A commentator explained: "Georgia plays better when they have a chip on their shoulder—when told they can't do something."

Before we knew it, the quarterback had been sacked again and Georgia scored yet another touchdown, this time tying up the score, 31–31.

As the lights flickered on, the sun began to set, and the sky turned purple and pink. The crowd was restless. Georgia fans barked whenever Oklahoma received the ball. A tall brunette in front of me, a Georgia fan, crowned with red roses, talked stats with an Oklahoma fan behind her.

Oklahoma had possession now, but not for long. After the standard Georgia barks, the Georgia defense line intercepted a pass. Then Georgia scored again.

They were winning!

My mom's school, home state of Jimmy Carter!

My team!

I stood up.

Steven stood up.

The score was now 38–31, Georgia.

But with only eight minutes left in the third quarter, Oklahoma tied it up again. It was 38–38, anyone's game.

The teams took a break. As the sun edged below the upper rim of the Rose Bowl, it looked like Kevin's red Mohawk helmet in the skate park.

But it also reminded me of something else.

* * *

WHEN WE PLAYED TOUCH FOOTBALL one-on-one, with my dad alternating as quarterback, we'd get into a huddle and he'd draw a play on his stomach. Sometimes, when he did this, I noticed crescents of red on his nails. He was a sloppy eater—he invariably had mustard or ketchup ingrained in his fingers, so I assumed it was that.

But sometimes when he came to pick us up on a Sunday he also had remnants of lipstick on his mouth. One time I asked about it. "Ahhh," he said, smiling, "she got me good last night." The mere idea prevented further questioning.

He did a poorer job explaining the black around his eyes.

I told my mother each time this happened. Finally, when I was eighteen, she decided I was old enough to know.

"You should ask him," she said, "but I think your father may be a cross-dresser."

I knew my dad sang in piano bars. I didn't know he wasn't always dressed as a man when he did.

By the time he met my mom in 1974, what my dad did was illegal in thirty-four states. The day my mom discovered it, he'd been hiding it from her for ten years. He'd been going away "on business" for one too many weekends, so she asked my grandfather, my dad's father, about it. My grandfather suggested he was going on drinking benders, though my dad barely drank. He told my mom to check the back seat of my dad's car for bottles. She wasn't prepared for what she found. A box of women's clothes, some of it hers. Photos.

She drove us to her sister's house. When she confronted my dad on the phone, he pretended what she'd seen was nothing. Then he asked for a divorce.

Seven months later, one month after moving out, my dad changed his mind, she told me after he died. He wanted to stay married, after all, he'd said, but only if he could keep some of his whereabouts private. My mom couldn't live with this lack of openness—and she worried about our reactions if we saw him "dressed."

The divorce two years later wasn't what either had wanted. Which was why they both seemed sad. They resolved not to tell Dave or me what really happened until we were old enough.

But when I was eighteen, and my mother told me, I immediately wished she hadn't.

Great, now I have this *to deal with*, I thought.

"This doesn't take away from his being a good dad," she said.

"But how could he hide so much of his life from us?" I asked her. "Who are these people who see him like this?"

Do they matter more than we do? I asked myself.

My mom said he'd always been an "entertainer," that he'd always been *on*—that this had made it hard for her to connect with the real him.

But that hadn't been *my* experience of my father.

My dad was the most real person I knew.

My father died believing he had successfully hidden this from us. He never told me himself.

But I still carried his secret, even if he no longer did.

* * *

I closed my eyes and said a silent prayer. The tension in the crowd was thick. I asked God (and my dad) to help Georgia win. A ridiculous request, and I didn't stop there. I asked that they make the final score the age my father was when he died.

The game was tied up 38–38 with only one quarter left. I knew enough about football to know what I'd asked for was impossible.

Six minutes into the fourth quarter, Georgia's star player dropped the ball, and Oklahoma recovered it and scored. The Oklahoma band played the same dirge they'd been playing.

"Talk about a game of momentum...oh my gosh!" one of the commentators said.

As the cameras panned up and down the stands, faces showed up on the large TV screens, most with hands covering their mouths.

The score was 45–38, Oklahoma.

"It's not looking good for Georgia," a commentator said.

But after a bad punt from Oklahoma, Georgia received the ball only twenty-nine yards from the end zone. The Georgia coach called a timeout.

Back on the field, with less than a minute left to play, Georgia's quarterback threw the ball to Javon Wims, who missed it. But Oklahoma's defense accrued a penalty, so Georgia got the ball again. This time, Nick Chubb scored. The score was tied again, 45–45.

"I almost can't take this tension!" I told Steven.

The Georgia band, on the other end of the stadium, played "Glory! Glory! Hallelujah!"

"We've been spoiled by a great game," a commentator said.

For the first time in history, in its 104th game, the Rose Bowl went into overtime.

I finally understood what my dad and brother meant when they called athletes "warriors"—the bond they'd shared when they watched their team win.

Oklahoma won the coin toss and opted for Georgia to take possession. The quarterback's pass was incomplete, so all Georgia could do was kick a field goal.

It was now 48–45, Georgia. But then Oklahoma kicked a field goal, too. It was tied up again, 48–48!

For the first time in history, the Rose Bowl went into *double* overtime.

"This is pretty great," Steven laughed.

"Do you like football now?" I asked.

Oklahoma won the coin toss again and took possession.

"The pass is intercepted by Georgia!" the commentator yelled.

All Oklahoma could do now was kick a field goal. They could still win by three points. But then, the unthinkable happened: A Georgia linebacker leapt through the air and with the tips of his fingers, blocked the kick.

The Georgia quarterback kept calm. He looked around as the ball was hiked, then threw.

Touchdown.

"Georgia wins!"

The rose-crowned girl in front of me jumped and hugged her friends, then turned around and hugged me, too. She even hugged the Oklahoma fan she'd been debating with.

Red confetti shot out of cannons and rained on the stadium.

Football wasn't boring. It was the most exciting thing in the world.

I cried. I hugged Steven, and then I remembered. I glanced at the scoreboard.

The score was 54–48, Georgia.

My dad was fifty-four when he died.

When my dad's Raiders won the 1977 Super Bowl, which was played in the Rose Bowl Stadium, it was because John Madden coached them to be creative. He wanted them to think for themselves. This was how my father coached us, too. Like the Georgia coach, Kirby Smart, he taught us to relax.

The spectators who left that Rose Bowl game left happy. It didn't matter who'd won. They'd witnessed an amazing display of sportsmanship.

Two months later, my brother and three stepbrothers included me on their football text exchange for the first time. Our home team, the Philadelphia Eagles, had made it to the Super Bowl.

"Brian Westbrook," Dave wrote. "Today is for Brian Dawkins. Randall. Jerome Brown. Eric Allen. Duce Staley. And Jim Johnson. Champions without a ring. Home team."

"Today is for fans like us who have suffered for years," Drew wrote. "For all Eagle fans who congregate together every Sunday and bond together over the team they love. Today is for our kids who will know what it is like to be a champion. Bring it home!"

"This is for my dad," Dave added, "who introduced me to Merrill Reese on the radio. This is for all the tortured memories of what should have been. It ends. Today."

"Today is the day," my stepbrother Scott wrote. "The Eagles will be Super Bowl champions. Home team!"

"Just glad I became a football fan in time to experience it," I wrote. "Sorry it took me so long."

"Hey," my brother said, "you're here now."

I vowed I would write my book after all. And if I sold it, I'd give half of my royalties to good causes.

It would be good enough, because it would be my words, I decided.

My voice matters, I thought.

And my dad's voice mattered, too.

CHAPTER 7

Help Laura Win a Scholarship

I am nine years old. We are spending Christmas at my aunt's house in Pennsylvania. I've been permitted to play pool in the basement, which we usually do at my grandmother's house, though those games devolve into chaos, my cousins' hands squished by heavy stripes and solids, rolled with force into corner pockets; my itinerant maternal grandfather plodding downstairs to yell at us to knock it off.

My mom has dressed me in a gray velvet mid-calf skirt with a white oxford top, tied at the waist with a pink satin sash. As I scan the table, studying my next move, I hear a low chuckle. Something is wrong. I scratch my first shot, then hand my wooden cue back to my uncle, standing next to the two other men playing. This is what's wrong. I am a little girl playing pool with grown men. I am confused. We play pool at my dad's apartment every Sunday, just Dave, Dad, and me. And there, I sometimes win.

I tell my uncle I'm tired and walk back upstairs.

* * *

THE MORNING I'D MET my literary agent, the final scene of *Teen Wolf* entered my mind. I hadn't thought about that movie in twenty years. But there was Michael J. Fox, sweaty and smiling—relieved—after making his game's winning foul shot.

By February, I still hadn't written the one hundred pages my agent had requested.

I *had* joined a writers' group. A freelancer at work, Gabrielle, read my blog and asked if I'd like to join. I told her I would think about it.

But then, the first weekend in February, I found myself sitting in Gabrielle's one-bedroom apartment in Brooklyn, staring at her climbing plants on her industrial wall of windows, reviewing her friend Anna's Russian novel. My turn would be in a month.

I'd developed chronic heartburn, mostly at night. I was still trying to check off "have a twenty-seven-inch waist again," but instead I'd gained an inch—maybe from all the fried food while traveling. I usually stayed thin by forgetting to eat when work got busy. But this method, plus the coffee I drank, seemed to make the heartburn worse.

Steven's best friend, Craig, a homeopathic healer, said the heartburn symbolized my desire to write. "Your heart burns to tell the truth!"

Steven suggested I visit a doctor.

* * *

My dad's hearing, in September 2003, came a month after his death.

On August 8th, a seventeen-year-old had turned off the highway at an exit and made a phone call at a traffic light. She'd driven through the next light, which was red, still on the phone, plowing into my dad's car as he turned left—at least that's how the newspaper described it. Seven people saw it, all of whom came to the hearing. The state-appointed lawyer said he'd never seen so many witnesses show up.

The newspaper spelled it out, "Teen cited for talking on cell phone." On the stand, the girl claimed the traffic light had been green—that perhaps it had malfunctioned. But the police said it worked fine. The district justice fined her $200. This was the only repercussion for killing someone.

A lawyer told my mom and uncle they could file a civil suit, but it wouldn't be worth it—the legal fees would surpass any financial compensation. Plus, from appearances, the girl's family couldn't afford it.

Her father, dressed in a UPS delivery man's suit, walked over to us in the parking lot after the hearing. He told us they were an Irish family, too, that he also had a brother named Mick, my dad's name.

"She's a perfectionist," he added about his daughter, who'd taken the stand in a Catholic schoolgirl's uniform. "She's always mad at herself for making mistakes."

This had been a pretty big one.

The only compensation my father's death earned was a $100,000 settlement from his insurance. My uncle used $30,000 to cover funeral fees and my dad's debts. My brother used his $35,000 to pursue a master's degree. I used mine to stay in New York.

I quit my job at Outback Steakhouse a week after Steven and I drove across the country; one day I didn't show up. This was awkward because I'd found Steven a job there, too, in the kitchen. He worked there for four months, coming to my apartment smelling like Bloomin' Onions every night. He quit the week someone stole his shoes from his locker—the same week he'd made Employee of the Month. He started working in data entry. It wasn't easy to find a job without a college degree in New York.

Whenever I did score a journalism job interview, the subject of my father's death inevitably came up. I didn't get those jobs. I finally settled for being a slumlord's personal assistant.

Jerry gave me a good deal on a two-bedroom apartment rental in Manhattan, enabling me to move out of Jackson Heights. I soon found another magazine internship, where I was so good at fact-checking that they started paying me. This earned the respect of a college alumnus at the Associated Press—who gave me my first journalism job.

It had been two years since I'd moved to New York.

My $35,000 had just run out.

I found success as a writer at the Associated Press—my byline traveled around the world. But my grief didn't dissipate.

In the middle of researching a story for the technology desk, I started arriving late to work. I was devastated when I was fired, but I'd also been through this before.

Six months later, as my unemployment ran out, I took a job as a copy editor in Baltimore. I didn't make friends easily, mostly because I was sad about leaving New York—and Steven, who'd moved in with his parents while finishing an online art degree. I lived with a couple who were students at Johns Hopkins, the hospital where I'd gotten off the medications. It took months for me to tell them that story. Since my move to New York, I'd developed pain-dominant IBS, what my mom called "the family curse." Depending on what I ate, or how anxious I was, sharp pains burrowed into the right side of my stomach. I was in and out of the ER in Baltimore until it was diagnosed. Steven said it was where my grief went. Nine months later I lost that job, too.

Baltimore was a test for us. When we were in New York together, I'd broken up with Steven a handful of times. It was how I ended arguments. I had to leave him before he might leave me.

We moved in together in rural New Jersey after I was hired at a trade magazine. Four months later, I was laid off from that job, too—but this time through no fault of my own. Steven encouraged me to freelance at the women's magazines I loved—I'd always been afraid to because it wasn't a full-time job, what I'd been taught I was supposed to have. But at this point, I was willing to try anything.

After freelancing for *More* and *Ladies' Home Journal*, and commuting to the city two and a half hours by train twice a day, I got my first full-time job in national magazines, seven years after I'd started looking—at a celebrity tabloid.

One of the first issues I copyedited had a photograph of a dead Michael Jackson on the cover. I almost quit. My brother begged Steven, "You can't let her leave that job."

My brother and I were closer since our father's death. He'd moved to Boston and was acting in musicals. My mother, who'd lost an ex-husband, said she wasn't permitted to grieve. My brother seemed to express his grief through his shows—whether *Carousel, Company, Les Misérables,* or *The Birdcage,* his characters always had a tinge of Dad. In his playbills, he dedicated every performance to him.

Aristotle said good people have musical souls, and that was how Dave bonded with our dad. They were men of many voices, multiplied when together, each with perfect timing whether a joke, dance, or song. My brother inherited Dad's gift for bringing the fun.

The week I got fired at the Associated Press, I had already made plans to take the train up to visit Dave. I pretended I was OK with what had happened. He was living with three grad students, so I would sleep on the floor of his bedroom.

As soon as I arrived, I noticed a copy of *Hedwig and the Angry Inch.* Though I'd never seen the film, I knew it was about drag queens—my first landlady in New York, Jenny, had told me about it when I'd shared my dad's secret in a moment of weakness.

"Oh, like Dad," I said to my brother.

"What?"

Dave didn't know. I'd assumed my mom had told him.

I told him the story my mom had shared when I was eighteen.

As an older sibling, I'd often been Dave's teacher. After Dad died, Dave took on that role.

By the time I was hired at *Good Housekeeping,* my brother's creative career had seen a rise—he was regularly cast as leads. He'd always juggled acting while working as an accountant. But as he got busier on stage, he got tired of juggling. He'd scored a job at a biotech firm and loved it. But he never stopped singing.

I leaned on Dave's social life after Dad's death—a result of his having gone back to school. It was harder to make friends in New York. I focused on succeeding at work. I was driven to be something nobody thought I could. Unlike my dad, I thought, I would be remembered.

Working in the Hearst building felt like a dream. It was glamorous; no matter how tired I was riding up that escalator in that glass beehive each morning, and then the elevator to the twenty-eighth floor, often after having arrived home at midnight the night before, I'd pinch myself.

I felt this way still, seven years later, the year I started my dad's list. Despite my desk having been moved into a closet.

* * *

WHEN I RETURNED from the Rose Bowl, my chronic heartburn began making me miss work. I made an appointment with a gastroenterologist.

One of the days I missed was when my boss was on vacation. A limited-edition advertorial needed my department's eyes, and only one of us was available because I was at home.

Stacy, my boss, took me down to the cafeteria to talk about it when she returned.

"I don't want to lose my job," I said in the mirrored elevator. It felt robotic as it came out of my mouth, like it was someone else saying it.

"Don't worry," she said. "That's not what's happening."

As we sat down, Stacy said she was worried about me. They needed me to be more reliable, she said. Stacy was my *new* boss—she'd only just started. She had no idea how reliable I'd been for seven years.

"This is not how I usually am," I explained. "This list—and now writing a book—is a lot to juggle. And I haven't been feeling well. I will do better."

A week later, I woke up after an endoscopy in a happy delirium. I told all the nurses how wonderful they were. Laughing at me, Steven drove me home. It's a bad idea to interact with people while recovering from anesthesia. But once I was in bed, I noticed safe driving advocates talking on Facebook and joined in.

One post promoted "hands-free driving" (where a phone is used via Bluetooth). Another was for a campaign called Hands-Free Georgia. Someone had photographed a billboard that read "Hands-free saves lives."

What bothered me about this was that it wasn't true. Researchers and advocates knew that hands-free phone use was risky and caused crashes, just as handheld did.

It was the reason, at my father's hearing, in 2003, that the driver claimed she saw a light as green while seven others saw red. The girl wasn't lying. She thought the light was green because it was the last color she'd seen before her phone blinded her.

When I went to Chicago in 2016, the NSC told us the studies they shared with us, of where a driver's eyes went, weren't brand-new. Some had existed for a decade. And car companies had known the risks of hands-free phone use and not talked about it. For twenty years.

This was what compelled me to write about it. I was shocked by the cover-up.

Watching advocates help build another one shocked me more.

I wrote to the Georgia advocate. She said she worked for AT&T now, and they weren't interested in preventing phone call deaths, like my father's—they would now focus solely on preventing texting deaths. She called me selfish on her Facebook wall for caring about people killed by drivers making phone calls.

She said nobody used the phone for calls anymore anyway, that everybody texted. But the dial tones I heard in the cars on my street every day told me otherwise.

"We always make sure to add, 'Hands-free isn't risk-free,'" she said.

"But that makes it seem like hands-free is bad, but not *that* bad!" I wrote. "You know the risk is exactly the same. The people you're trying to convince don't know that."

She said saving all lives was impossible. She said we needed to settle for what we could get. The national hands-free campaign was a baby step, she said. Later down the road, we'd try to get phone calls out of cars, too, she promised.

I didn't believe her.

I knew from twenty years as a journalist that if you present the public with a lie, they're not likely to trust you again.

Later I mentioned this on an NSC conference call for advocates. I said I'd thought our goal was to get both texts and phone calls out of cars. An advocate laughed.

"You're asking for the impossible," she said.

I couldn't dispute publicly what was happening. My literary agent had instructed me to stop taking interviews.

My gastroenterologist diagnosed me with a hiatal hernia—a condition where your stomach bulges up into your esophagus. Nothing could be done about it, he said, but reducing stress, sleeping more soundly, and improving my diet could help.

"No more acidic foods," he prescribed.

The next day my boss invited me to a magazine event, a *Woman's Day* heart health benefit. Blondie performed "Heart of Glass." The décor was heart-themed—there were red hearts everywhere. I'd begun seeing hearts at least once a day since starting the list. I felt guilty going to the event—my old boss, Benay, wouldn't have sanctioned it. She stayed behind in the office and worked.

The next week Stacy and I both got calls from HR.

"It's business restructuring," Kim, the new managing editor, explained. I'd loved my previous managing editor, who was laid off after working there forty years. When Kim replaced her, she met with everyone in my department to introduce herself—everyone but me.

My company had purchased a smaller, failing company and absorbed its magazine titles. This meant they needed to blend staffs yet again. Instead of working on four magazines every month, my copy department would now work on five.

Benay, my former boss, would now run the department along with a copy editor from the new company, and they'd dispense the extra work to freelancers. Hearst was laying off Stacy and me.

"So, this isn't performance-based?" I asked.

"No," Kim said. "It has nothing to do with that."

I'd worked for *Good Housekeeping*, my dream job, for seven years. This meant my severance would be upward of $12,000.

My reflection surprised me when I walked into the mirrored elevator.

It was smiling.

On the train ride home—Kim let us leave early—I emailed and texted everyone I knew in journalism. I already had a job interview lined up at Condé Nast, our rival. The severance would kick in shortly, and the company was letting me work an additional two months in the office.

"This is great," Steven said, when I told him sheepishly after getting off the train. "Now you'll have time to write!"

"How could they do this to you?" my mom asked, sobbing, when I told her over the phone.

Losing my job made affording our trip to Texas to check off "see the NCAA basketball finals" easier.

My brother couldn't believe this was how I wanted to spend my fortieth birthday.

Four days before my first birthday, the most-watched NCAA championship in history aired on TV. More than thirty-five million watched Magic Johnson defeat Larry Bird, which set the stage for their rivalry—defining the NBA of my youth. Besides this, I knew next to nothing about college basketball. Or Texas.

My stepbrother Scott signed me up for his 2018 NCAA pool, and Karen, *Redbook*'s health editor, a blonde who sat outside our closet office, helped me pick the right teams.

"I'm from West Virginia," she explained. "It's against the law there not to love college basketball."

Thanks to Karen, I made top picks on my March Madness bracket, including Villanova, the closest I could come to a hometown team.

I based most of my picks on the players' life stories.

Villanova's star point guard Jalen Brunson's father had played nine seasons with the NBA and was cut nine times. When he was cut from the Philadelphia 76ers, my dad's favorite team, he told Jalen he was finished with the game.

"I don't want you to live how I've lived," he told his son.

Jalen was a star high school player when his father was arrested for allegedly sexually assaulting a masseuse. Though his dad was later acquitted, Jalen faced taunts about his dad not only from the other teams but also from his fans. His coach at Villanova, where the taunting continued, said Jalen developed a "killer mentality" to cope.

"He turns the taunts into fuel," he said.

We got off the plane in Austin on a spring Friday. We went through our routine: car rental, then coffee. On the door of the coffee shop a sign said something we'd never seen before: "Leave your guns outside."

Our first stop was Lady Bird Johnson's Wildflower Center. I'd joked that the only thing I wanted for my fortieth birthday was to lie in a field of flowers. March is bluebonnet season in Texas. When we watched the video about the former first lady's drive to "beautify" the United States, I cried. Lady Bird's motto was "Where flowers bloom, so does hope." She'd planted flowers along highways.

After more hours than Steven had wanted to spend frolicking, we stopped at a vegan barbecue truck then had afternoon tea at an old plantation. That night, in our hotel, we watched Villanova beat Kansas on TV over vegan pizza. This meant we'd be watching them play in person at the game on Easter Sunday.

My home team had made it into the championship.

Most people think Texas is a macho place. But in Austin and San Antonio, where we were, the Native Americans worship water—a feminine substance. Barton Springs—a public swimming hole—is infused with prayers, blown into its depths by the smoke of Native American women. This has been happening for thousands of years.

The next day, we paid our three-dollar fee and put a hotel towel on the grassy hill at Barton Springs. But Steven refused to get in. "I don't like how I look right now," he explained.

So I tiptoed down the smooth limestone myself. The water was cool. As I floated toward the middle, seaweed brushed my feet. A turquoise dragonfly skittered by, an insect who spends half her life in water and half in air. The dragonfly's a celebration of maturity.

If you see a dragonfly, your life is about to change.

San Antonio, where the game was held, is like Venice—lined with canals. That Sunday, after we entered the stadium, I found out Bill Walton, who'd cycled the Tour de Tucson in Arizona like I had, was there—and then I met him. I was even more amazed to learn that Clyde Drexler, my brother's favorite player, was there, too. We stood in line for his autograph.

"I know what I'll say when I meet him," I told Steven. "I'll say, 'Hi, Mailman.'"

"He might be confused by that," Steven responded, "because that was the nickname for Karl Malone, not Clyde Drexler."

My brother's conversations with our dad that revolved around basketball, around any sport, were the only ones I never tried to join. My dad loved Karl; my brother loved Clyde. They debated about who was better. I'd heard the conversation so many times, the two had merged into one.

Half the number one seeds in the 2018 tournament were from Catholic schools. My dad played basketball for a Catholic high school. When the game was invented, American Catholics were often working-class families clustered in the cities where these schools were. Basketball's field of play is inexpensive. The equipment's cheap, too. Part of Catholicism is looking after the less fortunate. And Jesuit philosophy is holistic: it's not only about caring for the mind and the soul, but about nurturing one's physicality. In short, basketball was created to help young men become good Christians.

It was strange watching this urban game in a place known for *Friday Night Lights*.

Though we remembered the Alamo, we forgot to have dinner. I promised Steven another trip to the vegan barbecue truck later.

The stadium was enormous, though only one-fifth the size of the Rose Bowl. I kept my eyes on Jalen Brunson the whole first half, mostly because Villanova was losing. But by halftime, they'd inched their way above Michigan by ten points.

Probably a good portion of the team, I realized, had made it to Villanova thanks to scholarships.

* * *

My dad coached me in basketball as earnestly as he coached my brother.

I played a year on the girls' team in high school and two in junior high. But before that, when I was twelve, I played in a YMCA league, where I was the only girl.

Every time we met at center court, the boys on the opposing team fought over who would cover me. Playing a girl was easy, they thought.

But my dad had coached me in man-on-man defense so tight that they'd never touch the ball. As the boys grew frustrated, he'd chuckle courtside.

"That Ken Morley has my daughter as a starter!" he'd say.

My dad called me "the female Bobby Jones" because he was the top defensive player in the NBA. But he was also a team player. Bobby Jones helped my dad's 76ers win the NBA championship in 1983. Charles Barkley once said, "If everyone in the world was like Bobby Jones, the world wouldn't have any problems."

* * *

The day before the NCAA championship, the coach of St. Joseph's said in the *New York Times*, "In basketball, it doesn't matter if you're Black or white, rich or poor, city or suburbs. And in the Catholic faith, you shouldn't be measured by those things...you should be measured by your character."

My dad never cared about status. He cared about character.

It was true—he hadn't saved for my college education. But I realized now this was partly due to his belief that he could help me earn one.

In the end, Villanova beat Michigan by seventeen. But Jalen Brunson, their star player, scored only nine of those points. It was a player from my home state, Delaware, who scored the most. In the second half, Donte DiVincenzo scored thirty-one.

"Delaware for the win!" a commentator yelled.

In this one game, Villanova had broken the record for the most three-pointers in a championship, the most points scored by a nonstarter in a championship, and the most points scored by any player in a final in three decades.

"This doesn't surprise us," Brunson told a reporter afterward. "It just shows you how much depth we have as a team, and how we don't care who gets credit."

Jalen Brunson hadn't overvalued his ambitions—he'd been a team player. He'd satisfied his father's wishes after all.

Two weeks later, back in New York, I packed up my office of seven years.

For nearly a decade, this building had been my life. I even slept on its floor sometimes, when it got too late to take the subway.

Steven took a photo of me in front of a wall of windows, the city skyline and Hudson River behind me. We compared it to the one he'd taken after I was hired.

I had worked so hard to get here.

We flew to Florida to see my mom the next day. I told her I planned to pursue book writing full-time for a while. I tried to sound optimistic.

But back in New Jersey, I cried. I hugged Steven in the kitchen, holding onto our nubby white couch blanket. Our cat, Pinky, rubbed her face on our legs.

Though my stepdad had said nothing about it, I feared he didn't approve.

"I don't know when you're going to stop caring what that man thinks," Steven said.

I set up my new writer's office in the living room. I gave myself a schedule. On Wednesdays I drove to jury duty—I'd been assigned to a grand jury for sixteen weeks. For seven years I'd postponed serving—my previous boss, Benay, had said our schedule didn't allow for it. But a job that doesn't permit you to be a full American citizen is a job that probably requires too much.

My new writer friend Gabie referred me for a freelance job at *Guideposts*. But I mostly spent my hours reading. For years my eyes had been too tired from copyediting to read books I loved. Now I read about everything I ever wanted to know. I read the authors I admired most. I felt like a scholar.

It was like my dad had helped me win a scholarship.

CHAPTER 8

Grow a Watermelon

I was born without peripheral vision in my right eye. Nerves that were supposed to develop in my mother's sixth week of pregnancy didn't. Doctors called it a spontaneous defect, though it happens more in families where people have lazy eyes.

But I don't have a lazy eye. My right eye is simply defiant.

It's mostly meant a life of turning my head to the right. It hasn't caused many problems while driving because I'm hyper-alert. When I've thought about being that seventeen-year-old driver, with my dad's car coming from the right, I've realized there was no way I would have seen him. My right eye would have made the phone distraction worse.

We named all of my father's cars. The green Oldsmobile was Kermit, the orange van was Homer. Once he won a car in a contest by keeping his hands on it the longest. I don't remember naming the car he died in.

Due to my right eye, I've walked into trees. I bump into strangers in crowds more than most. I've broken toes because of it.

In June 2018, my right eye struck again.

I was trying to check off "beat a number-one seed in tennis." My friend Craig, Steven's best friend, had coached tennis for twenty years. On a trip to York, Pennsylvania, Steven's hometown, Steven and I hit a few rounds at a local high school while we waited for Craig—that is, until

I needed a bathroom. I walked all over campus searching for one, my stomach distended.

When I came back, I found Steven running around the football field. His asthma usually stopped him half a mile in. But he'd been reading books for vegans about exercise. He believed running could cure his asthma—as long as he ate the right foods.

He was out of breath when I found him. I worried he might die. I forced myself to walk back to the tennis courts.

Steven was triumphant by the time Craig arrived—he'd run a full mile. He suggested he play his friend in tennis on my behalf, since I was sick. But I said no—I was determined to check off the list item.

Since I'd played on the high school tennis team, I was sure I could do this in one afternoon. Even if I only scored one point on Craig, it still counted as beating a number-one seed in tennis.

Steven and I played each other while Craig offered tips. Then Craig played Steven, and then me, promising he'd go easy.

Instead, he had me running all over the court.

* * *

MY DAD'S TENNIS LESSONS were similar to how we played football.

We played doubles versus single—my brother and me versus him. He put me on the left, in the backhand position—an odd choice, given my lack of right peripheral vision. Playing the left side meant I'd hit more backhands, and I'd have to hit them blind. My reflexes became automatic, like Luke Skywalker lightsaber fighting a remote.

Maybe his choice was no accident.

* * *

WHEN CRAIG LOBBED A BALL into the far-left side of the court, I leapt for it, confident in my blind backhand. But I landed hard on my left foot. I felt a snap.

Oh no.

For months I ignored my hurt foot. I taped my second toe to my third and hoped for the best. I took an official tennis lesson like this. I

128

ran a 5K. I walked to work at *Guideposts* in the city, at least a mile each day, with my foot taped up. I taped it for my family reunion in July.

"What happened to your foot?" my stepbrother Drew, the one we went surfing with, asked at my aunt's house.

My mom was planning a family trip to London in October, to celebrate her seventieth birthday. It was a place my dad had wanted to visit—it's item fifteen on his list. So everything I brought for the reunion was from a British bakery.

"You're not still eating meat, are you?" my cousin Jimmy's wife, Lizzie, asked. She'd just recovered from breast cancer. She was pescatarian.

"About twenty-five percent of the time," I said.

Steven did all of our cooking and had just started a blog of vegan recipes. It was easy to eat vegan at home. But I still ate "normal food" outside the apartment.

Besides being my cousin Jimmy's wife, Lizzie was also my favorite living author—she wrote a best-selling memoir in her early twenties. She was famous at an age when most people are still making terrible mistakes, so she made hers in public.

Meeting one's heroes is a bad idea; being related to one by marriage is worse. Watching Lizzie navigate my family was hard. Their collective response to her wit and proclivity for debate showed me there was little space in my family for such a creative woman—or maybe just for such a combative one.

Lizzie understood, like many writers, that too much reverence for dignity limits accepting one's humanness. It is only when we are comfortable in our skin that we are truly alive.

As I sat in my aunt's backyard, eating the last of my potato salad, Elizabeth Wurtzel asked how my book was going.

She asked if I was writing about my dad. "Everybody wants to write about their father," she said. She said it was only interesting if we'd had some conflict. Then she asked, "What about Jim? Is your conflict with him?" My stepdad was standing behind us. I didn't know how to respond. I told her I found the writing therapeutic.

"When I finished my first draft of *Prozac Nation*, I went to the movies and thought some kind of miracle had happened because I'd forgotten my glasses at home, but I could see the screen perfectly," she said. "I believed my eyesight had been cured because I'd healed myself through my writing."

"Wow!" I said.

"It turned out, I'd fallen asleep after finishing the draft with my contacts in, but forgotten," she explained. "It's not worth a damn how therapeutic writing is if it's not a good story. Make it a good story."

I stared at my husband playing lawn games in the distance.

"What kind of game is 'corn hole,' anyway?" she asked.

Lizzie had spent her entire life in New York; suburban pastimes bewildered her.

I took my potato salad over to the lawn. Somehow my dad's list came up in conversation; my sister-in-law Jessi and cousin's husband Shane wanted to know what was left. Shane, who'd just bought a house, sneered at "own a large house and our own land."

"Good luck with that!" he said sarcastically.

"I wish I could convince your stepbrother to stop texting and driving," Jessi said.

I found my stepbrother Scott behind us.

"Is it true?" I demanded. "That you *still* text and drive?"

"Sure, sometimes, man," he said.

"But you know the science!" I yelled. "You've seen my interviews."

"Science?" Scott asked, blinking.

"Of what happens to your brain when you use a phone while driving! I've dedicated my whole life to this. You were at my dad's funeral! You're a dad now, too!"

Shaking, I ran inside. I was so heated when I escaped to the bathroom that I couldn't even cry.

When I came back downstairs, Scott stood in the kitchen doorway.

"I'm sorry," he said. "Can't we talk about this? I'll never do it again."

"No, Scott," I said. "I'm not doing this. I can't have this conversation. This is as serious to me as a heart attack."

Steven and I hugged my cousins goodbye. After I reached our hotel, I texted them, apologizing for my display. Explaining that I had to be "an advocate first."

The next morning my stepdad dropped my mom off at our hotel. She'd agreed to go to an activism event with Steven and me, hosted by my mentor, Joel Feldman, to honor his daughter.

I'd become an advocate because of Joel. One day at *Good Housekeeping*, an article came across my desk about Joel and his daughter, Casey, who'd been killed by a distracted truck driver while walking to her summer job. She was only twenty-one. I had never talked about my father's death at work, until this article appeared. I called Joel the next day.

Joel's daughter had been a star journalism student. He encouraged me to write about my dad's death. The first essay I wrote about it was for Joel's website. I spoke alongside him in a local high school. I raised funds for his foundation when I ran the New York City Marathon.

Casey loved animals, so Joel honored each anniversary of her death with an ASPCA cleanup. Steven was excited—this event combined my cause with his. I told Joel about being angry with my stepbrother. I also told him about the Georgia advocate who'd ridiculed me.

We sprayed the animals' cages then settled in for lunch—but all they'd provided was deli meat hoagies, which Steven, a vegan, couldn't eat.

"We love your daughter," Joel's wife, Dianne, told my mom. "She's been a good friend to us."

"Laura really lives by her beliefs," my mom responded.

I wasn't sure what she meant.

We drove off to find a vegan restaurant in Philadelphia. I told my mom over lunch how upset I was about my confrontation with Scott.

"How can I love someone if they're not showing integrity?" I asked.

"Integrity isn't a requirement for love," she answered.

After one bite of her chickpea tuna sandwich, my mom learned that it wasn't real fish. Her eyes widened. She closed her mouth and put the sandwich back on her plate.

The next few days, I was still bummed out. If I couldn't convince a loved one of the science behind distracted driving, how could I convince anyone?

"Well, I've educated you about the science behind factory farming, but you still eat meat," Steven said.

He was right. I had watched enough videos and read enough books to agree that the way animals were treated in factory farms was inhumane. It made me disgusted to eat meat, and yet still I did it.

My running was my last reason not to go vegan. But Steven had shared information with me all summer about vegan athletes—how eating vegan made them stronger. It was how he'd become a runner.

I realized I could not hope for anyone I loved to drive safely just because they'd learned about phone use from me. And I would probably encounter more situations like the one at the reunion if I continued like that. Instead of trying to change people, I needed to be the change.

I told Steven, not only would I go vegan, but I'd finish an Ironman that way.

I needed to live by my beliefs.

I befriended a twenty-five-year-old kindergarten aide at jury duty. Heather laughed at my attempts to get out of serving.

Heather was generous, despite having seemingly little, and talked about Native Americans and ghosts and how much she hated Donald Trump, defending her Latino friends (she volunteered in Ecuador once a year and often burst into Spanish, though she was white). She shared on our second day of jury duty that she took the bus instead of driving because she was losing her eyesight. She'd be blind by the time she was forty. "That's why I try to have as much fun as I can *while* I can," she said. I volunteered to drive her home every week.

I feared the list was making me more like my dad in bad ways. Though he usually worked in advertising sales, he sold many products in his life: liquor, bottled water, phone books. He worked as a taxi driver briefly, placing my brother and me in the cab, which made my mom nervous. Toward the end of his life, he worked as a substitute teacher. Every job felt temporary. Every transition had no explanation.

When I asked my spiritual coach friend Christina if doing my dad's list was a mistake, because I'd lost job stability, she said, "Always keep your vibration high! Thank the universe for bringing *abundance* into your life." So I recited silently every Wednesday on my drive to jury duty, *Thank you, God, for the abundance.*

After my agent failed to sell my book, the year before, I lay in bed one night and asked my dad in my mind's eye, "What am I supposed to be learning from this? Because this is really hard." Behind my closed eyes, I sat in the back seat of my father's car in front of my mom's house, where he dropped us off twice a week.

Abundance, not scarcity, I heard.

An image of the rat race in New York entered my mind. I shared a fear with many that you must work hard to make sure you have enough...that if I didn't get that prized job, the other guy would take it. This is a scarcity mindset: a belief that there are limited opportunities.

The truth is, the possibilities in life are endless. There is always enough for everyone.

I realized that if I looked at my life through a filter of abundance, I could shift from taking to giving. God would provide—it was my job to provide for others.

My gifts weren't there so I could compete. They were there so I could give.

The day I started writing my book, I also planted four watermelon seeds to satisfy "grow a watermelon." They were sugar baby watermelons, no bigger than a bowling ball. I didn't have a backyard, so I needed something I could grow in a pot on my fire escape. I planted four seeds and said a prayer.

In the last week of jury duty, Heather asked how my watermelons were doing.

"OK, I guess," I said. "Only one has sprung up."

"It'll happen," she said.

I'd killed plants all my life. With the hours I normally worked, I didn't have time to take care of them. But now, suddenly, I did. And I had time to take care of me, too.

My apartment was always clean now. When cleaning out my home office, I discovered old notebooks of my dad's. They were to-do lists—he'd categorized them by year: "1976 to 1978," said one. It included items like "paint baby's nursery" and "buy milk" and "get my religion straight." He'd placed existential projects alongside mundane chores.

"Wow," I told Steven. "He was organized!"

"Yeah, reminds me of someone...." Steven said.

On the first page of one notebook, he wrote, "*A Pledge to Self, According to the Principles of Napoleon Hill.*" It was my father's vow to become a writer, composed at age twenty-two. What was eerie about it was how much it resembled a pledge I'd written at twenty-six—on the one-year anniversary of his death.

In another notebook I found an inscription: "*I dedicate this book to Laura and David. They are two beautiful, shining lights in my less than brilliant life. Thank you for letting me love you. Love, Dad.*" The rest of the book was blank.

When I started my manuscript, I wrote about the hardest times in my life. I took Steven to Beach Haven afterward, where I hadn't been since skydiving. But when he accused me of taking too long to get ready in the hotel, I overturned a chair.

Lying on the beach, crying beneath a straw sunhat, I peered at him. He was sculpting a funny face with a long chin he called "Sand Leno." I said, "They should have protected me." I meant my mom and stepdad. It was the first time I realized I was angry about the hospital.

I was beginning to enjoy my quieter life. Every day, when I wasn't working in the city or headed to jury duty, I had the same routine. I'd wake up at 2:00 p.m., take a shower, make the bed, do the dishes, drink coffee, smudge my crystals, and write. I'd started a collection after the rose quartz I found on Mount Atalaya. As I smudged them with smoking sweetgrass, I'd say: "I love the truth" (for the rose quartz), "I see the truth" (for the clear quartz), "I speak the truth" (for the lapis lazuli), and "I know the truth" (for the amethyst). My green aventurine was the biggest, in the shape of a heart, so I smudged this one last, saying, "I feel it all with my whole heart." I held the stone up to my chest when I was afraid.

On our honeymoon, in Sedona, during the part when our family was still there, Jaime and I were perusing a crystal shop when Steven and Dave left to get the car. I explored the computer in the back that photographed auras. I was too skeptical to pay for a photo but too curious not to look. As I played around with the mouse, a woman with long, dark, wavy hair emerged through a beaded curtain. I apologized for fooling around where I shouldn't. "That's OK, you've almost got it," she said. When she clicked the mouse, my portrait showed up on the computer screen, engulfed in yellow. "This is the aura of a writer," she said. "You're trying to write a book, but you're afraid it won't be good. Your solar plexus chakra is blocked. Do it anyway, because what you're writing is the truth."

"I think you are a real writer now," Heather said at jury duty, after my weekly watermelon update.

"Why do you say that!?" I laughed.

"Because you used to talk about *Good Housekeeping* all the time," she said. "But you haven't said one thing about being a copy editor in two months."

On our last night in Beach Haven, *High Noon* had been on TV. Gary Cooper says to someone after being stripped of being sheriff, "I'm the same man without the badge."

Maybe I was, too.

In late summer, Steven and I ran our first trail 5K, which went wonderfully for him but terribly for me. Running downhill was hard. My injured foot couldn't do it. As Steven congregated with friends at the finish line—we'd run in his hometown—I wandered around the farm, trying to walk off the gnawing. I made an appointment that week with a podiatrist.

Since Beach Haven, I'd been picking fights. I worried the life choices I was making would drive Steven away—despite his encouragement. Surely my dad felt discouraged from being a full-time writer for a reason. The emotions writing stirred up were volatile. Steven and I were intimate less often, and I took this as a sign he would soon leave.

One night, I drove off to a hotel—at midnight. I packed a bag and left.

We don't run away from our marriage, I heard my dad say as I lay in the hotel's king-sized bed.

But you did! I thought through angry tears.

You're right, he said. *I'm sorry. But you don't have to be like me.*

Suddenly I heard my own voice—it was the real me, the higher me: *I love you, Laura. I'm so proud of you. We're going to be OK.*

I'd never heard her before.

I called Steven and apologized.

As a new vegan, there wasn't much I could eat at the hotel. So I drove to Target the next morning and bought spinach, balsamic dressing, baby carrots, vegan meatballs, trail mix, dried mangoes, and dark chocolate. I spent the next two days reading and writing whenever I wanted. Nobody asked me what I was doing or when. I had space of my own. For the first time in my life.

Even in the hospital I'd had a roommate.

After I checked out, I stopped at McDonald's and ordered a Big Mac. Going vegan was hard.

When I reached our back door, I saw that each watermelon seed had sprouted. A week later the seedlings flowered, and then, on the anniversary of my dad's death, one of the flowers fruited. We named the fruit Audrey II.

Later that night, a great green grasshopper appeared on the window behind our sofa. This would have been less strange if it hadn't shown up on that window on the anniversary of my dad's death the year before.

The grasshopper is an animal that can only move forward.

The next day at *Guideposts*, I Googled "cross-dressers' support group" and a name popped up: Pat Cross. At first, I thought it was his real name. I explained in my email that my father had been a cross-dresser and I wanted to understand it better. Pat agreed to meet in a Dunkin' Donuts.

Pat looked like Wilford Brimley. As soon as I sat in the booth, he handed me a sheet of paper listing the things a wife worries about when she learns her husband cross-dresses. It filled the entire page.

"You know who wrote that?" Pat asked.

"Who?" I asked.

"Me."

Pat was like a den mother for cross-dressers and transgender women. Whenever someone wanted to dress in public, even if it was just a gas station, Pat would be their guide. If someone considered suicide, the most common cause of death for transgender people, Pat was the one they'd call.

He clicked through photos on his laptop of himself in drag, usually on battleships, his hobby; sometimes he was dressed as Wonder Woman ("for Halloween," he said); and sometimes he was wearing a woman's bathing suit by a motel pool.

His nails reminded me of my dad's, which often looked like they could use a trim. I now wondered if that had been on purpose. But when I asked Pat about them, he said, "Oh, these? I keep them long for my job."

Pat was a locksmith.

"I never got to have this conversation with my dad," I told Pat, crying. "You are giving me a gift today."

"He was trying to protect you," Pat said.

Pat explained what a torturous experience the desire to dress was. Straight men who cross-dress do it because they like the texture of women's clothing or they feel more relaxed when dressed as a woman. It doesn't mean they want to stop being a man. "Imagine how confusing it must have been for him," Pat said. When my dad was a kid, cross-dressing was forbidden even in films. He couldn't have seen an example of it, except maybe on Merv Griffin or Bugs Bunny. And my dad was Catholic. The Bible says God detests those who dress like the opposite sex.

Maybe my dad wasn't being selfish by hiding this. Maybe he was being selfless. Hiding this much of himself meant sacrificing time with the two people he loved most.

Maybe he didn't want his children to be tortured, too.

Suddenly I noticed the TV propped up by the ceiling. It was playing *The Little Mermaid*'s "Part of Your World."

I'd finally been let in to my dad's.

All I'd needed was a locksmith.

After I drove home, I told Steven what I'd learned. How grateful I was for Pat's help. Steven had been nervous about our meeting. I cried, talking about it, for an hour.

"But what if you helped him, too?" Steven said.

Pat had teared up a few times. He was sensitive and witty, like my dad. He didn't take himself too seriously. His eyes moistened readily—it was like the vulnerable part that gets dulled in men had never left him.

"Yes," I said. "Maybe I did."

Our London trip was coming up in two months, and by the time we went to the Catskills for Labor Day, we had mostly paid for it. Over Steven's birthday dinner we reflected on how nice it was to take a trip just for us (and not for the list).

The Indian restaurant was dimly lit. Steven said he felt OK eating extra birthday cake because he'd lost so much weight from running. It was the first time I'd ever heard him say he was happy about his body.

"Wait a minute," I said. "Can I ask you something?"

"Sure."

"Do you feel 'healthy'?"

"Yes!" he said.

"How about 'young'?"

"My doctor said my blood work was that of a twenty-five-year-old!"

"So all that's left is 'happy' and 'handsome,'" I said.

"What do you mean?"

"'Make my wife feel happy, healthy, pretty, and young all her life.' My dad wrote it on the list."

"Oh, so this was *your* doing?" Steven joked.

"No..." I said, laughing. "But maybe my intention helped?"

That fall, as I wrapped up my first week of working freelance for Condé Nast, I met my friend Mary Latham in a café on the Upper East Side. I couldn't believe I'd scored work at *Vanity Fair*.

Mary was midway through a three-year mission, traveling the country in her mom's honor, collecting stories of small acts of kindness. After she'd visited all fifty states, she'd compile the stories into a book for hospital waiting rooms, where she was when she learned of her mom's sudden death from cancer.

Mary understood my mission. I could text her at any hour and she'd answer, no matter where she was. When we parted ways in front of the café, I gave her a big hug and wished her luck. I walked a few blocks to my old Upper East Side apartment, where I'd lived my second year in New York.

* * *

ONE DAY IN THAT FIRST YEAR after my father's death, I found myself alone in my Jackson Heights apartment, reflecting on how disconnected I felt.

I was sitting at my landlady's desk—none of the furniture in that apartment belonged to me—in the middle of the day, with Oprah on the TV behind me, my computer screen in front of me, when this idea occurred. In my yearning for connection with my dad, I couldn't discern what part of him still existed and where. And for a moment I felt, well, how different will it be when someday, I, too, am separated from my body?

I wondered if there was an emotion more expansive than grief. Mine knew no bounds. As a young person, I'd often wondered what life was like from other people's eyes. Now I realized I'd never needed my eyes at all.

In my five short months living in Jackson Heights, that once vivid fuchsia, that bustling street of busy Indian men, those Our Lady of Guadalupe candles flickering with promise and light, the Empire State Building, a sliver of hope through my kitchen window, all of this had turned, changed, into a cavernous eggplant room, solemn men on the streets, candles blown out and sacred, everything had this air of the empty and the sacred—the Empire State Building now as religious to me as a cross.

Everything had changed, and in the mornings, when I woke to another day of applying for jobs, I looked across the street, at the arched tops of the buildings. I sat up in bed, imagining they were the tops of a beach house in Delaware—I imagined I was home. It brought me comfort in what had become at last a cold, distant land.

Gradually the solemnity gave way to spirituality. I learned my Muslim neighbors prayed three times a day. I pictured them kneeling and worshipping on a blue rug, in front of a window, and suddenly I felt part of a congregation. Even the Empire State Building made me feel that way in time. After all, he stands there all by himself, inspiring the masses.

But the worst part was that in the midst of my grief, my heart was being forced open by someone more each day, as though doing this would keep me alive.

The depth of my disappointment that I could no longer fully feel what I'd felt for Steven pained me in a way I couldn't explain—it was like the feeling you get as a child, when you've discovered a beehive or butterflies or a nest of baby birds, and then you come back the next day to find sweet, smashed honeycombs on the ground, monarch wings on the pavement, or cracked eggshells next to a robin with a broken neck.

It was like *I* was that robin, and I'd finally found the courage to fly, but then my nest had been destroyed.

Steven could have run away after he joined me in New York, too jarred by it.

But instead, he cradled my little robin neck and lay there on the ground with me.

Sometimes I woke in the middle of the night, and in the seconds between sleeping and waking, heard Neil Diamond's song "Turn on Your Heart Light."

Once when I was four, my dad showed up at my preschool to surprise me. Dressed in his business suit, he'd just come from work, and I felt so important as he took me away from the classroom and out to see the movie *E.T. the Extra-Terrestrial*. Afterward, we stopped at Howard Johnson's for lunch, and then he took me back to school. It was an exciting day.

At the end of the film, before the alien returns, his heart begins to glow, and he tells the boy who's become his friend, "I'll be right here." It's a common misconception that he points to the boy's heart when he says this. But Spielberg insisted he point to Elliot's head.

Whatever planet my dad had returned to, he really was still "right here," but it would take some time for me to see that.

It would take turning on my heart. And it was by that light that I could see through the dark, however faintly. And then it grew brighter.

I kept it lit with the help of a man who didn't fear dark skies, who when he himself was four, ran around the classroom during a thunderstorm, telling his little friends not to be afraid.

Because the truth is, there is an emotion more expansive than grief. Love.

* * *

I WALKED TO THE PARK beside the East River and searched for the Peter Pan fountain. After I moved to the Upper East Side, I walked down there many nights. It was a proxy for my dad, who used to say he was twelve on the inside. He loved Peter Pan.

I looked up at the fountain.

I'm done with you, I thought.

After I rode the train back home, I climbed the stairs to my apartment. It was dark.

I watered my plant and noticed something strange.

My watermelon had grown into the shape of a heart.

CHAPTER 9

Visit London

I ate Audrey II on the train to the airport. My sugar baby watermelon fit in the palm of my hand.

We'd be traveling the first two weeks of October, which included my sister-in-law Jaime's birthday. She and my brother had booked us an Airbnb in Notting Hill the first few days. Then Steven and I would go with my mom and stepdad to their timeshare, an old country estate in Canterbury, while my brother surprised Jaime with an overnight trip to Paris. We'd reconvene in Dublin then drive to Ireland's West Coast.

Anytime I mentioned trip ideas to my mom, she said, "Your brother doesn't want us to plan anything. We can all discuss it the first night."

I couldn't comprehend not planning what we wanted to do.

But my mom didn't seem bothered.

"How do you think this will go?" Steven asked on the plane. Wondering what might go wrong is a normal state for him.

"We'll make great memories!" I said.

But secretly I was nervous.

I talked to my brother less often lately. My mom encouraged me with the list now, but our last family trip like this, to Paris nine years earlier, hadn't been free of shenanigans.

* * *

WE VISITED THE CITY OF LIGHTS in 2009, combining vacations with my aunt's family's. Most of us were still single, and those of us who weren't couldn't afford to bring partners, so the trip made us feel like kids again.

My brother, who'd just broken his ankle, arrived in Paris alone in a walking cast because Steven got stuck in New York traffic driving my mom, stepdad, and me to the airport. My mom was distraught when we just missed our flight. I felt guilty this had happened, though it hadn't been my fault. I calmed my mom as we rescheduled for the next day. We had no way to reach Dave when he was mid-transit, but somehow my mom convinced the airline to pass a note through a flight attendant. My brother spent his first night in Paris with his cousins and aunt and uncle, without us.

After we finally arrived, we visited Notre Dame and the Catacombs. Only my cousin Jimmy and I could speak French, but half of Jimmy's was somewhat made-up. He became our de facto guide, marching through Paris with the same pace he'd developed in New York, his parents and aunt and uncle struggling to follow.

Emily, Jimmy's younger sister, got so frustrated with him that when Steph, their youngest sibling, and Dave and I wanted to climb the Eiffel Tower, Emily refused. She sat on a bench. It took restraint on Steph's part to leave her there. I couldn't believe my brother managed to climb all the way down.

The last day we each decided to do our own thing—Dave and I toured Montmartre while my mom and Jim visited Musée d'Orsay, meeting up again at the Louvre. Even in a walking cast, my brother moved faster than me. Jimmy wasn't with us at dinner, so I got my chance to order for everyone. They were surprised my French was so good. For most of the week, I'd listened to them ask slowly and loudly, "DO YOU SPEAK ENGLISH?" The gelato vendor had responded, "Sometimes."

By the last day, Dave and I were fed up—though this might have been his broken ankle talking. I didn't have that excuse.

146

* * *

THE LANGUAGE BARRIER wouldn't be a problem in England. But my cousins and aunt and uncle weren't coming this time. We'd have to juggle our parents' wants with our own. It was the first time the six of us would be in one place for so long.

Already, we were each trying to do things our way.

As I watched the sun set on the plane, I found myself praying. And asking my dad for advice.

How will this trip go? I thought.

Be your brother's friend. It's not your job to tell him what to do.

I'm sorry I haven't been doing that, I thought. *And what about Jaime?*

Loving your sister-in-law is part of being his friend, he said. *And give your mom a kiss on the cheek for me, she'll know who it's from. Tell her she's doing a great job.*

I asked what he thought of my progress as a writer and saw an OK symbol with his fingers. *Stop being so hard on yourself,* he said, *but full steam ahead when you return.*

Why is it I can hear you? Am I going crazy? I thought.

Because you want to, he said.

I asked him for advice about Steven, and I saw him shrug.

Not my area! he said. *But you are a grown woman, making decisions just fine. You live by your beliefs, you can't do any better than that, Laura Bara.*

A tear streamed down my cheek. I'd forgotten his nickname for me—from "The Name Game" song.

Realizing this seemed like a rare opportunity to contact the dead (which I wasn't sure was real), I thought bolder questions: *Anything else you want to tell the world?*

Yes, he said. *Stop wasting life being so serious and worrying about everything. Life is about loving and hugging and running and singing and dancing...well, not you at the moment....*

He was mocking my hurt foot. My doctor had given me two shots of cortisone to get through the trip. I'd scheduled surgery for when I got back.

147

How do I know this is really you? I thought.

Well, who the heck else would it be? he laughed.

This window might close, I realized, so I went deeper. *Are you OK where you are?*

I'm fine! I'm pure love now. You'll see. I will be running to meet you. You have to trust me. People are being brought to your doorstep. They are channeling me. I am making this happen. I am pulling the strings. I have the ability to give you now what I couldn't in life. Also, remember how lucky you are that your mother sees you, that she believes in you. Give her her due. As for your stepdad, you can't teach old dogs new tricks. Luckily for you, you are a young dog!

I'd read somewhere that spirit communicates in idioms.

A calm overtook me. I stopped crying. I felt at peace.

Thank you, I thought.

He gave a comical samurai bow.

What had happened was strange. The things he'd said I couldn't have imagined. They were trademark him....

I didn't plan on telling anyone about it.

After we deplaned in London, I rested my head on Steven's lap on a bench. I'd done a good job memorizing my London map, but not so well with mass transit. My stomach hurt. Vegan sandwiches from London's equivalent of 7-Eleven helped.

"Wait, vegan sandwiches in a bodega?" I asked Steven.

I'd forgotten—veganism was invented here.

We rode a red double-decker bus to the Airbnb in Notting Hill, then went out for dinner at a pizza place down the street. This suburban side of London only gave us a glimpse of what the trip had in store. My mom and stepdad were full of stories from their week in the Cotswolds, which mostly seemed to revolve around Irish butter and cheese.

My brother leaned back at the table after ordering and glanced at me.

"So, you don't drink, you don't smoke...what *do* you do?" he laughed, quoting the song. It was his job in life to tease me—and I loved it. It had been a while since we'd caught up.

"Do you think you'll be vegan forever?" Jaime asked earnestly.

"Well, never say never," I said.

In the morning, Steven woke early to run—this was his new routine. I walked through the mist to a Tesco for breakfast and snacks. In 2018, it was hard to find anything vegan in convenience stores in the United States.

The Brits take breakfast seriously, which was a relief, because breakfast in the States was also anti-vegan. And I really missed breakfast.

I picked up crumpets, jam, vegan butter, vegan sausages, and oat milk and brought it back to the Airbnb. My family was surprised to find me awake so early, like they'd never seen it happen before.

"Vegan breakfast!" I explained.

We discussed what we hoped to do and on what days. My mom anticipated seeing Buckingham Palace. But as soon as we walked outside, things began to fall apart.

We somehow ended up at the wrong train station and had to leave Dave and Jaime behind while they waited for tokens. My mom worried we'd be late for her scheduled tour.

"You were supposed to study this!" she told me on the train. I blushed. My mom had never spoken to me like that.

As Steven and I escorted my mom and stepdad off the train at Buckingham Palace, my mom picked up her pace. Pretty soon she was five blocks ahead.

Dave and Jaime reached the palace not long after we did. I tried to convince Steven to tour it with us, but he said he had no interest in royals. He left to photograph Hyde Park. I knew him well enough now to know that his not joining wasn't a reflection on me. But it was still awkward. Especially since Dave and Jaime seemed to do everything together. They got through the palace in less than half an hour and were off. My mom and Jim toured at a standard pace. I finished in an hour and a half.

When I reached our meeting place, my phone wasn't working. I called my provider and fixed it and saw I'd missed my brother's text that he and Jaime had gone to Harrods, the famous department store. I noticed on my London map that my favorite author Mary Shelley's house was on the way, so I convinced Steven, who'd rejoined us, my mom, and Jim to walk to Harrods, which ended up feeling a lot longer than twenty minutes.

The more we walked, the more impatient my mom grew. My brother was moving from place to place now. When we reached Harrods, he wasn't there anymore.

I'd reserved a table at the Victoria and Albert Museum for high tea. We'd caught up with my brother, who suggested a different place for lunch, but I had my heart set on high tea with my mom. Now we were arriving at an off time, and the café had barely any food. Jaime and Dave disappeared. They were dealing with a stressful situation back at home that I didn't know much about—and it required their sometimes disappearing. I took it personally. I ran to the bathroom and cried.

Jim needed to rest, so just my mom, Steven, and I toured the dark, vast museum, which we mostly rushed through because we still needed a decent meal.

In my London research, I'd learned about Sunday Roast, a traditional weekly repast, and that some restaurants served it vegan. So I reserved Sunday Roast at a place near the Airbnb. But when we arrived, the restaurant had no record of any crazy Americans. Jaime came up with a new plan—a place that served vegan pizza a few blocks away. My mom and Jim seemed disappointed.

After dinner, Jaime said, "I found a vegan breakfast place called Farmacy a few blocks from here." It was a place Steven had been begging me to visit.

"Yes, I know about it—we want to go," I said. "But I'm afraid my mom and Jim won't like it."

The next morning, Steven and I had breakfast with Dave and Jaime at Farmacy, a beautiful Notting Hill restaurant, its front door adorned with roses. We'd invited our parents; they'd declined.

I blamed desperation. As a new vegan, I hadn't eaten pancakes or an omelet in months. I told Dave and Jaime my vegan origin story over breakfast.

My mom and Jim planned their own morning: They would visit the Shard then meet us for a boat tour on the Thames. But they ended up taking the boat tour alone because we screwed up mass transit again. My mom told us later that she sprained her ankle when she got off the boat.

London was gray and beautiful by the river. From our boat tour, we saw the Ferris wheel (the London Eye) and Westminster Abbey. We stepped off the ship at the Tower of London, where we waited for my mom and stepdad. Dave and I toured the crown jewels and armor while Jaime and Steven waited outside, uninterested. They liked newer exhibits.

As we watched the changing of the guard, my mom and Jim joined us. She was limping.

The six of us made a plan to meet for dinner at the top of the Sky Garden at sunset. Dave, Jaime, Steven, and I toured Shakespeare's Globe Theatre, which my mom had already seen, then split up: Jaime, a *Harry Potter* fan, wanted to find Diagon Alley; Steven wanted to tour the Tate—it was the only request he'd made for the week.

I'd never seen a sunset like the one we saw over London, from a penthouse restaurant above the city. It was like the beginning of *Mary Poppins*. Everybody in the place had their phone out, photographing it. But I was too tired to look at it for long.

My mom and Jim spent the next day at Kensington Palace while Steven, Dave, Jaime, and I toured Carnaby Street. Jaime and I browsed the beauty boutiques while Steven and Dave ostensibly talked about movies outside.

I'd known my sister-in-law for four years, but I didn't know her well. She was gracious when it came to sharing about herself—she preferred to listen. She was more feminine than me and younger.

Jaime had been a stylist at Bloomingdale's when she moved to New York to try Broadway and had become an Instagram influencer: She'd created a lifestyle juggernaut from scratch, every day posting photos of their rustic home, painted in whites and neutrals. An only child, she'd grown up with her mother and grandmother—which made me assume her voice had been heard, whether or not I was right.

Jaime's suggestions were always good ones. She paid attention to what people liked. My favorite things I'd done on the trip had been her ideas.

In one of the boutiques, she saw me testing a lotion that I didn't buy because I couldn't afford it. A few days later, she gifted me the lotion.

After lunch, we shopped at Liberty of London. Dave had three other surprises for Jaime's birthday (she'd already guessed Paris): *Hamilton* tickets, a fancy dinner, and a trip to an Instagram-famous bakery.

We parted ways.

Steven and I had made a deal: a modern art museum for him, a classic art museum for me—or as Steven calls it, "the boring stuff." We headed to the National Gallery.

* * *

ONE OF MY FAVORITE THINGS is teaching Steven about classical art. Though he missed a formal liberal arts education, his eye is impeccable—and was when we met. We'd draw each other, draw cartoons on the train. We were always drawing or writing or creating something.

We broke up five times our second year in New York, always initiated by me. My job at the Associated Press caused the first breakup. Steven had enrolled at the Art Institute online to get his graphic design degree. He'd finally chosen a major, at the age of thirty-one. He still worked data entry full-time, so while he needed to be home doing homework at night, I wanted to go out with my new friends.

"So, this boyfriend of yours is imaginary, right?" my new reporter friends joked. After he couldn't be convinced to come out enough times, I ended it—I thought for good.

For a month I dated someone else, a guy I met online. But when I stayed over at Zach's apartment, I threw up. I'd only known Steven two years. But the thought of being with anyone but him made me ill. This was how I knew he was my soul mate.

When we got back together, the condom broke. I took Plan B and worried for weeks—mostly that I'd be punished for going to such lengths to prevent a pregnancy.

Now I was forty. What if that had been my only chance?

* * *

As we strolled through the National Gallery, which was arranged by century, Steven followed me, letting me explain the periods of art. Afterward we listened to street musicians in the twilight. Our recent lack of intimacy again came up.

"What's wrong with me?" I asked. "What more do I need to do?"

"I can't talk about this anymore!" he said. "There is clearly something wrong with me. *I'm* the problem."

We sat on folding chairs on the side of the crowded square. As I wiped my tears, a homeless kid, dusty blond with brown eyes, sat next to Steven.

"Make sure to put your wallet in your front pocket, 'ey," he said in a thick accent. "There's loads of pickpockets 'round here."

"Uh, thanks," Steven said warily.

I needed to not be near Steven. We'd had a wonderful time in a gorgeous museum, but my compulsion to compare my life with my brother's had made it not good enough.

I walked over to a street guitarist, who was playing "Tears in Heaven." The homeless kid dropped change in the guitar case.

"OK, he's going to kill us—and then rob us," Steven whispered behind me.

"What?" I said. "He just gave that guitarist money!"

We ran down to the Underground and double-checked the map—the first stop I saw was named Angel. What I believed the homeless kid was.

"Nope, that guy was a grade-A thief," Steven said.

We walked for what felt like hours to the British Library, where I found the only remaining manuscript of *Sir Gawain and the Green Knight*, the oldest work of English literature. Then we discovered the homes of British authors—Virginia Woolf and Charles Dickens—and ate a romantic meal in a Japanese restaurant.

On the way back to Notting Hill, we saw a fox in an alleyway, staring at us.

The fox symbolizes diplomacy.

The next morning was Jaime's birthday. We gave her presents over breakfast and wished her and my brother a nice time in Paris.

Steven, my mom, Jim, and I took an hour-long train to Windsor, where Steven rented a car for the rest of our journey.

Windsor Castle, gray stone and medieval, is where Queen Elizabeth II lived primarily. My favorite part of our tour was St. George's Chapel. After our tour, I finally got to have my high tea with my mom—in a cute café. The pace of the trip seemed to be slowing.

On our way back to the car at dusk, we stumbled upon a bevy of swans in the Thames. There had to be fifty of them. Steven took photos for an hour.

It was what the Irish call a "thin place." They say heaven and earth are usually three feet apart, but in a thin place they're closer.

My brother's request that we not plan anything was a magnet for them.

You can't ever set out to find thin places.

Thin places have to find you.

Broome Park, the timeshare we stayed in the next few nights, was two hours away. It was dark by the time we got there. We laughed as Steven drove us through cornfields in the Sussex countryside on the wrong side of the road. Finding our cottage was a comedy of errors, as all four of us searched the grounds and yelled to one another. We'd somehow rented the only cottage without a clear number labeling it.

The next day we toured the Cliffs of Dover and Dover Castle, the oldest and largest castle in England. Its chapel is where Sir Gawain was buried, if Gawain was real. This would have been my dad's favorite part of our trip—he loved King Arthur.

Thin place.

While exploring the white Cliffs, we were separated. I walked back to the car, to meet where we'd said, but my stepdad was the only one there, so I sat on a log next to Jim in silence. For the first time in my life, I didn't resent it. It was more relaxing than the planning and re-planning and meeting up and who-didn't-make-it and where-are-we-going-next and oh-but-I-want-to-do-this-instead happening the rest of the trip.

Thin place.

The next morning Steven and I set out for Winnie-the-Pooh's Hundred Aker Wood while my mom and Jim toured Canterbury.

"Have you ever seen ducks walk through the forest before?" I asked. Two of them strolled squawking by.

"Definitely not," Steven said, bemused.

We searched for the houses of Pooh, Eeyore, Owl, and Piglet, my favorite characters as a child. Then we found the house of their creator, A.A. Milne—it was a quaint mint green cottage. The sun streamed across the thin trees, cloaking them in sparkling light.

We climbed the hill for a grander view. My grandmother gave me those books. She also sang about ladybugs, so the ladybug became her totem after she died.

As we hiked back, a loveliness of ladybugs swarmed us.

Thin place.

We rejoined my mom and stepdad for dinner in Canterbury, where we toured the Cathedral—and I snuck into the crypt.

The next morning, we caught a plane to Dublin, where we'd meet Dave and Jaime. When we left the hotel, I realized I'd forgotten a stuffed animal—Piglet—I'd bought in a store near the Hundred Aker Wood. I cried over having forgotten it. I'd regressed. I blamed Steven for rushing me and leaving it behind.

After we landed in Dublin, we met up with Dave and Jaime at the boutique hotel Jaime had chosen. They took my mom and Jim out to dinner. Which meant Steven and I had the night to ourselves. We found a vegan fast-food joint across the street from our hotel—and ordered it twice in one evening, staying in to watch movies. Suddenly having a night to ourselves, in a brand-new city, we felt like we were in our twenties again.

Our intimacy problem resolved itself.

The next day we met Dave and Jaime for coffee and heard about Paris. They wanted to explore Dublin's shopping district, so we agreed to meet up again at the Book of Kells.

Steven and I spent most of Dublin alone—ordering vegan dough-nuts, touring the Francis Bacon installation, visiting the Oscar Wilde statue—while everyone else drank beer in the pubs.

But we did rejoin my family to tour the Leprechaun Museum.

My dad convinced us as kids that leprechauns lived in his shoes. I told my brother I was OK with not seeing the Blarney Stone, because no Carney would ever need to kiss it.

"Why, what's blarney?" Dave asked.

"A way with words," I said. "I certainly don't need to kiss it."

"Oh, and modesty's your *best* quality," he countered, laughing. He was quoting our dad's favorite Jack Benny joke.

"Blarney means being long-winded!" I explained. "The Irish talked the ears off of the British who came over to take their land, making things up as they went along, until they relented. That's blarney."

Our dad was full of it.

"Is that really all Steven packed?" Jaime asked, pointing to his small backpack the day we left. My brother and Steven stood several feet away at a counter, discussing the car rental contract for the rest of the trip with an agent.

"Yep," I said.

"Most of these are actually your brother's," she said, pointing at their suitcases.

Dave turned and grimaced at us every few minutes to make us laugh. It took him and Steven an hour to negotiate car insurance. Scraped fenders and worn tires are common in the Irish countryside, where tourists drive on the left side of winding roads at top speeds.

As Dave drove off with Jaime and my mom, Steven chauffeured Jim and me. It was dark when we arrived at the cottage hours later.

"If anything happened, I just prayed God would take me first," Dave said.

The next morning, we set out for Cong, the setting of my mom and dad's favorite movie. My mom and I toured the *Quiet Man* museum alone. She pretended to play the piano while singing the movie's theme song, "Isle of Innisfree," wearing the shawl Maureen O'Hara wore—or a convincing replica.

As I wandered among the monastery ruins, I contemplated my parents' romance. I didn't know if my checking off my father's list was helping or hurting her grief.

I found the monastery ruins in a field of yew trees. The yew is the only tree whose branches dip back into the ground, then re-emerge as new trees. The Druids called it the tree of life and death.

Thin place.

Steven felt the most comfortable on the roads, so he became our driver—though he hated the roundabouts.

We left early on our last day together for the ferry to the Aran Islands, which is the best place to go if you want to see ancient Ireland. The place is filled with square stone enclosures, green squares of grass, and roaming horses, cattle, and sheep.

After the ferry docked, we ate in Inisheer's sole restaurant. The island is only two square miles. "Good luck finding vegan food here!" my stepdad yelled.

After lunch, my mom and stepdad took a carriage ride while the four of us meandered. The map had nothing on it but a ruined castle and magical wells.

Thin place.

Dave and Jaime wanted to go back to the restaurant, but Steven and I wanted to hike, so we agreed to meet later.

As we crossed the island, we saw it in the distance: a "Blath N'Graine, the most Western vegan restaurant in Europe," the sign boasted. We sat down for tea with oat milk and a vegan strawberry cake—freshly baked.

When we found my family, they couldn't believe it.

Thin place.

We toured the Cliffs of Moher at sunset, and everyone seemed at peace. We dined in Doolin, the closest to an Irish pub I'd experienced, with a fire going and Irish music. My dad would have loved it. Not only did it serve vegan dishes but also nonalcoholic beer. Jaime had picked it.

Thin place.

My mom and stepdad flew home the next day. Dave and Jaime left for a night in Galway.

Steven and I explored my father's homeland.

It was spitting rain when we woke up.

After driving two hours north through County Mayo, we stopped at Killedan Cemetery, built in the eighth century. When we parked, the biggest rainbow I'd ever seen spread across the sky. This was how I knew we'd found it. Steven choked up.

Thin place.

The Carneys lived on a farm in Kiltimagh, which still looks as it did seventy years ago—a two-room thatched-roof house for a family of ten. I couldn't know how difficult living conditions were, but I'd heard that my great-grandfather, the first to immigrate to the United States, never wanted to go back.

Anthony Raftery, Ireland's most famous *seanchai*, or traveling storyteller, came from Kiltimagh. The ancient Irish had no written language, so the *seanchai* kept history in their heads, their stories blending myths with reality. They traveled the countryside, telling stories for room and board.

They were what I now realized my father was.

And maybe what I was, too.

The Raftery statue stood near the church where the Carneys married. A tombstone for Thomas Carney stood on the church's front lawn. My grandfather's name.

In the distance stood Croagh Patrick, a pyramid shape at the end of the road.

"Let's go climb it," I said.

Fionnan and Becca, who owned the vegan café on Inisheer, had warned us the hike was difficult. St. Patrick was a hermit here—exiled for forty days, taken prisoner by the Celts. Even so, Patrick petitioned the Church to let him return, to convert Ireland.

Steven crept up the mossy, rocky paths ahead of me, slipping in the streams, trying to get a good photograph of black-faced mountain sheep. Because of my foot, we only climbed halfway. As I rested on a rock, admiring Clew Bay, I heard rustling. A black-faced mountain sheep and I froze, ten feet apart, staring at each other.

Thin place.

On our rainy last day, Steven and I toured Thoor Ballylee, the medieval tower W.B. Yeats called home. We walked its haunted halls, one room devoted to a jackdaws' nest. A sign encouraged guests to write a poem. I couldn't think of what to write. Instead I asked a question. If it worked with my dad's spirit, why not a famous poet's?

Do you have any advice for a young writer? I thought.

Just as the soldier protects his country, the writer must save souls, I heard. I shuddered later reading a book of Yeats poetry when I found this: "*It takes more courage to examine the dark corners of your own soul than it does for a soldier to fight on a battlefield.*" Maybe I'd read the quote before. Or, maybe the real spirit of Yeats had communicated. His wife held séances in Thoor Ballylee.

Steven thought the guide and his henchmen were out to kill us when they suggested we explore the park around the tower alone. I thought they were being nice.

We drove to Coole Park, Yeats's artists' enclave, to find the Autograph Tree, an old copper beech signed by Irish writers. As we left, we spotted five red stags resting by the park's entrance.

To the ancient Celts, stags symbolized legacy.

Thin place.

I was sad to leave Ireland. I coped by stocking up on crumpets and jam and tea and salt-and-vinegar chips, my dietary staples for those two weeks. I followed my dad's advice and got back to writing.

One weekend my writers' group held a retreat, at Hayley's house in upstate New York. We went for a hike on the second day. As the browning leaves tumbled we came upon a wrecked car in the woods. I believed it could only have landed there one way. I sped up as my friends laughed and explored. Gabie ran after me.

Gabie has long, wavy brown hair and grew up in the South of France—so her accent is French, despite being born in California. She's quirky, funny, and smart. Her laugh is infectious. She yelled after me, "I should have realized that would upset you!"

"It's OK," I said, fighting back tears. "I understand why they'd see it as an adventure. It's just, someone died in that car."

Gabie convinced me to walk back. The closer I got, the more I hated the car.

When we found Hayley and Anna, I started yelling, tears rolling down my cheeks.

"I don't want this in my life anymore! I want to erase it!"

Gabie said she understood. There was a time in her life she wanted to erase, too.

My surgery to repair my torn tendon was in November. My podiatrist hadn't warned me about the recovery. I couldn't walk without an Aircast for three months.

I rewrapped my foot in gauze each day. I propped it up on pillows on the couch, which became my bed. Steven served me meals and often helped me to the bathroom so I wouldn't have to redo the Aircast. I'd hop on one leg and let him lead me. I hated that he was seeing me like this.

Dressing was a pain, but showering was worse: I bathed while seated on an upside-down bucket, my left foot hanging out wrapped in a bag. When the Percocet wore off, I believed I was in hell. I found out later my antidepressant shouldn't be mixed with it.

"This is the worst I've ever felt in my life," I moaned, as Steven lifted me into our bed one day for a change of scenery.

"Really?" he replied. "That seems unlikely."

I couldn't believe how frustrated immobility made me. By Christmas, I was distraught. I hadn't worked in two months. My severance was nearly gone. I couldn't go anywhere to buy presents or send cards. I didn't know if my surgery had worked—I feared I might never run again.

"This is too hard!" I yelled to my dad one day. I asked him for a sign that doing this was still right.

An hour later, I received a Facebook message from my uncle Jim, my dad's brother. An old roommate of my father's had just written him, and he'd forwarded it to me.

Happy Holidays! Hi, Jim, I hope that all is well. I was cleaning out my desk area at home and found a piece of memorabilia from Mickey from

1979. It was his first newsletter about his "Sports and Leisure Club" that he wanted to start in 1979. He was recruiting members. He was way ahead of his time. It was part Facebook, Pinterest, and Amazon Prime. I would like to share this with you and his family if there is any interest in the almost 40-year-old entrepreneurship. If there is interest, send me your mailing address and I will post it shortly.

My uncle gave my dad's old roommate, whom I'd never met, my mailing address.

The Sports and Leisure Newsletter (S.A.L., for short) was a means for family and friends to save money on sports via group discounts, whether played or watched. My dad had organized game nights and cocktail hours. The focus, he'd said, in the introductory letter, was to have fun.

No matter how much I was struggling, no matter how uncertain my future seemed, I realized I could be sure of one thing.

These last two years, I'd been having fun.

Thin place.

CHAPTER 10

Make More Money
Than I Need

I am eight years old.

I stare through the rainy window at my babysitter's house, at the reflection of the soap opera on the TV behind me. It's getting dark earlier. I have on my coat and shoes. I am ready to leave.

But my mother is late.

My brother changed a baby's diaper today, though he's only six. Mrs. Jamison also made him eat brussels sprouts, a fact I'll learn later and not believe—this kid won't even eat green beans.

I feel a longing I can't explain in this smoky living room. I know without knowing why that my life will be different than this.

* * *

IN THE WINTER OF 2019, as I tried to figure out what I'd do to make ends meet, my brother was buying a brand-new four-bedroom home in New England. I was happy for him but couldn't stop comparing my life with his.

I tried not to worry about it and focus on what I was doing. Which was a lot for a miserable invalid.

Part of why I'd fallen in love with New York had been the multiple locations it provided, the multiple roads one took to get there, and the exciting walk it would be—not drive. But now, when asked if I wanted to go somewhere, I had to calculate if it was too far for me to handle.

As I started physical therapy, I was still on the couch but in less pain. Gabie got me another gig, at a magazine called *Bumble*—we'd copyedit their launch issue together. Getting myself ready to hobble to the train station and into the city twice a week distracted me from the fact that the magazine was owned by Hearst, my former employer.

On my first day, a wave of anxiety washed over me as I limped into the glass beehive. *God is with me always*, I said in my head, over and over, praying I wouldn't run into anyone I knew.

This was inevitable, though, and one day in the subway station below the building I ran into the research team, some of whom I'd been friends with. One asked about my progress with my book and who my publisher was. "My agent couldn't sell it yet," I said. "But he will! I'm writing my first one hundred pages."

I was. I'd written about my dad's funeral for the first time while stuck on my couch. My physical powerlessness had helped.

The most remarkable thing about working at *Bumble* was my boss, Kathy, who was so intrigued by my project to finish my dad's list that she sat and asked me about it for an hour on my first day. At my old job, I'd trained myself not to talk about the list too much. But here it was possible for me to work as a copy editor and also be my full self.

My first day of physical therapy scared me. Except for my doctor and Steven, no one had come near my foot in months—well, except for my mom, who accidentally walked into it at Christmas.

A married couple owned the therapy center. First, I met with the wife, who massaged my foot tenderly. A week later, I met with the husband.

Oscar, a former soccer player, kept telling me how great it would be to get into stilettos for my husband again. He accused me of having a type A personality. At "a certain age," we have to slow down, he said. I regretted telling him I'd run marathons.

"This injury happened from a wrong move on a tennis court," I explained.

"The tendon was weakened from too much use," he insisted.

I cried when Oscar demonstrated stretches to get me prepared to run again.

"You don't understand," I said, in exasperation. "I've only been running for five years. And now I'm afraid to walk!"

I went everywhere in my Aircast now and grew tired quickly. At a nephew's second birthday party, it made for an excuse to leave early. We missed a family member drinking and then trying to drive.

I'd separated myself from safe driving advocates. Whereas I'd once said yes to any request for help, I now had to consider their definition of "distracted."

A researcher at an advocacy group explained why advocates' focus had shifted to promoting hands-free.

Though most universities who'd studied the effects of phone use on the brain agreed that phone calls were too much of a load for anyone to drive safely, a few found something different—and the largest one had been funded by the Automakers' Alliance. Their study said hands-free phone use was safer, so the carmakers could point to this to defend their new dashboard technology. "Millennials need tech," a carmaker's PR person told a reporter friend. She said they were trying to fill that need.

The researcher said this development had been why she'd stopped working in the field. The federal government also had helped fund the the largest university's study. One day in a conference call, a government representative told the researcher's group to stop defining hands-free as equally dangerous. When the researcher protested, her superiors said she was "asking for the impossible."

I asked her why she was telling me all this.

"Because maybe you can do something with it," she said.

I shared her information with my advocate friends, but most didn't want to hear it. I sent it to a reporter at CNN but never heard back.

In February, the National Safety Council announced in an email to advocates that they'd rewarded a grant to their "star supporter," General Motors. I emailed to complain.

"How can we police carmakers if we are aligned with them?" I asked.

Representatives for the NSC called me and paid lip service, but I was already done. I sent an email to the rep who'd always been kind to me.

"It's not you I blame," I ended it, "but your organization."

The advocates had been like family to me.

Now I was on my own.

At the start of spring, my podiatrist in the city removed my Aircast. I could almost walk normally and would soon be able to run, he said. I told him I was grateful to have such a wonderful doctor.

"It's patients like you that make it worthwhile," he said, chuckling. He wasn't accustomed to gratitude.

"Is there any chance of my reinjuring it?" I asked.

"Only if you do something extreme," he said.

I pondered what that meant.

It was hard to determine what I could check off from the list since I still couldn't move much. So I tried "play piano or guitar." My friend John Myung, an Asian American guitarist who was blinded by a speeding driver, offered me a lesson. He was the one who'd heard *Back to the Future* in the hospital when he woke up.

* * *

MY DAD DIDN'T PLAY AN INSTRUMENT. He pretended to play harmonica and guitar. He'd blow once, strum once, slap the guitar, and sing. He sang in a folk duo with a female friend through college. Once they performed the Beatles' "Norwegian Wood," a scandalous song for its time, in a nursing home. My dad's idea.

His specialty was ballads. His voice had a warmth that could be soft or loud. He never had training. But when he sang, it was the truest expression of who he was.

* * *

As John taught me where to place my fingers on my father's guitar, I closed my eyes. I wanted to experience music like John did. He taught me four chords and how to play a scale. But the strings hurt my fingers, and I strummed like a piano player—staccato. "It should feel like you're tickling a cloud," Steven said. By the end of our lesson, John had taught me the four-note riff to "Under Pressure" and the two-note theme to *Jaws*.

"Those are songs!" he laughed. "Check 'play guitar' off the list!"

John and his wife were headed to New Orleans in a few weeks, and we were going at the end of April. It was my next list item.

New Orleans was the first travel destination my dad wrote down. Music was the only reason I could find, so we bought tickets to JazzFest. Started in 1970, my dad would have known about it.

Just as my gig at *Bumble* ended, another one started—copyediting college textbooks. The managing editor had Googled "copy editor" and "anthropology" and found me—I'd copyedited an anthropology textbook ten years earlier.

It was a strange feeling, not trying to replace my old full-time job with a new one.

By my forty-first birthday, I'd lost eighteen pounds—mostly due to lying on a couch for three months, eating oatmeal. On a hunch, I measured my waist and saw it had lost four inches. I had a twenty-seven-inch waist again! That was a list item! I'd been trying to check it off for a year.

On my last day of physical therapy, I lifted weights with my back in the weight room. Lifting the weights required squatting.

"Oscar, this isn't very ladylike," I joked.

"You're not a lady," Oscar said. "You're an athlete."

By April 2019, I'd completed what my agent had requested. I'd finished writing my first one hundred pages. In fact, I'd written two hundred fifty. I'd told myself that once I was done, I could open my dad's brief-case. It was the last piece of him I had left.

I gingerly placed it on my bed and undid the brass latches. I assumed I would find more of his writing, like I'd discovered all along.

Instead, I found mine.

My dad had kept every term paper, every poem, every news article, every short story I'd ever written. It was like walking into a retrospec-tive, curated by my biggest fan.

Next to my writing was an envelope of photos—mostly girlfriends I'd never met. But one was ripped in half, of a man in drag. I wondered if the other half had been him.

My beta readers sent me reactions to my 250 pages. My oldest Carney cousin, Leif, was excited. He'd been absent most of my life. We'd reconnected on Facebook, and since the start of the list he'd promised to help me with the musical items.

I made my readers' edits, said a prayer, and emailed my draft to my agent.

We woke at 3:30 a.m. the day we flew south. My unemployment had completely run out, as had my pay from *Bumble*—I was living on checks for my textbook copyediting, but by late April I'd only received two. Steven convinced me to apply for a credit card—something I hadn't done since age twenty-five. Since thirty, I'd been debt-free.

Taking this trip didn't make sense financially, Steven reminded me at the airport. I told him I didn't need reminding.

We'd booked the most picturesque yet reasonable hotel we could find in the French Quarter, the Maison Dupuy—an 1800s-style estate with a Spanish courtyard. In the middle stood a fountain, café tables, gardenia trees, and string lights. After we checked in, we left for a ghost tour of St. Louis Cemetery.

I'd binged Ken Burns's *Jazz* for weeks, so I knew a lot about the place—even sometimes correcting the tour guide. By the tomb of voodoo queen Marie Laveau I looked up and saw a chem trail—it was one big cross and twenty smaller crosses. By the time I snapped it with my phone, most of the crosses were gone.

The cross or *veve* is a voodoo symbol. When voodoo-practicing Africans were enslaved and shipped to the United States, they brought their religious beliefs with them. Catholics believe the cross is where Jesus's spirit left the world, but voodoo practitioners believe the *veve* is where spirits *enter* the world. Drawing a *veve* is an invite—for the spirits to join. In a voodoo ceremony, when the spirits have done their work, the *veves*, or crosses, are erased.

As we left the cemetery, I asked our tour guide about other haunted spots in the city. I asked about the voodoo offerings at Marie Laveau's tomb. "Do you have to make an offering to have a wish granted?" I asked. She said because Laveau was a hairdresser, tourists often left hair. My hair had accidentally shed all over the cemetery.

"What happens if people make a request?" I asked. "Does it come true?"

"With voodoo, it's usually a little of what you want and a little of what you don't," she said.

I posed for a photo in what had once been Storyville—where Jelly Roll Morton played piano in Lulu White's brothel. He'd orchestrated his arrangements to match the lovemaking. The music was initially called "jass," after the jasmine perfume the working girls wore.

New Orleans is a romantic city. There's a reason writers like Sherwood Anderson, Tennessee Williams, and William Faulkner lived there. It's an ocean of curiosities with almost no rules. You can be whomever you want. And there's a new sound and a new smell around every corner. Maybe it's that ghost who smokes cigars in the Bourbon Orleans, maybe it's lavender soap from that French shop on Royal, or incense floating out of Marie Laveau's House of Voodoo. It's hard to say, but spring's the best time to find out, when it's all mixed with a breeze and jasmine.

We walked down to Café Du Monde, bypassing raucous Bourbon Street, only to learn the famous beignets off the Mississippi River weren't vegan, so we bought black coffee instead then stopped in a vampire shop. The clerk invited us to a speakeasy later that night. "It's quieter," she said. Her skin was preternaturally white. I unconsciously clasped my neck.

Back in our hotel, I looked at the photos Steven had taken and saw a strange dark splotch on my black tank top in the Storyville shot.

When I zoomed in, I saw a woman's face.

"What is *that*?" I shrieked.

A ghost's face was on my shirt, and I didn't know what ghost. After Googling I realized it resembled Lulu White, the owner of the former brothel I'd posed in front of (which is now a convenience store). No photo trickery could explain it, though it could have been pareidolia, the tendency to see faces where they aren't.

New Orleans is the most haunted city in the U.S., mostly because its dead people aren't buried—the water table is so high that floods push corpses to the surface. To solve this problem, they are placed in tombs. Mourners dance at funerals in New Orleans as brass bands parade the streets, celebrating a soul's transition. It's the only thing a people can do, when death is always around.

Steven woke up the next morning before me, as usual, and bought us iced chicory coffee for our long walk. Walking or biking the two miles to the music festival was recommended online since it attracts 500,000 people.

We took a shortcut through Louis Armstrong Park, to find the statue of the first original American singer. Armstrong's trumpet spread the influence of jazz worldwide. As Steven and I crossed the cobblestones I heard drums in the back of my mind. This park had once been Congo Square.

During the 300 years millions of enslaved Africans were brought to this country, they weren't permitted to keep their pasts. If they survived the voyage, they were given new names. And then split from their families.

By the late 1700s, when we were supposedly free, this was still happening, despite founding fathers (who also owned humans) protesting it. The United States outlawed the international slave trade in 1808. But it would be another sixty years before all Americans were free. By then, nearly every other nation had already banished slavery.

Because New Orleans was French until 1803, it wasn't subject to mainland laws. Ownership of the colony had also passed through the hands of the Spanish, who treated enslaved people only slightly better. In New Orleans under Spanish rule, enslaved people could buy their freedom. And on Sundays, they had the day off. They sold wares from their personal gardens in Congo Square, played music, and danced. When they met there, it was often a family reunion.

Every form of popular music in America originates from this place—from the drum circles of Congo Square. Their pasts had been erased, but not their music.

My foot survived the two-mile walk. When we were given our bracelets and entered the festival, we were overwhelmed by options: jazz, gospel, Cajun, zydeco, blues, R&B, rock, funk, African, Latin, Caribbean, and folk, on over a dozen soundstages. It was the greatest collection of American musical styles ever in one place. By the entrance a group of Mardi Gras Indians—not to be confused with Native Americans; these are African American dancers—chanted in a circle, their red, blue, and yellow feathered headdresses jostling. We landed on festival regulars Bonnie Raitt, the Marsalis brothers, and Van Morrison.

Jazz Fest is like a Disney World exclusively for adults: the attendants swayed slightly in the sun, in Ray-Bans and straw fedoras, sipping beer.

I knew now that guitar is terribly hard—Bonnie Raitt made it look easy. As she sang "I Can't Make You Love Me," my mind drifted to my father's tapes. We recorded ourselves singing with him every year. According to him, this song was my best number.

Steven and I found ourselves swaying before long.

After an hour in the Marsalis tent, we walked back over to the main stage for Van Morrison. As the sun set, we drifted from the masses of old white people and back onto the streets, by the jasmine-lined sidewalks, the palm tree–filled front yards, the open porches, through Tremé, along Louis Armstrong Park, and back into the French Quarter for a 9:00 p.m. dinner.

My foot felt just fine.

As we ate vegan gumbo in the historic Gumbo Shop, a brass band marched by the open front of the restaurant, at 10:00 p.m. at night.

"Funeral?" Steven asked.

"Wedding!" I responded. A bride marched triumphantly down the street, her congregation a bunch of bead-wearing skeletons hanging off wrought iron balconies.

"I bet those skeletons stay up year-round," I said.

"Those are last year's festival-goers," Steven joked.

After dinner, we stopped at the hotel where Tennessee Williams lived when he moved to New Orleans. He wrote home to his mother, "Here surely is the place I was made for." New Orleans is a natural home for writers. I was beginning to learn why.

We took the next morning slowly. After a self-guided tour of haunted hotels, we rode a trolley through the Garden District, where we ate vegan *etouffé* and beignets. After lunch we climbed back on the trolley, disembarking at Audubon Park, named after the famed painter and naturalist. There is a lake in the park where hundreds of birds nest. And a tree that is one of the largest live oaks in the world.

We spent most of our day searching for this tree. Believed to be 500 years old, its trunk is thirty-five feet in circumference, and its low-hanging branches reach 160 feet. I followed my Google map down an alley of live oaks, dripping with Spanish moss, to the Étienne de Boré oak at the end—the Tree of Life.

The Druids believed the oak tree was an entry to a sacred world. It's the tree most likely to be struck by lightning and also most likely to survive it, handy in a place attractive to hurricanes. The Celts called the oak tree "the father of the woods."

As I stepped across its knobby rising roots, I considered climbing it—many do, in hopes of spotting a giraffe in the park's zoo. But I didn't trust my foot. So I sat at the oak's base with my knees pushed together and feet out to either side. Clasping the raised roots by my sides with both hands, I felt like a child on a throne.

The park was so large that it seemed pointless to retrace our steps, so we searched for a new trolley stop.

"C'mon!" Steven yelled. I was lagging behind, not just because of my now-aching foot. I had my nose buried in jasmine bushes.

"It's like it's a sickness," Steven complained.

We went for a swim back at the hotel. The pool sat in the courtyard in the hotel's center, next to the fountain. Steven and I raced each other.

After I ran upstairs to get ready for dinner, I discovered stunning news in my bank account: my last paycheck for the textbook hadn't come. And it was my fault—I'd written the wrong date on my invoice.

I tearfully told Steven what happened. I'd used the last of my credit card to help pay for plane tickets. We'd yet to pay for the hotel. I needed $1,000. And I didn't know where to find it.

Steven and I kept our bank accounts separate, mostly because I didn't trust men with money. He'd paid for most of the plane tickets and everything else on this trip and hadn't put aside anything extra. He suggested we ask his parents for a loan.

"I can't believe I've put us in this position," I said, crying.

Steven was irritated but not angry. He arranged for the loan and said, "It's taken care of. We can pay it back next week. Let's enjoy the rest of the trip."

I slipped on my striped sundress and fastened my hair into a low bun, applied red lipstick, and sprayed jasmine perfume for dinner on Frenchmen Street. We ate at a vegan restaurant called 13, which struck me as fitting because New Orleans was the thirteenth list item, and thirteen was my dad's favorite number.

Thirteen isn't unlucky—it developed that reputation because of the Bible (the thirteenth apostle), because of astrology (twelve signs), and because of sexism (women have thirteen periods in a year). It's a lunar number. It's the number of rebirth.

As we left the restaurant, we walked by a jazz trio playing in the window of the Spotted Cat to a crowded room. Then we took our own ghost tour, down darkened streets, ending at voodoo queen Marie Laveau's house.

Marie Laveau was half Creole and half Black, a free woman who owned her property at a time when that was uncommon. She consulted with the most successful businessmen in town. Her predictions probably derived from gossip—her circle reported what they'd overheard in their homes, then she'd repeat it. But many believe she had real voodoo powers. And that her spirit still resides in that house.

Taking a chance that it did, standing there in the dark, I asked Marie Laveau's spirit if my book would be successful.

Yes, I heard in my head. *But don't mistake success for happiness.*

A week after the trip, Steven and I paid his father back. My dad wrote "pay back my dad $1,000 plus interest" on the list. Years later, he crossed it out and wrote "failed." Which meant my grandfather had died before my dad could afford to repay him.

It also meant he hadn't been holding out on us all those years.

"*I feel like I'm a fool,*" I wrote in my journal. "*And yet I'm a brave fool. And that's better than never letting yourself be a fool at all.*" I was nervous waiting to hear back from my agent. It had been a month.

My brother invited me to his thirty-ninth birthday party in Massachusetts at the end of May. But I'd sunk into a depression. I told him I might not make it. The anxiety about what my agent might say was too hard. I couldn't handle my guilt over letting Steven owe his parents money. And I envied my brother's financial security and feared our growing distance.

Steven told me as I lay in bed that it was like I was in a cave, and he had to pull me out.

"I don't understand what makes you believe in me so much," I cried.

"Because I can see what's ahead for you, even if you can't see it yet," he said.

Steven didn't want to make the four-hour trip to Massachusetts—and didn't think I should, either. So Steven stayed home, and I hitched a ride with my brother's best friend, who lived in New York.

His new house was more beautiful in person—filled with light. As I got ready for bed in their all-white guest room, I felt like I was lying on a cloud. I was happy I'd made myself go. My brother's life was full—he was on his own path, and I was proud of him.

I hoped my dad could see it, too.

A week after my brother's birthday, Steven and I celebrated our third wedding anniversary. At 11:00 p.m. that night, already in bed, I reached for my phone.

My agent had emailed me.

Most of his letter pointed out the problems in the 250 pages I'd sent him. He no longer wanted to represent me.

I bolted out of bed and ran to the bathroom.

I curled up on the floor by the bathtub and cried from my heart, clasping it. In my mind I was back at my babysitter's house, sitting and waiting for my mom to come.

Dave and Jaime came for a visit to New York a week later, and I shared the news with them over lunch.

"So, what will you do now?" Dave asked.

"I'll keep writing my book," I said. "I'll find another agent. Dad was rejected by an agent, too, but he gave up. I'm not giving up."

The items my dad had successfully checked off were "do a comedy monologue in a nightclub," "give a radio interview," "see a World

Series game live," "help my parents enjoy their retirement," and "own a great record collection." I inherited half the records—my brother got the other half, designating a room in his house for them. But I was surprised my father hadn't checked off "develop an impressive library." He'd often said whenever he entered someone's house, the first thing he did was look at their books.

As I restarted my summer job at *Guideposts*, my mom visited. The last time she'd come, just after our wedding, I'd cried in an IKEA after she tried to convince us to buy a bigger bed. She'd suggested one with drawers beneath it because we "had too much stuff."

On her first night of this visit, she asked if she could choose a book from my bookshelves. "Wow, Laura," she said. "You've certainly developed an impressive library."

"What did you say?" I asked.

I loved when list items checked themselves off.

On her last morning, we took her to our new brunch spot.

"If you had to describe yourself in one word, what would it be?" she asked after our dishes were cleared and we sat sipping coffee.

"Gentle," I said.

My mom said "teacher." Steven said "champion."

"See, I think your word is 'writer,'" my mother said. "That's the word your father always chose when I asked him."

In the car on the way home, the radio played the old song "Moonlight Becomes You."

"This is the song your dad serenaded me with," my mom said.

She hummed along in the back seat, her eyes welling up.

By mid-summer I had more freelance jobs than I knew what to do with—my official count, since leaving *Good Housekeeping*, was eight. All of them had discovered me, not vice versa. I now also had more money than I knew what to do with. I worked around the clock, but I didn't mind. I would be able to check off "go to the Super Bowl"—I'd pay for my $5,000 ticket in two parts. The old me never would have bought something so frivolous.

But the new me had more money than she needed.

Now that she no longer cared about money.

CHAPTER 11

Go Sailing by Myself

"He's given you a gift," Steven said about the agent. "Use what he said as constructive criticism."

Everything he'd said in his email was what Steven had said all along.

All summer I reworked the pages in my mind, creating outlines, studying character and plot in my favorite books and films.

"What is the isness of the story?" a friend at *Guideposts*, who once worked for a literary agent, asked me one day.

"The 'isness'?" I asked, squinting.

"Yes," she said. "What *is* it?"

In July Steven and I ran my first 5K since surgery. I now ran sixteen-minute miles. But at least I was running. I cried with joy the first time I made it around the loop in the park down the street.

In a year's time, Steven had gone from running 5Ks to running a half marathon, which had happened by accident: When vegan ultrarunner Robbie Balenger ran across the country—3,275 miles in seventy-five days—Steven joined him for the New Jersey leg. He'd planned to only run three miles but lasted thirteen.

When we ran with Craig in York, Pennsylvania, Steven's hometown, I told him getting injured on the tennis court with him that day was exactly what I'd needed. "It forced me to slow down," I said. "I was overwhelmed by all I was doing. Now I think more clearly because I've had to simplify. I react more slowly because I don't have the energy to freak out. It forced me to depend on Steven in a way I never had before. It taught me to trust him."

"That's great!" Craig said. "But wouldn't it have been better to learn that an easier way?"

"What do you mean?" I asked.

"If you could have stopped yourself from playing tennis that day, none of this would have happened. In life there is always an easy way and a hard way to learn."

"Well, I think I usually choose the hard way!" I joked.

One morning, I felt strong enough to play tennis again, which Steven and I play every Fourth of July. I joked about how bad I'd be.

"You're the number-one seed in our house now!" I told Steven. "Wait a minute...maybe I just have to beat you!"

I took my father's list out of the frame my sister-in-law placed it in and realized the paper had folded, obscuring part of the tennis item. It didn't say "beat a number-one seed in tennis." It said "beat a number-one seed in a tennis tournament."

Beating Craig in one day wouldn't have counted.

Two of my dad's tennis trophies were won playing doubles with my mom, who gave up on tennis after they wed. On weekends as she worked on renovating the house, usually basic maintenance, my dad would ask her to play tennis. My mom told me they replaced the den she'd set up for his trophies with my nursery.

In July, my friend Mary Latham was interviewed on the *Today* show about her mission to collect stories of kindness in all fifty states, in her mother's honor, and compile them into a book for hospital waiting rooms. I was envious—I hadn't done an interview in two years because of my agent's ban on publicity. But I wrote a social media post promoting her anyway. To make myself feel better, I wrote a post in a women's triathlon group on Facebook, about my goal to complete a half Ironman as a vegan athlete (Steven had convinced me a full Ironman was too much).

A young woman in the group wrote that she had been hit by a texting driver that weekend and she'd suffered a concussion. It was her third concussion since college—her swimming career had ended because of hitting her head against the pool wall. She told me privately that she wanted to finish a half Ironman too. Danielle and I vowed to train together.

I met my friend Melissa Blake for dinner in New York a week later. I'd emailed Melissa in 2017, after she'd written an essay about her late father in *Good Housekeeping*.

At dinner she told me not to worry about losing my agent.

"Don't forget, only you can tell your story..." she said.

"...because I hold the pen," I said. It was a quote I'd posted online.

That week President Trump tweeted, "Rep. Elijah Cummings has been a brutal bully, shouting and screaming at the great men & women of Border Patrol about conditions at the Southern Border, when actually his Baltimore district is FAR WORSE and more dangerous. His district is considered the Worst in the USA. Cumming District is a disgusting rat- and rodent-infested mess. If he spent more time in Baltimore, maybe he could help clean up this very dangerous & filthy place." When people complained about his tweet, he fired off another one, calling Cummings, a Black man, "racist."

Melissa wrote a story for CNN suggesting Twitter ban Trump. A week later, she discovered a YouTube video of Trump supporters angry about her op-ed, attacking not only her credibility but also her appearance—a casualty for female journalists. They said Melissa should be "banned from posting selfies because she's so ugly."

Melissa was born with Freeman-Sheldon syndrome, a congenital condition that affects muscles of the face and skull and often the joints of the hands and feet. She has been in a wheelchair all her life.

She responded by posting three selfies, vowing to post a new selfie every day, starting with her photos from New York.

Melissa became Twitter famous overnight. She was offered a book deal—from that one viral tweet. Just as I'd envied Mary Latham's success, I realized I envied Melissa's. I didn't like the person I was becoming.

Melissa welcomed her followers to post selfies. So one day I did.

I wrote, "Per Melissa's request, here's one thing I love about myself: my curiosity. It helps my research, my storytelling, my ability to take risks, my creativity, and my willingness to speak up for causes that need it. Not once has it occurred to me to tell a jack-of-all-trades that he is 'too complicated,' 'thinks too much,' 'is unrealistic,' offers 'so much info,' is 'sprawling,' or 'overwhelms me.' So why do we tell ballsy, brainy, diverse women the same? I've been told all these things, most in the past week, and was even manhandled in the workplace when a man was trying to make a point, even after he'd been told it made me uncomfortable. He said his reaction was spontaneous. I said so was mine. That's why this is my best selfie—my curious, outspoken face is my best face. You're welcome, gentlemen. Stop trying to tamp down unruly women—they probably know what they're talking about. Melissa Blake sure does."

My supervisor at a freelance job rubbed my shoulder every time he left my desk and sat on my desk, facing me, when he needed to tell me something. One day he absent-mindedly stroked a cup of coffee I'd placed in front of me. He shared stories about ex-girlfriends, adding, "we were in bed together at the time." When I complained to female editors, someone told HR, and he was reprimanded. So now when he rubbed my shoulder, he'd do it saying, "I'm sorry, I know you don't like this."

A PR person I'd met four years earlier, who'd called me after she read my first essay in *Good Housekeeping*, saw my Instagram post and messaged me. Susie asked if I had a literary agent. I told her about losing mine. She said she could recommend a good one.

The agent said she'd like to read what I had.

This had happened purely because I'd supported a friend.

My dad had wanted to "golf in the 70s a few times." Rohan Mohanty, the reporter who went skydiving with me, explained this: "Yeah, that one's gonna be tough—that's Tiger Woods–level golf!"

I signed up for lessons with a PGA professional, Roger Stone, at the local driving range. Golf was a sport for old, wealthy white men, as far as I was concerned. But it turned out, I loved it. And I wasn't half bad. As I took Roger's lessons to heart, I got better.

Golf is a game of the mind. Your main opponent is yourself. If you're relaxed, your swing reflects it. You can't swing at a ball in anger. The swing is like a pendulum—up through the thighs, the hips, and the core. It's a natural sport for a woman's frame. Golfers have strong arms, but it's their sturdy legs that make the difference.

I had a tough time focusing at my third lesson—the supervisor at work was still groping my shoulder, and I didn't know how to make it stop—so I tried shutting down my mind. And then I remembered, *Dad didn't like doing things that were hard. He liked doing things that were easy. I'll just pretend this is easy.*

And then it was.

In the fall, I restarted my regular freelance work at Condé Nast. I added Monday nights at *People* to my jobs. I now worked for nine places. But every weekend we drove up to Connecticut to play golf.

The first time Steven and I played with my mom and stepdad, I scored in the nineties, though it was only nine holes. It had also been seventy degrees out, so I decided this qualified as "playing in the 70s."

The next time, I improved my score by twenty points, meaning I technically played in the seventies—but again, it was only nine holes. My mom gave up halfway through, not happy with her performance. As she walked back to get a club she'd lost, my stepdad and I finished the game. Jim tallied up the scores and was excited by mine. It was strange to be alone with him and doing something together, an organized activity. I couldn't remember the last time this had happened.

I hoped to check off my third time playing golf in the seventies in San Diego, another list item. I liked to double up when I could.

"It's always seventy degrees in San Diego," I told Steven.

My mom was invited to a wedding near San Diego, the same time we were going. She suggested they join us in golf.

Steven said he couldn't afford another trip. He hadn't recovered from New Orleans. I wondered at what point he'd be fed up by my selfishness.

So I offered to pay for his trip. Doing so could mean checking off "send [my spouse] on a $1,000 shopping spree," I reminded him. "You'll be in California, your favorite place. What better shopping spree could you want?"

Steven wasn't sure he agreed yet.

In October, I drove to a hotel again, but not to run from my marriage. This time I was running toward writing.

For four days I reworked my manuscript to send to the potential new agent. I made it the way I'd wanted it from the start.

Most people I knew didn't understand staying in a hotel, away from my spouse, to rework a book I might not sell. But that didn't matter—I was writing my book for me, because I needed to write it.

I called Steven one night to update him. I began to sob.

"What's wrong?" he asked.

"I realized just now that I've forgiven my dad for everything, and I've forgiven my mom and Jim for the hospital, but there's still one person I need to forgive."

"Who?" Steven asked.

"Me."

I needed to forgive myself for how I'd treated my dad. When I'd told him in the car that day that he had no right to lecture me if he wasn't funding my education. When I'd thought him irresponsible for going after his dreams.

"I was mean, and I was wrong," I said, crying even more. "I regret that now. And it's too late. He'll never hear my apology."

"He just did," Steven said.

After I hung up the phone, light flooded my room. Gleaming lights, bigger than streetlights, had come on outside. Stadium lights.

I'd accidentally chosen a hotel next to the golf driving range.

I sent my writing to the new agent the next day.

The first thing we did after we got off the plane was drive to Mission San Juan Capistrano. Laid out in the shape of the cross, Capistrano is called the "jewel of the missions." Red roses and lavender surround its fountains, and lime trees and palms line its sandy paths.

In 1769, Father Junipero Serra, a Franciscan monk, established the first of twenty-one missions up the California coast: Mission San Diego de Alcala. He'd done so on the orders of Spain, who'd discovered this part of the world 200 years earlier but neglected it, under the impression there was no gold. But now Spain hoped to settle the land to prevent Russia and England from taking it.

Father Serra planted crops from his mother country at his missions, even though the land had provided everything Native Americans needed for thousands of years. San Diego was the first where he planted wine grapes. Mission San Juan Capistrano was the second.

Capistrano was the most industriously successful of the early missions, but it also required the most slave labor, which was what the Kumeyaay and Tongva tribes became.

The padres lured tribes with beads and trinkets. But once in, they couldn't leave. They'd take children over the age of eight, and then they'd take their mothers, who feared for the child's safety. This, in turn, drew the men.

The padres thought they were doing God's bidding. They viewed the Native Americans as stupid heathens. Because the padres worked without pay, using the same methods they'd been subjected to in Spain, they didn't believe they were doing anything wrong.

Mexico set the Native Americans free, but similar to the plight of Black sharecroppers, they ended up ranch hands, working for little pay. Or dead: Over one hundred years, more than 200,000 Native Americans died of small pox from the missions. When the United States established California as a state, they attempted to preserve a system and people in ruins.

But in their heyday, the missions were a source of income for Spain, producing among other things thousands of barrels of wine per year.

Monks have a long history developing wine, a necessity in the Catholic Church. Unlike farmers who hoped to turn a profit, early monks grew grapes purely for their use—this, plus the nature of their days, meant they had time to get it right.

The earliest successful grapes sent to the Americas were *vitis vinifera*, the mission grape. These cuttings made their way from Peru to Mission San Juan Capistrano.

Mission wine wasn't great. But the vines are still found all over the state. I was on a mission now to find the oldest one. I was checking off "teach a class about wine." My dad was an American wine expert, and this was where it was born.

When we toured Mission San Juan Capistrano, I was happy to find one of the vines still there. But then I learned the grapes weren't two hundred but fifteen—planted by a nearby vineyard. A sign said "please don't pick our grapes," so I picked one up off the ground and ate it.

Mission San Juan Capistrano is most famous for its cliff swallows, which return every year. And its Serra Chapel, the oldest building in California. I entered a side chapel designated for St. Peregrine, the patron saint of cancer, and said a prayer for my mom's best friend, my aunt, and Lizzie, my cousin Jimmy's wife.

We checked into a Best Western in San Diego that night. I had an early lesson the next morning, to check off "go sailing by myself."

San Diego is famous for sailing—it has more naval bases than anywhere in the world. Before we left New Jersey, I'd Googled "sailing lessons for kids," because I wanted the easiest (and cheapest) experience; I'd found a sabot class at a marina on Mission Bay. A sabot is a boat the size of a bathtub—it's Dutch for "little shoe."

Most importantly, a sabot can only fit one person.

As I entered the sabot class at Mission Bay Aquatic Center, I scanned the room: three men and one woman. A bunch of rope sat on everyone's desks. Kelsey, our instructor, taught us how to tie sailors' knots, each with its own purpose. We had to get these exactly right,

Kelsey said, because sometimes the boats needed to be docked at a moment's notice.

The parts of the boat were heavy—a sabot weighs ninety-five pounds. We carried all of our sabot's components down to the dock, then constructed the boats ourselves: the mast, the sheet, the boom, the tiller. This is called "rigging." The knot-tying lesson had been about vocabulary, too. Once we were done, Kelsey told us to loosen the knots and push off from the dock. The five of us sailed figure eights for an hour.

When a sailboat turns windward or leeward, the boom—the bottom part of the sail—shifts from one side of the boat to the other. But because the sabot is so small, this required ducking beneath it and shifting my body to the opposite side. Each turn was a series of this, sliding from one side to the other.

On the dock, after we'd tied off, the only other woman in the class complained of back pain, telling Kelsey she might not return.

The next morning's lesson was early. The woman didn't come back. Kelsey asked each of us to tell the class why we were there.

A classmate asked why my husband hadn't signed up. Steven was spending my sailing hours trail-running in Tecolote Canyon.

"Because," I said, nervously laughing, "the list item said 'go sailing by myself'!"

After lunch, the same student asked Kelsey what we should do if our boat capsized.

"Oh boy," she said, smiling, "I was hoping we could avoid that bad juju...."

She said if the boat "turtled," we were to wave one arm for her. It's challenging to turn a sabot upright from the water alone.

The wind picked up in Mission Bay when she took us back out. I almost asked, "Is it OK to be out in this?" but I didn't because I was too busy gripping my sheet and becoming vertical while my boat nearly toppled over. I rode the current like a windsurfer.

I'd never been so thrilled in my life.

But my boat collected so much water that I had to bail out, and as I did, I watched one of my classmates capsize. I sailed by to ask if he was OK, but skimmed a stranger's boat. The stranger shoved me away, and I capsized, too.

I remembered Kelsey's instructions.

Kelsey was busy helping Mitch, the one who'd capsized. A man sailed over and asked me to climb onto his boat, but Kelsey stopped him just in time. "It's OK," she said. "She's my student."

Kelsey yanked me up by my armpits onto her motorboat and grabbed my sabot by the sail with one hand. Then my boat capsized again.

In the next thirty minutes, as Kelsey tried to right it, my little boat capsized three more times. I said, "This seemed easier when Mitch did it." "Well, Mitch is really strong," Kelsey said.

Once my boat was upright long enough, I climbed back in, and Kelsey towed me to the dock. On the way we found Mitch sitting in a boat filled three-quarters with water. Kelsey pulled me back up along with him, and then both of our boats capsized three more times as we tried to upright them.

This all happened amidst a regatta—there were fifty sailboats rushing around us.

* * *

ONCE WHEN I WAS ELEVEN, I visited my uncle and aunt, my mom's sister, in their brand-new home. The neighborhood was new, too, and much of the land not fully developed. I went for a walk with my little cousin Steph. When we came across a muddy patch, a future pond, I stepped onto it. And started sinking.

The mud was like quicksand. Soon I was up to my thighs.

Scared, Steph ran back for her father.

I tried pushing with each palm into the mud to pull myself out, but the harder I pulled one leg up, the deeper the other one sank.

Eventually I realized that if I pushed hard with both hands at once, I could pull both legs out slowly.

As long as I relaxed, I could get myself free.

* * *

"I JUST WANT YOU TO KNOW, I'm having a great time!" Mitch shouted to Kelsey from the back of her motorboat, as she tried to keep both sabots steady. He told me he was in the Navy, so he'd been in worse disasters.

My dad probably wrote "go sailing by myself" because his friend was a champion sailor. In his briefcase I'd found an ad for her book, *Sailing Is Fun*, which he'd published with his short-lived publishing company. He likely got the "by myself" from a sailing race around the world that happened in 1968. Nine men set out to single-handedly sail a vessel south from England, below the southern tip of Africa, across the Pacific, under the southern tip of South America, and then north back home. After ten months, only one sailed back.

Most of the men who didn't finish called for help halfway through. But one, who'd reported himself in third place the whole race when he was actually somewhere near Brazil, in a boat full of water, vanished. Family believed he'd ended his life, unable to face the repercussions of his lies.

This should be evidence enough that sailing isn't meant to be done solo. Though I'd saved myself from quicksand mud at eleven, I couldn't do that in Mission Bay.

I had to rely on others.

After Mitch and I climbed back in our boats, Kelsey towed us to the dock. He kept sailing, but I told her I was done.

Of course, I wasn't completely done. I still had to take my boat apart. And help the other students take theirs apart, too.

When Steven picked me up, I asked him to take a photo of me with my new friends. Because how could these strangers be called anything else?

That evening we moved into our residence for the next few days, a timeshare courtesy of our Los Angeles friends Kelly and John. I texted

Kelly after we checked in. She asked if I'd been scared sailing. I told her fear hadn't occurred to me.

We met my mom and stepdad for dinner in Little Italy, along with their friends whose daughter had just wed. Jim revealed that he'd once taken sailing lessons. He spoke so infrequently when I was growing up that every time he shared something new now, it was like I was meeting a whole new person.

The next day, we met my mom and Jim and their friends in Balboa Park, a group of museums and gardens that rivals Central Park in size. We explored the Japanese Friendship Garden and saw the tiniest trees—bonsais—many of them 200 years old. As they left for an early dinner, Steven and I walked to the largest tree in the park, the Moreton Bay Fig, which was there when the park held the 1915 World's Fair, the Panama-California Exposition. After I smelled every rose in the award-winning rose garden, we hiked to the international cottages, another remnant from the World's Fair. We found the Ireland house next to the Polish one (Steven is Polish).

It was twilight, and the only house still open was the Denmark house. The blond man inside said he liked to stay late to play the piano—a Steinway, which was playing by itself. He asked why we were in San Diego, so I told him about the list. He poured us coffee and asked where else I would travel. He gave me tips on what to do in Vienna, where he'd once lived.

"Go during ball season," the man implored. Ball season in Vienna is when everyone dances the waltz.

I said, "How funny that we found the Denmark house! Yesterday I went sailing in a sabot, which is Dutch for 'little shoe.'"

"Ah, Holland is a nice country, too," he said, laughing.

I'd booked us a tee time at the ruggedly beautiful Rancho Bernardo Inn the next morning. As we took practice swings at the driving range, my mom said she wouldn't be playing.

"I'll be the ranger," she said, a golf term I thought she'd made up.

My theory about it always being seventy degrees in San Diego hadn't proven true—on the day we'd chosen for golf, it was ninety-five.

"Dad is somewhere laughing," I said.

* * *

MY DAD KEPT HIS BAG of golf clubs in his trunk at all times. Someone theorized this was what he'd been doing when he died.

Usually we played mini golf, but once, when we were teenagers, he introduced my brother and me to the real thing. "Mulligan!" he'd yell, chuckling every time I missed the ball. He eventually relegated us to putting. He had a novelty putter shaped like a Champagne bottle. He'd watch as I focused on the hole, as I focused during any sport—on the balance beam, shooting hoops, at home plate. I'd develop laser focus. I always took my time.

I did the same thing years later, after he died, playing beer pong at a party with my brother. Steven and I were up against the strongest contender, and as my Ping-Pong ball circled the red Solo cup, I watched my brother jump up and down, his arms waving wildly in the air, screaming. He was so proud of me.

It was only beer pong. But it was something more to us.

* * *

MY STEPDAD SUGGESTED we play Best Ball, a game where everyone advances to wherever the golf ball closest to the green lands. The best ball was usually Jim's or Steven's, so I got to see what it felt like to hit par on every hole. But it was my putt that got us par for the first time all day. A putt I focused on for ten minutes.

My mom cheered for my every swing—even the bad ones.

"Mom, that one was terrible," I shouted.

"I'm just excited that you can do this!" she said.

When we were four holes from the end, I realized we needed three 3s and a hole in one if we hoped to score "in the 70s."

"Yeah, that's it!" my stepdad said as he watched the sun slip beneath the mountains. "It's too dark. I'm done!"

We still had one hole left. Steven and I continued playing in the dark, but when Jim said he was done, our score was seventy-nine.

Which meant we'd played golf in the seventies.

I found out later Rancho Bernardo was where professional golfer Sally Little had broken the record for the lowest score in a final round—she did it the week I was born.

We had dinner with my mom and stepdad at Cesarina in Ocean Beach after golf. Steven called it the best vegan meal he'd ever had. The waiters sang "Happy Birthday" to seven different tables, which had my stepdad covering his ears and my mom singing along.

"You don't even know *Italian!*" my stepdad laughed.

Steven and I spent our last day in San Diego in the mission. This was where the first revolt occurred. Then we hiked Torrey Reserve with our spritely wedding photographer Joni on our way back to L.A. Joni had been a nomad most of her life—she specialized in destination weddings. Oceanside was the first place she felt settled. The Torrey pine can't survive anywhere in the world but in that reserve. Joni reminded me how much of my fulfillment I owed to marrying Steven... that I was like that Torrey pine, and he was my Oceanside cliffs.

After a double date with Kelly and John in Los Angeles the next night, Steven and I prepared for our race. I'd signed us up for the Day of the Dead 5K.

I averaged just under twelve-minute miles, the fastest I'd run in two years. Steven slowed down toward the end. "Rich Roll lives right around the corner," he said. Roll was an ultrarunner.

"I don't run for Rich Roll," I huffed. "I run for me."

I cried and kissed Steven after we crossed the finish line—the first we'd crossed together.

Afterward, we found part of the "mother vine," the oldest mission grapevine in California. It comes from the one at Mission San Gabriel— and is over 200 years old. I asked the museum docent on Olvera Street if it was OK to eat the grapes. She said she wouldn't recommend it. But it was too late.

On our last day, we visited Mission San Gabriel. By the 1830s, the vineyards there produced 50,000 gallons of wine a year.

The original mother vine is as big as a tree trunk, fanning out atop an arbor into three other vines. I tasted its grapes, too.

They were the best ones yet.

When we got home, I checked off "be invited to a political convention," which I'd been working on for months. I'd written to every Democratic candidate for president, but nobody wrote back. So I emailed a college friend who worked for a Delaware newspaper. He said he could get me invited to the state convention. I laughed and cried at the same time. If my dad had checked this off, it would have been in Delaware.

Before Thanksgiving, an old college friend wrote to me on Instagram. Adrian, a photographer, said he wanted to help with the list.

I immediately knew which one. "'Own a black tux,'" I said. "Maybe if you photograph me, I'll feel like I'm truly *owning* it."

I was surprised by Adrian's interest. He'd been the cool guy at my college newspaper I was sure didn't see me. Once I'd spotted him on the subway in New York and was too self-conscious to say hi.

Adrian said his father had recently died, from brain cancer. He conducted our first interview on a tape recorder in the cafeteria below *People*, just before my Monday shift. He wanted to know my biggest lesson from the list, he said. My commitment to the mission impressed him. It was an area in life where he struggled.

I told him that when a list item worked out, it was never all my doing. That as long as I focused on the gratitude I felt for these miracles, the miracles continued.

"There but for the grace of God go I," Adrian said. It was something his dad had told him. Adrian emailed me his eulogy for his father that night. This line had been the most important part.

We spent Thanksgiving at my mom's house, after Steven and I ran my first five-mile race since surgery. My mom said my brother wanted to host Christmas.

I wondered if Steven and I would ever host a holiday.

The next week, I came home from work and sheepishly asked Steven as he cooked dinner, "Hey, would you say you enjoy our standard of living?"

"Are you kidding?" Steven said. "All we do is travel, and that's what I love most!"

"Would you say then you are 'comfortable' with it?"

"Yes," he said.

I'd just made my final payment on my Super Bowl ticket. I had zero dollars in my bank account. But I realized all I needed to check off this list item—the second on my dad's list—was my family's assessment of whether I provided a comfortable life.

And Steven was my family.

Photo by Adrian Bacolo

CHAPTER 12

Own a Black Tux

By December 2019, I had thirty-one items on the list completed. Adrian suggested I post the whole list online. "Why is it a secret?" he asked. So I did.

I worked all the time now. After searching for weeks, I found my black tux—in the front window of the boutique below my apartment. I popped my head in.

"Is that a women's tuxedo?" I asked.

The storeowner said it was and she only had one left.

It was exactly my size.

She gave me a discount when I told her about my project.

Later that week, I tried on the tux with a white tuxedo shirt I'd had for years and Steven's long black tie. I studied myself in the mirror, misty-eyed. Doing this, as a woman, was deemed perfectly fine in society. But what my father had done was not. I was experiencing a freedom he hadn't.

The first year of the list, we didn't put up a Christmas tree. We were traveling for the Rose Bowl, and there wasn't time. In the second year, we skipped a tree again. I was couch-bound from my foot surgery and didn't trust Steven to handle it. Our Christmas decorations sat dormant in the back of our walk-in closet. And boxes had piled in front of them.

If I hoped to have a Christmas this year, I had to clean out the boxes.

I'd avoided dealing with them for three years because of what was in them: our wedding supplies, items from my desk at *Good Housekeeping*, and a box of my dad's stuff.

But in the first box I opened, I found a smiley face drawn by my dad: "*Warning: Peace of mind may be helpful to your health,*" he'd written beneath it. It was a sketch he'd made for the back cover of his book, *The Why? Generation*.

That night I wrote a list of life goals. Following my dad's lead, I hid it.

We drove up to Dave's house the weekend before Christmas; our Christmas Day would be spent with Steven's family in Pennsylvania.

When he opened my Christmas gifts, my stepfather cried. I'd given him expensive golf clothes. And a nice card. I'd wanted to celebrate finding something we could bond over.

Steven and I drove down to his mom's the next day and then stopped by three more houses the day after: my cousin Leif's, my stepbrother Scott's, and my cousin Steph's.

Leif was helping me check off "have five songs recorded."

It had been many years since we'd talked—never in person as adults—and we had the same communication style. It was like talking with my dad.

He mentioned hearing a rumor that his father, my uncle, had fathered another child. Leif had two younger sisters, his dad's second family (Leif was born when my uncle was in high school), but he said supposedly there had been another.

"Should I tell him?" I asked Steven in Leif's kitchen.

Back when I'd published my article about checking off my dad's list in *Good Housekeeping*, I'd received an email from a woman who claimed to be my cousin. I didn't believe Kristin until she provided photos of my uncle—Leif's dad—holding her at her christening. It was the only time she'd met her father.

On my mom's advice, I'd been keeping this a secret for two years. I'd told my aunt on my dad's side, and she'd assured me she'd tell Leif and his sisters.

But she never did.

I told Leif that the rumor was true. He cried. He'd just been presented with the existence of a whole new human.

A human his father had similarly neglected.

Leif's birth name was Tim, the same as my uncle's. But after turning eighteen, he'd changed it. He'd chosen "Leif" because it meant "life."

Four years older than me, Leif knew more about my dad's family. The most I knew was how my grandmother had yelled, "Tommy, Jimmy, Mickey, Timmy, Robby" at dinnertime. We theorized that she probably knew about Kristin but kept it to herself after witnessing our grandfather's reaction to Leif's birth. For an Irish Catholic cop, having a grandson conceived by a teenage son wasn't ideal. My dad had just met my mother when this happened. My grandmother died of a heart attack in her early fifties, just a month before Kristin was born.

Grandpop Carney made it his life's mission to educate all of his sons, and he included his first grandson in this. He constructed a plan for Leif's life. Leif knew from an early age what high school he'd attend and what college, even what career he'd pursue. Leif was rarely present at holiday get-togethers. I didn't know he was often with our grandfather the rest of the time.

When quoting him, Leif adopted my grandfather's gruff, scary-sounding voice—one I recognized right away. One so different from my dad's.

"Your dad was the creative one," Leif told me.

When Leif became a musician as a teenager—and ended his base-ball career, to my grandfather's disappointment—he ran into my dad once in a guitar shop.

"How'd you like to buy an ad in the best circular in town?" he'd overheard my dad ask the man behind the register.

When he recognized Leif, he commended him on his music.

A few years later, when Leif's father died suddenly of a stroke, my dad greeted Leif and his mother at the airport in Florida. Leif had cut his long metal-band hair—in fact, he'd shaved his whole head.

"Nice to meet ya," he said, putting his hand out. "Mick Carney."

"Uncle Mickey!" Leif said, laughing. "It's me!"

"That's just like you," Steven interjected. I always introduced myself with a handshake.

"Your dad was the reason I survived that funeral," Leif told me. "It was awkward, being with everyone again. He kept me laughing."

He did the same for Leif's younger sisters, who were only six and four, and had witnessed their father's stroke. He'd jumped on the trampoline with them all afternoon.

It was hard to remember my dad had just lost his brother.

"I'm sorry I've kept this from you," I told Leif. I'd seen one of his younger sisters, Ashley, when she visited New York and said nothing. "I understand better now how my parents kept my dad's cross-dressing from me for twelve years."

"Oh, so you know about that," Leif responded.

Once as a preteen Leif visited my grandfather, who'd developed dementia. My dad had moved back in—this was just after the divorce. My grandfather told Leif a story about finding my dad in his mother's clothes and stalking him to a piano bar. He'd confronted him about it in the parking lot, he said, calling him a gay slur.

Leif said it was during this fantastical story that he realized his grandfather no longer knew who he was. He came home and told his mother about it. "Oh, is Mickey still doing that?" she asked. She explained that this was why my parents divorced.

"Wait..." I said. "Did *everyone* know?"

When my mom and brother cleaned out my dad's apartment after he died, my uncle Jim had removed any evidence of cross-dressing. But he'd brought along his son. So that cousin knew, too.

Leif told me he and his sisters had wondered for years if I knew. He said this was why he respected that I knew a secret about his dad but hadn't told him.

"Well, what *else* don't we know?" I said, laughing.

Leif revealed that once our grandfather had struck him because he wasn't at church as an altar boy. He said our grandfather had hit our fathers—that he'd picked on them the most.

"This only makes me more grateful that my dad was who he was," I said. "I had no idea he was intentionally being the opposite of someone."

Both my mom and dad had made a point of explaining to us that they were against spanking.

"Your dad took after his mother," Leif said. "She was the warm one."

I'd never known my paternal grandmother. She died before I could talk.

Every New Year's Eve, I came up with a word for the next year. My words for 2020 were humility and faith.

After midnight, I wished "Happy New Year" to my family and friends, and my cousin Jimmy texted back. I asked if he could call me.

"Lizzie's in the hospital," he said. "She doesn't have long."

My cousin's wife, the writer, had beaten breast cancer the year before, but suddenly in December a brain tumor was detected. He was there in the hospital now.

I regretted not responding to a chain email she'd sent at Thanksgiving. I hadn't known she was still sick. Apparently neither had she.

That weekend, Steven and I drove to Pat Cross's support group. He'd told his friends about me, and they'd agreed to let me attend. As Steven drove I texted my cousin Steph, who now also had breast cancer. She'd had a double mastectomy before Christmas.

"I wish I could go back in time and take away my dad's shame," I texted her.

"Well, you can't," she texted back, "but by taking away yours, he will feel it."

The cross-dressers met in a church every Sunday about an hour from my apartment. A song my dad serenaded me with when I was a kid came on the radio. "I Just Called to Say I Love You." My brother had danced with me to it for my father-daughter dance.

"Do you think Pat will be dressed as a man or a woman?" Steven asked.

When we arrived, we saw that each man was "dressed," in a wig, makeup, dress, and heels. Some weren't men at all but transgender women. And some were transgender men.

Pat walked us into the church, and I heard the voice in the back of my mind again.

Beaming.

After we met everyone and were given nametags, I left for the bathroom and cried.

I realized the voice had always been my dad.

Most of the cross-dressers had "L" names—Lori, Leah, Lauren—so I joked that it would be a confusing night.

"We should change yours to Stephanie," Leslie told Steven.

Pat had provided delivery pizza. As we stood in line to fill our plates, I mentioned that I believed my dad had performed in drag locally. My hands were shaking.

"Oh yeah?" Leah said. "Maybe I can find out where that was."

We sat around the table eating pizza, and the temperature of the room was no different than if I'd been sitting with my brother and stepbrothers. All they wanted to talk about was football. But this was OK, because it was mostly me talking. They were dressed as women, but they were still men.

The men all went by "she" or "her." Some were closeted, some not. One explained her wife was OK with it as long as she only dressed outside the house.

"My daughter and her friends think it's so cool, though!" she said.

"That's how I would have felt, too," I said, "if given the chance."

As I listened to them talk about their lives, I remembered all the times I'd sat in therapists' offices as a teen, complaining that there was something wrong with me. "I'm different somehow," I'd said. Some told me it was my sensitivity. Others blamed my parents' divorce. But for the first time, sitting with this group, I knew what it was.

Even though I didn't "dress" like my dad did, and even though he'd never told me about it, I'd absorbed the feelings his life gave him. I'd absorbed his shame. Which he had for no reason. There was nothing wrong with what he did.

Though I didn't dress, my self-esteem was that of a cross-dresser.

It finally made sense.

We stopped in a diner on our way home. After we were seated, I left for the bathroom. I cried in the stall. As I washed my hands, my reflection gave me pause.

That's a beautiful woman, I thought.

I had the freedom to express this feminine side while the men I'd just sat with didn't. I realized I'd always unconsciously suppressed it.

That night I'd given that freedom to my dad, too, who consciously suppressed his.

I could finally let myself be.

When I sat back down at the table with Steven, I reached for his hand. I felt a closeness I'd never felt with him.

"Thank you for bringing me tonight," Steven said.

I'd worried he'd resent this. Instead, he treated it like a gift.

When I got home, I prayed. *Thank you, God, for my life*, I thought over and over.

Leif met his sister that week. They were planning a camping trip to Yosemite. My text back to him surprised me.

"Can I go, too?"

On Tuesday, Lizzie died.

I didn't find out from my cousin first. I found out from the editors in my office at Condé Nast and from national news.

After Lizzie's private funeral, we stood by her gravesite in the cemetery. One of the traditions at an orthodox Jewish funeral is for mourners to throw a shovelful of dirt on the grave. Watching my cousin do this was painful. I linked arms with my cousin Steph, his sister, whose experience of Lizzie's death was muddled by her own breast cancer diagnosis. I wrapped my arms around Steph and Em as we shivered in the snow.

When it was Steven's turn, he shoveled dirt in more than once. He kept shoveling dirt for a good three minutes.

"Oh my God," I sputtered. "He's not stopping."

"I can't believe you did that," I said once we were back in the car.

It was the most powerful display of love I'd ever seen.

"I couldn't let Jim watch that any longer," Steven explained. "Besides, you know how blue collar I am."

That Friday, as I sat in the Condé Nast offices, I closed my eyes when the new agent said over the phone that she loved the pages I'd sent, that she hadn't been able to put them down. She said she wanted to sign me.

I heard Lizzie's voice in the back of my head.

Let's see how you *handle it.*

When I called my mom with the good news, she said my cousin Steph had just learned she needed chemo.

I resolved not to tell any other relatives. The terrible news my cousins were dealing with was more important.

Cleaning the closet again that weekend, I found the last card I'd received from my dad—a valentine. It said, *"I've loved every moment of watching you grow from a sweet little girl to the wonderful woman I'm so proud to call my daughter—and my friend. With love always, Dad."*

The next day I signed my agent's contract.

In the airport on the way to Florida for the Super Bowl, I received emails from the *New York Times*, who wanted to cover me doing a list item; from Adrian, about our upcoming tux photo shoot; and from my college alumni magazine, who were writing a feature on my project. Steven joked that I'd become a celebrity.

We stopped at my mom's Florida home for a few days before the big game.

"Don't you feel..." she started when we walked in the door. I knew what came next: "...nervous about spending so much money?" But she didn't say that part.

My mom and I stayed up talking until 4:00 a.m., like we usually did. I confided in her about the cross-dressers' support group.

She remembered a phone conversation she'd had with my dad's girlfriend a year after he died. She didn't know my mom knew about his "dressing." Which meant my dad kept the cause of his divorce a secret from everyone.

His girlfriend said when he was getting dressed, it was the happiest she ever saw him. She said sometimes if he hadn't been able to dress for a while, he'd lie in bed depressed for days.

Over a Chinese dinner the next night, my stepdad expressed regret over the distance in our relationship. "You just want to help people," he said. "You're selfless. I never understood that until now. I'm the kind of guy who thinks, *What's in it for me*? But you don't function like that. I'm so sorry I couldn't see it."

My eyes watered, but my face stayed calm. I wanted to let my guard down, to accept his compliment. But I couldn't.

We left for the Super Bowl early on Sunday so we could stop for lunch in Miami beforehand. Plant was the best vegan restaurant I'd ever been to. The dishes were presented to us like works of art, as we sat on a veranda surrounded by palm trees. Steven dropped me off in front of Hard Rock Stadium. I imagined I was the only woman attending the game like this—alone, like I was headed to school.

I'd been tasked by *VegNews* magazine to write a vegan review of the Super Bowl, but all I could find in Hard Rock Stadium was an Impossible Burger, and they ended up giving me a regular one anyway. In line an Asian American man asked what it was—he was standing with his son. When I sat in the stands, Julian, the bald drunken man to my right who'd won his ticket through a lottery, sat with his teenage son. The preppy twenty-something to my left, Kyle, who'd just had a daughter, was there with his dad.

I told them my dad was with me, too.

A band of red and yellow formed as the sun set outside the stadium, and the magnitude of where I was filled me with awe.

Thank you, God, for my life, I prayed.

* * *

MY DAD ALWAYS SPENT extra time with me during sporting events. If my brother had a T-ball game, he'd pull me to the side of the bleachers and play catch.

When the San Francisco 49ers played the Cincinnati Bengals in 1989, in Miami, my brother stayed glued to the TV while my dad and I ate Chinese food in my grandfather's kitchen.

He noticed the fortune was half out of my brother's fortune cookie.

"Do you think you can fish that out of there?" he asked. "You have thin fingers."

I did, and then he asked me to grab a pen.

"Write on the back, 'A fool and his money are soon parted.'" I reinserted the fortune and, giggling, brought the cookie to my brother in the living room.

It was the first Super Bowl they'd placed money on.

Later that night, my brother groaned when John Taylor caught the winning touchdown.

* * *

THIS MEMORY WAS THE SOLE REASON I now rooted for the 49ers, the team that would become my brother's favorite after that childhood Super Bowl.

At halftime I prayed for the game to liven up. Then the tide turned against the 49ers. Patrick Mahomes, the Kansas City Chiefs' quarterback, was just too good. Julian and Kyle explained how this could happen, as though I needed a primer in football. I'd told them why I was there, but they didn't understand that being female didn't prevent me from knowing the game.

My favorite part was the halftime show, Jennifer Lopez and Shakira. I was surprised to learn the next day that people were offended by it. It's impossible to understand the athleticism of the performers when you watch it at home on TV.

Everything is different in person. When you remember the people you're watching are people, too.

This was the fifty-fourth Super Bowl. My dad was fifty-four when he died, there were fifty-four list items, I'd cycled fifty-four miles in Tucson, the final score for the Rose Bowl had been fifty-four.

Maybe instead of focusing on August 8th, the day he died, I should focus on the number of years he lived, I thought.

Super Bowl fifty-four was Super Bowl LIV. It was spelled out right before me, in big bright letters. *Live.*

When Steven picked me up after the game, I was on a high, just from the experience. My team had lost, but I didn't care. The crowd meandered like ants, some climbing a fence when they couldn't get out. I relaxed when I found our rental car. So did Steven.

"I told a guy in the hotel elevator my wife was at the Super Bowl," Steven said, laughing. "He said, 'When's the divorce?'"

Like jet-setters, we flew to St. Thomas the next morning.

The Caribbean was a popular destination in the 1960s and 1970s, mostly due to the freedom many of the islands finally experienced. They'd been under British, Danish, or French rule for centuries. My parents went to the Bahamas for their honeymoon, but I had no idea why my dad wanted to visit St. Thomas—except that he loved *Treasure Island*, and St. Thomas is basically that. The Virgin Islands were hideouts for pirates during the settling of the United States. Some say there's buried treasure there still.

Mine came in the form of my friend Mary Latham, who'd just finished her mission across the country to honor her mom and was staying in St. John. We made plans to meet up on the beach the next day.

Our hotel had a Mediterranean roof, similar to those in San Diego and Los Angeles, but the walls were painted bright blue. Roosters roamed the parking lot. I couldn't believe the view when we checked in—five sailboats that looked like pirate ships crossed the harbor, a panorama visible from our balcony. We fell asleep that night to the sound of lapping waves.

We took the ferry to St. John the next day, and as Mary and I lay on the beach watching the clear blue-green water, I asked how she felt now that she was done.

"Tired," she said.

She said she was depressed. Collecting stories of kindness had healed her because she'd learned she wasn't alone in her grief—the people she'd met had gone through terrible things. But her mission had felt like a thread of connection with her mom. The mission's ending meant she had to let it go.

Adrian had asked in an email what I would do once my mission was done.

"I've written my own list," I said. "And I plan to complete a half Ironman."

It struck me as the perfect wrap-up—during the list, I'd run ten miles straight, swum in open water, and cycled fifty-four miles through the desert. I'd already basically completed the 70.3 miles of a half Ironman.

Now I just had to complete them in one day.

To justify the training, I turned it into a list item. This was how I'd check off "own a $200 suit." Triathlon suits cost that much.

We stayed in tropical St. Thomas three days—not long enough. Steven and I were exhausted. We kept getting into stupid arguments.

He was stressed by the driving—on the left side of the steep and winding roads. I was stressed because I'd been doing too much.

"Wouldn't it be great if we could move to an island and not see anyone we know?" I said. "Like at least for a year...."

"Yeah," he said. "I need a break. I want to start living normal life again. I respect what you're doing with the list. But we need to take more trips just for us."

A week after we returned, I drove to the University of Delaware for my magazine photo shoot. I stopped to see my cousin Steph after her first chemo session. The next day, my uncle lent me his bow tie and cummerbund. While talking to him and my aunt, they suddenly remembered that a former coworker had been at my dad's funeral. They told her they hadn't known she knew my dad. "I don't," she explained. "I'm a fan."

I wondered if my dad had attended a group like Pat's. There had been two cross-dressers at his wake. I hoped he had friends he supported, like Pat did. He'd probably brought them joy—both on stage and in that world. How could he not have?

It's what he did for everyone else.

The next week I took the subway into Brooklyn early. I was getting my makeup done professionally at noon. And at 1:00 p.m., I was posing in a black women's tuxedo.

I'd told Adrian I worried I couldn't pull it off. I feared the tuxedo would wear *me*.

So I was surprised to find as I sat on that stool beneath the bright photographer's lights that the tuxedo felt like the most natural outfit I'd ever worn.

Adrian asked me to pose holding the list.

"You know, I'm just now noticing that my dad listed 'own a black tux' after 'make money on the stock market,'" I joked. "Every list item gets more expensive after that. I appreciate that he at least wrote 'start a charitable fund' before 'drive a Corvette'!"

Adrian asked how I'd celebrate when I got home.

"The list item *is* the celebration," I said. "I'm doing it right now."

Adrian's assistant accidentally knocked out the glass in the list's frame on the subway. It was fixed easily enough, but once I was home, I flipped the horseshoe inside of it.

When Jaime gave me the frame, the print that had come with it was in the U-shape position. I made it the arch shape instead.

The next day I was sick—I was in bed for ten days. I attributed it to walking around barefoot in an industrial photo studio.

When I'd recovered enough to take the train in for a dentist's appointment, I couldn't get over how empty Times Square seemed. The same thing happened two days later when I rode in for my annual mammogram.

I met Steven on the sidewalk when he came home that day. He was home from work early.

"We're all supposed to work from home now," he said.

A disease was infecting people in the city, to the point where New Yorkers had to stay inside. Nobody knew why it was spreading so quickly, but hospitals were filling up.

I texted my loved ones as Steven drove us to the grocery store.

"How's everyone doing with all this craziness? We can't go to work anymore."

Nobody texted back.

They hadn't heard of coronavirus yet.

CHAPTER 13

Plant an Apple Tree

I am ten years old.

My brother and his wild friends like to explore a creek on the south end of the neighborhood, an activity my mom has forbidden, but on this day I'm babysitting and my brother has convinced me to let him. I say he can do it on the condition that I go, too.

We stay in the creek far too long. When we return home, I'm surprised to find my mom not there—but her car in the driveway.

Running back down to the creek, I spot my mother, several feet away, roaming the streets in her panty-hosed feet, heels in one hand, yelling our names.

"Laura! David! Laura! David!"

She is sobbing.

When I run to her, we embrace.

"We're OK, Mom," I reassure her. "We're OK."

* * *

I WAS GRATEFUL WHEN THE PANDEMIC started that I'd been on the mission to finish the list. Everyone kept talking about uncertainty.

It was as though they'd believed their lives had been sure, and now they couldn't be sure anymore.

215

Before finding my dad's list, I had taken jobs where I wasn't treated well, where I worked too many hours, just so I could have certainty. It was what I'd been taught to want.

But it had also meant that if something great happened, I'd wait for the other shoe to drop. Because at least that would feel familiar.

People fear change. Even if it's good.

I realized I was in a position to advise people. I started writing posts on my blog and on Facebook, to lift people up.

Steven's asthma prevented us from seeing anyone we knew and going anywhere. We ordered our groceries on Amazon and never went to restaurants. If we did order out, I always picked it up, wearing a mask, and washed my hands when I returned.

I couldn't believe what had seemed like the easiest list item—"Live a long, healthy life at least to the year 2020"—was proving to be the most difficult.

I beat myself up about my list deadline. I'd wanted to finish by December 31, 2020, because of that first list item. My dad knew my biggest insecurity in life was being late. But the four-year deadline I'd set couldn't be met—two items required travel to Europe, which was banned.

The deadline I'd set had been arbitrary, I realized. I'd created it, so I could change it. I made my new deadline December 2021.

Since I was stuck at home, I prioritized homebound list items.

I invested in the stock market. I picked a stock my uncle, an expert, suggested. In March when the stock market tanked, after Trump banned travel to China, my stock went up ten cents.

Playing tennis in our town had been banned. So Steven bought me a portable Ping-Pong table. This was how I checked off "have my own tennis court."

Steven started growing a beard. And breakfast took on new meaning. If I had that meal to look forward to, I'd have a good reason to wake up. I took a mirror selfie each morning, too, documenting our lockdown. I felt like a prisoner, ticking off days.

When my birthday arrived, I missed my family. But I was grateful just to be able to go outside again. Even public parks were a scary place.

On April 6th, the grocery delivery services shut down temporarily. I woke up to find Steven yet again working on an Amazon order. We'd been trying for two days. Next we tackled the laundromat. We'd have to pay them to wash our clothes. We couldn't risk going inside.

After a month of working from home, we grew restless. I bought soaps, shampoos, candles, and lotions we'd discovered on our list travels, so I could at least smell like I was going on list trips. We wanted the feeling of travel without traveling, so we ran every street in our town.

Steven got the idea from an ultrarunner in San Francisco, Rickey Gates. I was nervous to embark on such an ambitious project. But our running turned every day into an adventure.

The states reopened in all different ways by late May. Each had varying levels of infections, none as plentiful as ours. Where I lived, the citizens clapped for frontline workers at 7:00 p.m. The hospitals had so many deaths, they turned shipping containers into freezers. I didn't just see this on the news. I saw it on our runs.

Where I lived, it felt like the apocalypse.

I couldn't believe any Americans thought the virus was overhyped. Or not real.

By May 27th, New Jersey was the only state still on lockdown with no plans to reopen.

When my *University of Delaware Magazine* article came out, I was surprised to find my story on the cover. And the editor in chief had written her editor's letter about my mission to finish my dad's list.

Steven's mom called him crying over the story.

My mom was excited, too—she'd told all her friends to look for it.

Soon I was publishing articles again and going on podcasts. My words of optimism were suddenly welcome. I believed we were experiencing something temporary with the pandemic. And I'd developed such a love of life that I'd do anything to protect it.

Of course, not everyone felt like this. Most people had a hard time staying away from each other.

The pandemic triggered grief for my father—I feared losing another loved one suddenly—but it also triggered my hospital experience. Being locked in was a situation I'd avoided. It was why I'd moved to New York, why I'd worked and traveled so much.

The World Health Organization announced after the Fourth of July that the virus was airborne.

We were still running every single street. My town is full of mansions, whose gardens inspired me. On my fire escape, I planted black-eyed Susan seeds sent by a local park—they called them "seeds of hope."

Then I planted apple tree seeds. A list item.

I used the same bucket my watermelon lived in. As I had with the watermelon, I named the seeds after my mom, dad, brother, and me. The Laura seed emerged first, a little green ball in the soil. I cried in wonder but then overwatered it. A raccoon ate the other seeds.

I moved my desk to our fire escape to watch over my plants. After one hundred days, I'd grown tired of staring at my bedroom walls.

As we finished running the 148 miles of our town, I came up with a new challenge: hiking the Appalachian Trail. We could hike the portions in New York and New Jersey on weekends, I suggested. Camping was the only safe way for us to travel.

I ordered a purple backpack and named her Bertha. It surprised me how much harder hiking was with twenty pounds on my back.

Our first night in Harriman State Park, we ran into hikers who warned us they'd seen a bear. I yelled "Yahoo!" with each step to scare it off. Before long, the sun had set. We put on headlamps and hiked in the dark.

"Are we there yet?" I asked a few times, though I was the one holding the map.

Steven took us down the wrong path. "No, it's that way!" I said. "Let's go back!"

"Look," he said, "there are no bears out here. We're going to get there soon. You're going to have to calm down."

"OK," I told him. "I trust you."

As soon as I said it, I realized what I'd done.

I'd never said that to him before.

I'd said "I trust you" to a man.

Steven had purchased a large tent—one for three instead of two. I watched from a rock while he set it up, our little home. Our big home.

We'd checked off "own a large house with our own land."

"How's that again?" Steven asked.

The tent was extra-large, as was the view of New York City and the pines around us. And the dictionary definition of "house" is shelter. When we ran every street, we'd owned our land—we knew where everything was now. Montclair was part of us. Before the pandemic, we'd merely slept in New Jersey.

The roads we ran were once Lenape trails.

The Lenapes didn't believe in land ownership.

The clothing I bought now was for camping and running. I gave up on makeup. I gained back ten pounds, half of the inches I'd lost from my waist. We never went to the doctor. And I cut our hair.

When the Democratic National Convention aired, I realized I much preferred watching it socially distanced on TV, over the phone with my mom, the person I wanted to see most. There was Joe Biden, accepting his nomination in my Delaware high school, of all places. Wherever my dad was, he was laughing.

In September, I trained for a virtual marathon. Steven and I had signed up to run in Big Sur before we locked down. But the most I could run was thirteen miles.

219

I planted a fresh batch of apple seeds, from a Gala apple I'd been eating. I named them Peace, Justice, Love, and Grace. I bought a wire cloche to protect them.

Within a week, all of them had sprouted.

On our second camping trip, in October, we slept in a huckleberry field. I cried happy tears when I learned we were on the Appalachian Trail.

I was checking off the first item from *my* bucket list.

When we learned painters were coming to fix the cracks in our ceilings—a state inspection required it—we were so afraid we'd get COVID-19 that we locked ourselves in our living room, wearing masks twenty-four seven, even while we slept.

Since the start of the pandemic, we'd watched movie series I'd never cared about—first it was James Bond, to understand my dad's tuxedo goal. This led to Mission: Impossible, and this to every Marvel movie. By summer we were watching only old films—Katharine Hepburn, Cary Grant. By October, this had bled into Universal monsters.

We watched old horror movies the entire time we were locked in the living room. It was one of the best days of my life.

I was nervous when Biden won the election. My neighbors sang and ran through the streets, exposing themselves to the virus. It seemed unnatural for anyone to be this happy about a president. But even more unnatural when President Trump said he'd won.

A news article said that even though we had our first female vice president, the number of college-aged girls who'd considered public office had gone down. The girls said the sexism they'd face wasn't worth the effort. So when I began training for my half Ironman, I also raised funds again for Girls on the Run.

We celebrated Thanksgiving over Zoom. Steven loved that he didn't have to drive anywhere. And could enjoy a Tofurky from home.

By day 272 of our lockdown, we hadn't stepped inside any building but our own in nine months—save for the infrequent times I picked up takeout. I was beginning to feel like a mad man locked in a cabin. The number of American deaths had surpassed the total number of spectators at the Rose Bowl, NCAA Final Four Championship, and Super Bowl I'd attended combined.

We'd spent the previous Christmas in the homes of five families. Now it was just us.

Christmas morning reminded me of when I was a child.

* * *

MY DAD ALWAYS SAVED THE STAR on the tree for me. When Jim moved in, he and my mom bought a new tree-topper. At thirteen, the replacement saddened me. My dad said this was because I loved tradition like he did.

When Steven and I moved in together, and shopped for ornaments for my Nana's hand-me-down tree, I spotted a gold filigreed star like my dad's. I told Steven we had to buy it.

The star never really fit on our little Charlie Brown tree, no matter how much we twisted and turned it. One Christmas Eve, I let Steven decorate the tree while I wrapped presents.

"I left the star for you," Steven said when he was done.

As I placed the star, a beam of light came through the window then bounced off the star and into my eyes. I thought it was my dad saying hi.

"Wow," I said, stepping back, "the star stayed on. That never happens!"

"Maybe there's something under it," Steven said.

He'd fastened an engagement ring to the top, like an ornament. I hadn't noticed he was halfway off the couch, on one knee.

* * *

ON NEW YEAR'S EVE, I celebrated having made it through 2020. I'd checked off that list item. My word for 2021 was wonder.

Then the capitol was attacked.

So much for 2021 being better.

The previous year, though devastating globally, had been one we'd managed to make great. I'd been given the space I needed to write. For the first few months of 2021, I pretended I was in a hotel again until my book proposal was done.

For most of my life, I hadn't been a homebody. For most of my career, I'd worked late nights. In high school, I was often at a friend's house. But now, I cleaned our house for us, not for company. We grew our own vegetables in an indoor vertical farmstand. I'd even learned to cook. Being in the kitchen so often was strange—in my efforts to avoid my stepdad growing up, it had become a room I disliked.

For the first time, every room in my home felt like mine.

I was invited onto more podcasts. In a pre-interview, one host said, "So I assume you've given up on having a family." I told Steven later, which led to a conversation I didn't want to have.

Though Steven had wanted kids when we met, he'd changed his mind, especially with the way the world was now, he said. I sobbed. I hid my face in my pillow. I told him I viewed the world differently.

He said he was 80 percent against it; I said I was 80 percent for it. We decided to pick up the conversation again after our Ironman, which he'd agreed to do with me.

But I didn't know if I had that much time.

One day in February, we separated the apple trees. They'd lived in the apartment all winter but were now overgrowing their pot.

I'd named them Peace, Love, Grace, and Justice, but they were really still my family of origin.

Repotting them in my living room with newspaper on the floor, I saw my dad's tree had fused at the roots with mine. I teared up as I pulled them apart.

"You have to let her go now," I said.

After Steven and I were vaccinated, we rejoined the world. First, we visited his mother, and then my stepbrother Scott, in Delaware, stopping to buy our new bikes.

When I came home, I ordered my triathlon suit.

By summer, Steven had injured his Achilles. He'd run four miles every four hours in one weekend, wearing his ankle out. My friend Danielle was in the hospital, coping with her mental health. It looked like I'd compete in the Ironman alone.

When we saw my mom and stepdad again, we toasted to my book proposal's near completion. The day I finished writing it, "Zip-a-Dee-Doo-Dah" played on the bells at the old church.

My first memory is of skipping as my father sang this song.

Our first social outing in sixteen months was a weekend camping trip with my cousin Em and her husband Lee.

I entertained Anna, their precocious six-year-old, and her younger brother, Eli. We drew together in the tent while the adults talked outside. When it started pouring, I created games to play while Steven manned the grill. Em and Lee had been cooped up with these kids, homeschooling them, the entire pandemic.

The next morning, as we prepared to leave, Lee said, "You know, you guys deserve a million dollars for watching those kids. Thank you."

"*What did you just say?*" I asked.

I'd checked off "sell a million dollars' worth of merchandise."

I should have known the merchandise would be my love for children—the priceless gift my parents gave me.

I finished my first sprint triathlon in Atlantic City. In September, I finished my first Olympic-distance tri. It took me five hours, and I came in last place.

On my next visit with my mom, I invited her to go with me to Vienna. I'd planned to travel to Berlin, Dresden, and Vienna in December, per the advice of the man in the Denmark house in San Diego. She seemed excited. But later she said she couldn't go due to balance issues and because she didn't want to leave my stepdad behind.

Steven and I couldn't afford for both of us to go. Partly because I'd owed him $2,000 for most of the pandemic. Partly because our cat had kidney disease.

The waiting to hear back from book editors was excruciating. One day I determined I'd let God do the big stuff while I did the little things. I channeled my energy into swimming, cycling, and running.

For nine months I worked out five days a week—some weeks for up to ten hours. As I rode my bike on bitter November nights, I remembered riding my bike as a kid. *It doesn't matter if anybody buys my book*, I thought. *I'll self-publish if I have to. It's my story, mine to tell.*

My mom sent me a check to help with Vienna, which I applied to my plane tickets. But a week later the State Department discouraged travel to Europe again. A COVID-19 variant had emerged—the most contagious yet. I rescheduled my trip for the spring.

The first week of December, we flew to Florida for my half Ironman. This was supposed to be an easy course. But the normal seventy-degree temps shot up to ninety degrees that December, and after forty-two miles on the bike course, the heat slowed me down so much that I missed the time cutoff. The race director kicked me out.

Steven and I spotted a rainbow in the distance after he found me in transition. I found congratulatory messages on my phone. It didn't matter that I hadn't finished the race. People were applauding my courage to try. I resolved to try again.

At Christmas, my family got together for the first time in two years. I handed out copies of Steven's Christmas present—as I'd trained for triathlons, he'd secretly redesigned my dad's book. *The Why? Generation (in a Why-Not World.)* was now available for purchase on Amazon. Forty-four years after it was written.

My dad's author photo sat on the last page, the rare time he had a mustache.

He looked optimistic for what his future held.

CHAPTER 14

Visit Vienna

I told a select few about my Zoom meeting with a potential publisher. This was the true gift of writing my book, I thought. That I'd found so many people I trusted.

When I signed my book deal a week later and received an advance, I finally paid Steven back. People asked me online why I wasn't smiling in my book contract signing photos. I said, "I'll smile when the book is done."

But really it was because I feared my dad was missing this.

I woke up the next day to an email from one of my dad's old friends—the champion sailor. We'd never met.

Hi, I was a friend of your father's at the U of D. We were in several American studies classes together. I was so saddened to hear of his passing so tragically. I have been cleaning out our house in preparation for a move and came across a poem your dad wrote (if I recall, it was an assignment for one of our classes). He was very gifted as a writer among other things. We lost touch several years after our graduation, but I think I met him and your Mom at a U of D football game sometime in the '70s (yikes!!). Anyway, I read the nice article about you in the U of D newsletter and thought you might enjoy reading it. I had told him how my ancestors on my dad's side came from England/Ireland, etc., and I named one of my sailboats "Abigail."

Anyway, give my best to your Mom,
Debbie Freeman Hoermann '71

'ABIGAIL'

by Mick Carney

From distant lands, the Freeman clan
traveled with the sun.
Through stormy seas, they set their sail
with freedom on the run.

At last they landed on bright green shores
in a land both wild and tame.
Their gallant ship survived the trip
to mark the family's fame.

This descendant of Old Glory
retells the story of persistent faith and love.
This ship it sails with liberty's flag
and asks for help from above.

You swift, sensuous ship,
approach the wind with that inherited
American Pride.
Set your course right, as
you float through the night with
the creeping crimson tide.

And when your young and talented master
gives you your command,
never let this Freeman fail.
For History sails in Debbie's hand,
Oh Mighty Abigail.

I cried in disbelief. Everything he'd written was what I needed
to hear.

Later that night, I Googled the name "Abigail." In Hebrew, it means
"my father is rejoicing."

In March, Steven ran his first official marathon—in Los Angeles. The same one I'd run with Kelly to start my dad's list. He couldn't believe he'd finished it when he was done. Before flying back home, we had breakfast with a film producer interested in adapting my book.

Once we were home from L.A., and my mom visited me from Florida for my birthday, we mostly talked about my travel plans. She said she'd be there with me for every step of the trip. She'd gone to Vienna as a teenager, with her sister. Her advice, along with that of my uncle David, who worked in Vienna once a year, was invaluable. I showed her the spot in the Montclair, New Jersey, café where I wrote. She acted like she was visiting something historic.

I bought a pack of Juicy Fruit, my dad's lucky gum, in the airport the day I left for Berlin. I feared it was the closest I'd come to vegan food for hours.

I couldn't find anything to eat in the Las Vegas airport, where I stopped for my connecting flight, but Chex Mix. But this lasted me until we landed in Berlin, twenty hours later. I watched *Wonder Woman* movies on the plane when I couldn't sleep.

What am I doing? I thought. *This is the craziest one yet.*

When we landed, I struggled to figure out the subway system. I was staying in the Almodovar hotel in Friedrichshain, the hippest neighborhood in Berlin, purely because it was 100 percent vegan.

I stopped for a gemüseburger (a German burger) on the way, dragging my suitcase on cobblestones. The sky was gray. I got lost four times. It didn't help that I barely knew German.

I sighed with relief when the Almodovar hotel appeared. The man at the front desk asked if my stay was for business or pleasure.

"Pleasure," I said, smiling.

After a quick tour of the spa-themed hotel, I called Steven—I'd promised I would each night—then finally slept.

I sat down the next morning for a leisurely breakfast in the Almodovar's restaurant, Bardot. They served vegan curried sausage, seitan, scrambled eggs, and a variety of fruits and breads. But what really dazzled me was their potato salad. And cut peppers, cucumbers, and tomatoes—not breakfast foods in the U.S. Every milk they served was plant milk.

The subway system was straightforward once I was downtown. I rode it to Märchenbrunnen, a garden of Grimms' fairy tale statues. From there, I took a tram to Marienkirche, one of the oldest churches in Berlin. As I walked across the square, I was proud of myself. I felt like I had when I'd moved to New York.

I toured Berlin Cathedral, the largest in the city and where the rulers are buried. It was damaged during WWII then later rebuilt. The climb to the top was filled with funny warnings, and the view, with the sun reflecting off the dome, was the most beautiful I'd ever seen. In the distance, a street performer sang "Shallow," from *A Star Is Born.*

I tried getting tickets to one of the many art museums, but all but one were booked. I settled for the Deutsches Historisches Museum, an exhibit on Wagner and Marx.

By 6:00 p.m. my feet hurt, and I was relieved to find a vegan fast food place—Swing Kitchen—and a vegan wiener schnitzel. I did my best to order in German, but wound up saying *"sprechen sie* English?"

At sunset I strolled the Unter den Linden and thanked God for my wonderful life. As the sky darkened, I toured Bebelplatz, where the Nazis burned books. The center of the square has a hole in the ground filled with empty shelves. I discovered a moment of hope in the Brandenburg Tor—a symbol of peace. Ukrainian flags and anti-war sentiment spread all over the city. It was a strange time to be in Berlin.

As I walked through the Memorial to the Murdered Jews of Europe, I sobbed. It was night now, and I was the only one there, walking amongst these rows upon rows of plain black slabs. It was designed to make you feel isolated and afraid. It worked.

The memorial was a block from Hitler's underground bunker, where he killed himself. It's commemorated by nothing but a sign— they built a parking lot over it.

On my second day, I got up early, though I'd had no sleep, and caught an 8:30 a.m. train to Dresden.

One of the best decisions I'd made was booking every train via an app in advance. All I had to do was get to a train station on time and make sure my phone was charged.

I was nervous about Dresden. I guessed my dad had wanted to see the jewel box of Germany that was bombed. But the Allies killed at least 25,000 civilians (some say 250,000), mostly women and children, and witnessing the aftermath even seventy years later struck me as morbid.

When my train arrived, it was brutally cold—hailing. I needed a warmer coat. My favorite store growing up—Esprit—still existed in Europe. I found one with a clerk who understood "it's cold" and an affordable faux leather jacket and cotton scarf and hat.

I got turned around on the tram system five times...I'd been trying to reach a place that served vegan brunch. I settled on Vietnamese pho. It was the first time in a long time I could remember having a meal in a real restaurant, all by myself. I felt safe because the hosts checked vaccine status before they let customers inside.

After lunch, I visited the Zwinger museum. I'd been eager to visit a true art museum but I couldn't help feeling I was missing out, looking at a bunch of old stuff in an old building. A guard said something in German in a panic.

"*Sprechen sie* English?" I asked.

"There've been technical difficulties. You have to leave," she said.

Because it was Sunday, not much was open. So I walked around Dresden, treating the architecture like art.

A lot of the buildings were charred. But Frauenkirche was still breathtaking—a cathedral destroyed completely in WWII and only just recently rebuilt. Our country bombed civilians here. It was strange to walk amongst tourists thinking about that. My cousin Leif had hinted that my grandfather might have been one of the bombers. I didn't know if my dad knew this.

But my dad was twenty when his favorite writer after Mark Twain, Kurt Vonnegut, published *Slaughterhouse-Five*, a thinly veiled autobiographical retelling of being in Dresden, underground, during the bombing. This book changed my father's life, and it changed mine at around the same age when he gave it to me.

And now here I was—in Dresden, satisfying my dad's dream, maybe witnessing my grandfather's nightmare, and reaching my own writing goals....

And so it goes.

In a café I'd ordered completely in German, even asking if they had oat milk, and was feeling proud, when suddenly the church bells rang...this went on for ten minutes. I texted Steven, who Googled it and learned the extended ringing was a call to prayer.

I said a prayer before the bells were done.

When I reached my hotel back in Berlin, I bought currywurst and frites from a place called Voner. I nearly fell asleep in the dark rooftop sauna, its ceiling lit to resemble stars.

The next morning, after a croissant and coffee, I hopped on an eight-hour train to Vienna. It was hard to focus on my travel books watching the German countryside go by, mostly backward.

I felt like I was in a film. I ordered a sandwich in the café car, then noticed something strange: balls of leaves at the tops of trees, which I later learned were mistletoe.

Kisses.

Thank you, God, for my life, I prayed.

It was nighttime when I arrived in Vienna, which made its majestic white buildings stand out even more. I texted a selfie to Steven.

"I'm here! I finally made it!"

It was my last travel list item.

I caught a streetcar to my hotel, surprised by how easy it was. Hotel Harmonie, decorated in pink satin, was designed for the city's esteemed ballet school. It had a dancer theme—even the artwork was ballerina footprints.

You should be dancing, my dad had said on my plane to London.

After exploring the hotel, I called Steven and my mom, who was still on my trip with me vicariously. I fell asleep watching a YouTube video of "I'm in Love with Vienna," what my mom couldn't stop singing on the phone.

The next morning I took a streetcar to Belvedere Palace, which is 400 years old. It was Prince Eugene of Savoy's summer home. It's also where Archduke Franz Ferdinand lived, before his assassination started WWI.

Its marble foyer is famous for a few things, but mostly Austria finding its independence in the 1950s. Its ceiling and sprawling gardens moved me to tears as I realized I was in fact finally here. I'd waited for Vienna for five years. Or, like the Billy Joel song says, it had waited for me.

List items didn't happen until I was ready.

The paintings in the Belvedere once belonged to the Habsburgs, so there were lots of old masters—but also some newer stuff.

What I most looked forward to was Gustav Klimt's *The Kiss*. This painting is special because, in true Secession style, Klimt took an everyday experience and elevated it to the level of religious icon.

Klimt captured the authentic inside of the faux saintly. There's no actual kiss happening in the painting—this is the moment before a kiss, which everyone can relate to.

Every moment I was in Vienna felt like this painting, anticipating authentic connection while skimming something sacred.

It was a whole new world.

I didn't enter the famous Vienna State Opera. I had lunch alfresco near it—in a Schanigarten, as the Viennese say. I ordered a *mélange*, a Viennese cappuccino.

My next museum was the Vienna art history museum, which greeted me with a jaw-dropping ceiling frieze, *Apotheosis of the Renaissance*, depicting Michelangelo, da Vinci, and Raphael—the museum housed their actual work, too. Titians, Caravaggios, and Rembrandts lined the museum's red walls.

After a stop in the Secession museum to view the Beethoven Frieze, I took the tram back to my hotel. My feet hurt too much to keep going. I was having fast food for dinner again, at Swing Kitchen, a few blocks away.

As I climbed the Strudlhofstiege (a staircase dedicated to the founder of the first art school in Central Europe), I stopped to appreciate the view. The last time I'd felt like this was when I was an art major in college. It was the last time my time felt like it was completely mine.

I looked out at the Liechtenstein Palace and asked my dad, *What is all of this for, looking at this art?*

It's because you need to understand that what you're doing matters, he said. *Someday people's feet will hurt from experiencing something you've made.*

Vienna is a place where an artist's life means something. It is not trivial, compared to other pursuits. Here I wouldn't feel the way I felt back home.

As I walked back with my dinner, I felt giddy I'd be having a sleepover basically with myself. *Movie night!* I thought, laughing. *And then tomorrow a palace and a concert!* Except I didn't just think this. I said it out loud. *I'm finally learning how to be my own best friend,* I thought.

A ladybug crossed my path—surprising in the middle of the city. I texted a photo of it to my cousin Steph.

"Hi, Nana!" she said.

"Be your own best friend" was the kind of thing my grandmother would have said. I tried not to cry too obviously on my walk to the hotel.

The next morning, I ordered a vegan *apfeltasche* completely in German.

I was off to Schönbrunn Palace, which was discovered by the Habsburgs, Vienna's ruling family, in the 1500s and served as their hunting lodge until Charles VI gave it to his daughter Maria Theresa as a wedding gift in 1723. The first Holy Roman Empress renovated it to be a permanent residence—its walls are Habsburg Yellow, a color that connotes wealth. It looked like Versailles, into which Maria Theresa's daughter, Marie Antoinette, would move.

Maria Theresa was nothing like her hedonistic daughter. Some say she's been lost to history because of her conservativism and religious intolerance. But Maria Theresa was one of the most powerful leaders of the eighteenth century—her empire thrived under her reign, though it had been expected to crumble under the leadership of a twenty-three-year-old woman.

My favorite part of the Schönbrunn was the gardens—all four miles of them. Some of it was still wild terrain, so I felt like Little Red Riding Hood. When I realized I was under mistletoe, I kissed my own hand.

I let myself rest in the Schönbrunn gardens. I took breaks on benches. *Rest is not lazy*, I learned. *Rest is smart.*

Three years before my brother found my dad's list, I'd started seeing Xs everywhere. I'd often wondered what they meant...but the definition that stuck was that they were a crossroads.

My soul was making me notice Xs because it was time to make authentic choices.

I came upon a crossroads, an X in the path, as I navigated my way to the Greek-columned Gloriette—a "monument to just war." As I turned around and considered the right path, I saw a statue of Heracles and Cerberus.

Capturing the three-headed guard of the afterlife was the twelfth and final of Heracles's labors in Greek mythology. With each task he advanced another step toward immortality. Each labor was deemed more difficult than the last.

No mortal had ever met Cerberus and left Hades. His three heads represented negative elements of the past, present, and future: regrets, overwhelm, and what ifs. His three voices could turn your time in the afterlife into hell.

So Heracles learned the secret to finding happiness in the after-life, just in case he never returned, and asked Hades if he could simply borrow Cerberus, not kill him. Heracles quelled the beast by grabbing his neck and employing a positive mindset: embracing the good of his past, being mindful in his present, and having optimism about his future.

This is the only way you can make authentic choices in life—the energy you bring with you affects the outcome. If you listen to Cerberus, fear can paralyze you.

It was the same thing I'd learned with my father's list. I was nearing the end of my journey, my most impossible tasks. As I tried to meet them, this was a good reminder that my greatest help and hindrance was always me.

On my way to dinner, I stopped in Michaelerkirche, Vienna's oldest church. I prayed in the Lady of Lourdes Chapel.

Please let me have a child, I thought. It came out of me like a dam had broken.

On the way out I learned Mozart's funeral was held there.

There are 150 coffeehouses in Vienna, a historic part of their culture (when coffee was introduced to Europe by the Turks is up for debate, but it caught on in Vienna in the late 1600s—taverns were the place for rabble-rousing, so the coffeehouse became the home for intellectuals).

I'd chosen Cafe Central, once called "the Chess school," which my dad would have loved. It attracted Freud, Adler, Hitler, Lenin, and Stalin. I ordered a Viennese *mélange* while reading the *New York Times* (newspapers from around the world hung on wooden poles). It felt like a time warp, reading about Russia attacking Ukraine, now and not eighty years ago, when news like that was more commonplace.

I was getting used to this whole "date with myself" idea. After dinner, I walked to Peterskirche for an intimate violin quartet, who played Mozart, Vivaldi, Borodin, Schubert, Bach, and Beethoven. As I walked in, I held my heart and let out a breath. The baroque interior was stunning. Enough to make someone pass out.

For three hours I listened to the music of Vienna in this dimly lit space, on warm violins, in an ornate, glimmering cathedral that suddenly felt small. A seat was left open next to me, which had happened a lot on this trip. I dropped my metal water bottle twice. But that absurdity, plus what the first chair announced in broken English—that their encore was "not by Mr. Beethoven, but from Ireland"—made me know my dad was there. Sitting beside me.

On the way to my hotel, I discovered the doorway Orson Welles emerged from in Steven's and my favorite old movie, *The Third Man*.

"Thank you, God, for my life," I whispered in the dark.

I spent my third day in Vienna visiting Salzburg—just a two-hour train ride away. This was where *The Sound of Music* was filmed.

With all the research I'd done on how to tour the movie sites on foot, it hadn't occurred to me that everywhere I'd turn, I'd run into the Alps.

I ate lunch at Heart of Joy Café, inspired by the work of Sri Chinmoy, who promoted compassion as a way of life. I explored Mirabell Gardens and the Do-Re-Mi steps, the part of the movie montage where Maria fashions clothes for the kids and they sing and dance all over town.

On my quest to find the convent gates, I strolled down Salzburg's adorable medieval streets, splashed water in the Residenzplatz fountain (where Julie Andrews splashed it), found my first heart of the day, and climbed up to Nonnberg Abbey. At more than 200 steps, it was twice as high as the famous steps in St. Thomas that Steven and I had climbed.

As I learned about the abbey, I understood why Maria was such a problem there.

The Benedictine nuns mostly work in silence, except when they are singing, which happens twice a day, and everything they do adheres to a strict schedule, so as not to waste God's time.

It was a bad fit for a *flibbertigibbet*.

As a notorious flibbertigibbet myself, I felt exalted up in those mountains, with those views. I'd hoped to hike up to the meadow where Maria taught the children how to sing, which required a forty-minute train ride to Werfen. But first I had to run back to the café where I'd had lunch to retrieve the water bottle I'd left there, and on the way, I got distracted by a heart on the ground and a unicorn sculpture I had to impersonate, so I missed the train I needed in order to do the hike and get back on time. It was only after buying my ticket and sitting at the terminal that I realized if I went through with the hike, I likely wouldn't make the last train back to Vienna.

Flibbertigibbet.

Looking after my own time on this trip was hard. The hike to Maria's meadow had been what I'd anticipated most eagerly. I called Steven in tears.

"Clearly this is not something I do on purpose," I said.

"I know it's not," Steven responded.

But in true Maria spirit, I'd had an incredible time wandering and finding things I couldn't have foreseen. That convent is 1,300 years old, the oldest in the German-speaking world, and I'd gotten to peek inside. The Gothic chapel was wooden and cold, and its views of the city took my breath away. My favorite song from *The Sound of Music* is "I Have Confidence," and I was walking in Julie Andrews's footsteps, where she sang it.

Because I missed the train to Werfen, I got to experience Salzburg at night, which meant *apfelstrudel*, pizza, and a stroll through altstadt searching for Felsenreitschule, the riding school where the von Trapp family performs at the end of the film. Once I'd found it, I realized this was more important to me than that silly hike up in the mountains, what I'd originally planned. My dad never would have taken that hike. He would have eaten apfelstrudel and a large pizza, then checked out where his favorite song from the movie was performed.

Back in Vienna that night, I did what my dad would have done—rewatched *The Sound of Music* over a Viennese chocolate torte and hot tea.

I cried during the opening scenes of the film—they pan over the Salzburg skyline, which I'd forgotten. It seemed majestic and foreign when I was a child. But there were the onion domes and St. Mary's chapel at Nonnberg. I now knew these were *real* places. I'd seen all of them in person that day.

First on the agenda on my last day in Vienna was the Hofburg Palace, to tour the Imperial Treasury. It's considered the most important in the world as it houses the crown of the Holy Roman Emperor; the Holy Lance (which supposedly pierced the side of Christ on the cross); the Holy Grail; and the Ainkhurn, or unicorn horn (a Narwhal tooth—it's at least six feet tall).

On my way out I passed the Hofburg Chapel, where the Vienna Boys' Choir sings.

* * *

WHEN I'D ASKED MY MOM at Christmas why my dad wanted to visit Vienna, she'd said it was probably because he'd loved the Vienna Boys' Choir, formed in the Middle Ages, who sang on the *Perry Como Christmas Special* in 1977. "I was pregnant," she said. "You were due in three months. I remember I was baking cookies. We loved Christmas." The choir's soloist was named Eric, and my dad loved his voice so much that he asked my mom if they could name their baby Eric if they had a boy—which they thought I was; the doctor had reported a strong heartbeat. This was before ultrasound. The next day, my parents picked up a Christmas stocking at the mall. On one side they printed "Eric" and on the other "Laura."

I spent the first six years of my life with this stocking, wondering who "Eric" was. I assumed when I was older he was the baby my mom had miscarried. But no—my parents were the crazy people who put both names on the stocking at once.

It made sense my dad would name his progeny after a child with a beautiful voice. I wasn't sure if I'd lived up to that.

But at least I was finally using mine.

* * *

I BARELY MADE IT to the university on time for a two-hour walking tour. For my last afternoon in Vienna, three women and I traced the steps of Dr. Sigmund Freud.

Our guide described what it was like to live in Freud's Vienna—as the City of Music adjusted to the Industrial Revolution, it also dealt with many cases of depression. Life was moving too fast for citizens' psyches to keep up. I'd heard of this before—the dysthymia experienced by American writers of that time, who headed to the Southwest—but not how Europe had experienced it. Until then, depression was believed to be caused by demons or genetics, or a character weakness. Freud was the first to recognize depression as a response to life.

Freud set up his office to resemble an Egyptian tomb. His patients lay on a Victorian longue in the main room as he sat in silence behind them. As they spoke, their eyes scanned the paintings around the room and the chestnut tree in the courtyard, undoubtedly gazing upon the small clay, wood, or bone statues on Dr. Freud's desk—his "old and dirty gods." Though they did not know it, they were replicating an ancient ritual.

Egyptian mummies were once entombed in connected rooms, similar to Freud's waiting room, office, and study. The corpse lay in one room while its worldly possessions lay in another—when the spirit arose to join the afterlife, the task would be less scary, Egyptians believed, because its possessions surrounded it. Mirrors, too, were used to assist the transformation because they reflected light. A small clay figure sat in the tomb as an effigy. This way, the spirit could come and go as it pleased—because its stand-in was secure.

This was the effect Freud hoped seeing the dolls would have on patients: their unconscious would open up and exit the body and do the work healing required. The rebirth of the psyche, enabled by a new womb. He believed seeing the antiquities made this more likely—as did the adjoining rooms and lying supine, like a mummy.

The office made me feel like I was walking in a temple. What I mostly found myself thinking, whispering to Dr. Freud, as I'd taken to stating thoughts out loud so often on this trip, was "thank you. Thank you for saving my life."

On the plane ride home the next day, I reflected on how most of my trip made me feel like Alice in Wonderland, a feeling I tried to cultivate almost all the time anyway. This was the place where I was happiest. At least once per day I'd thanked God for my wonderful life. I decided that the old adage was true, everything good was on the other side of fear. By facing mine, I'd found myself, which is always a worthwhile pursuit. And I was sure what my dad hoped to find, too.

I'd had to go to Vienna alone...to understand a married woman can still sometimes be solo. I was still my own person, not my family, I realized. I could be part of the whole, without being the whole. The list always had me doing the opposite of what's expected, and that's why it jolted me out of predictable emotions—it helped me assess things my own way.

I'd thought Vienna would feel foreign or isolating, but instead I felt like a native...to the culture and the art. Part of a family. I belonged. That's what the phrase "Vienna waits for you" means. It means you will always have a place somewhere.

Home was a place that lived in me. My life was a puzzle—I'd had to take it all apart to put it back together again in a new way, a way that made more sense.

In May, Steven and I celebrated our sixth wedding anniversary by competing in our own at-home triathlon. We also played tennis. Our third time playing that summer, I finally beat him in a set. We decided this counted as beating a number-one seed. I might not have beaten him at a tournament, but I'd beaten him *in* one.

I checked into my cheap hotel again, to finish writing my book.

In Vienna, I'd prayed to the Virgin Mary for a baby—but what if the baby was me? Writing my book felt like a rebirth.

By the end of July, I was competing in the New York City Triathlon and planning a ten-day backpacking trip on the John Muir Trail, in

California, with my cousin Leif—a result of my asking if I could go to Yosemite with him and his newly discovered sister. Leif took this trip every year. Steven thought I was doing too much.

I called my brother before my flight.

"So, if I have any major news, I should tell Steven and have him send you a smoke signal?" he asked. He thought I was hiking the John Muir Trail alone. He exhaled audibly when I told him Leif was going with me.

Steven reminded me that we'd never gone a day without talking to each other.

"I've been keeping track," he said.

My cousin had said not to worry about the hotel the first night. But when I arrived in Reno, I learned he'd reserved only one room. I used the credit card Steven gave me for emergencies to book my own. We had a fun night talking and catching up. We were excited for this trip.

But the next morning when we left for the five-hour shuttle to the trail base, Leif told me he'd left our maps at home. He said he could text them to me.

"But what if my phone dies and we get separated?" I asked.

"We won't get separated," he said.

I'd meticulously packed my backpack, Bertha, and even rewatched *Wild*. I'd trained all summer with Steven, with increasingly longer hikes and an overnight on the AT. After the shuttle ride, as the 10,000-foot peaks loomed over us on the drive up the mountains with Lone Pine Kurt, a courier for hikers, I felt like I could faint. It was the Paramount Pictures logo in real life.

After sunset, Kurt drove off. Leif threw on his rain pants and jacket. I put on my puffy coat over my hooded sweatshirt but was wearing shorts.

"Do you think I need bug repellent?" I asked.

"No way!" Leif said. "It's nighttime!"

As we trekked the first mile up the mountain, my cousin yelled. "Yes! I love you!" He was talking to the mountain.

I wasn't worried when we got lost. It was dark and hard to see what was beneath us. I sat on a rock while Leif found our way. Many of the trails were washed out. The town of Independence, California, had just seen a once-in-a-century storm. It never rained out in the desert. The little town didn't know what to do with it.

The second time we got lost, I stayed calm.

"These trails keep vanishing," Leif grumbled.

As he hacked through the bushes with his trekking pole, I saw my dad in the distance, in my mind's eye. I listened to the rush of the waterfall I couldn't see, looked up at the starry sky, remembered navigating the woods with my dad and my brother as a kid. I teared up.

"Thank you, God, for my life," I whispered.

Leif returned frustrated. He recommended we go back the way we'd come. But just as he approached the fork in the path where I'd sensed my dad's spirit, he stopped. "Wait a minute...is this...?"

He'd found the trail.

"That's so weird," I said. "When you were searching, I sensed my dad's spirit standing right there!"

"Thanks, Uncle Mickey!" Leif yelled. "Love ya, boo!"

The altitude hit me once we reached 9,000 feet. I had to stop every 100 feet to rest.

"We can stop here and set up camp," Leif said, "or we can keep going. The campsite is only half a mile away. Up to you."

There were two tents filled with strangers near the log where I sat.

"Let's keep going," I said.

I couldn't get over how enormous the trees were. I'd never seen trees so big, much less so close to my face. The higher we climbed, the fewer we saw. The terrain began to resemble a desolate planet.

Leif lost the trail again.

"There, there's another cairn!" he said.

"We're relying on *cairns*?" I asked. Cairns are Buddhist-like piles of rocks hikers leave to guide other hikers. Someone had been on this trail and found the way through.

This time I waited longer. It was nearing 1:00 a.m.

"I must admit," Leif said, "I am at a loss."

He suggested we climb back down and set up camp for the night. It would be easier to find the trail again in the daylight.

I'd asked Leif before our trip what kind of pajamas to bring. "LMFAO! That will weigh down your pack!" he'd texted. When Steven and I camped on the East Coast, I slept in long thermals.

I'd also left our big, three-person tent at home, on Leif's advice. "Too heavy," he'd said. "You can borrow my spare."

But his one-person tent looked like it had seen better days. As he unrolled it and set it up beneath a sequoia on the edge of a waterfall cliff, I asked how long it had been since he'd used it.

"About a decade," he said.

It was the size of a hammock. Or a coffin.

I wondered how I'd fit my air mattress in.

But this became moot as my bare legs were so cold that all I wanted was to get in my sleeping bag. I had no patience for blowing up an air mattress. Or for eating. I unrolled my bag inside the one-person tent and threw my body in. I didn't even take off my shoes.

"Good night!" I said.

Leif set up his tent several feet away. He'd given the prime location to me. But it didn't feel prime as I lay there shivering, the wind rustling the ancient hassock, held up only by two hiking poles, and just barely. *Just go to sleep*, I told myself. But I couldn't.

I was losing feeling in my fingers and toes.

Something was moving around outside. I froze. *What is that?* But then I saw Leif's headlamp. He was still setting up.

I wanted to go over and tell him, "I can't do this." I wanted to explain how cold I was, that I was worried my digits might fall off. But doing that would require climbing out of the tent, into the cold night air, feeling more exposed than I already felt.

"Everything all right?" he asked.

"Nope!" I said. "Things are not good!"

"What's wrong?"

He came over to the entrance of my tent.

"I can't feel my hands or feet!"

"Well, you're lying on pure granite!" he explained. "Why don't you climb out and let me blow up your heated air mattress. You can put on your rain pants to get warm."

"I can't," I said, crying. "I'm sorry, but I think I'm done."

So many things had gone wrong. I couldn't picture nine more nights of this, sleeping in this tent, in my short sleeves and shorts, which didn't protect me from the elements. Getting lost several times a day, with no maps.

"I feel trapped," I said.

I climbed out of the tent and sat on a rock with my sleeping bag wrapped around my legs, shivering—my teeth chattering, my whole body shaking. *Steven was right*, I thought, *I shouldn't have taken this trip.* Now I just wanted to get back to him alive.

"Why don't you do some jumping-jacks!" Leif suggested. I looked at him blankly.

I told him I was sorry I'd gotten upset, but I feared I was having a medical emergency. "What if I need a hospital?" I asked.

"The nearest hospital is a hundred miles away," he explained.

"Well, then, what do people do?" I sputtered. "Is there a helicopter that can fly down and get you?"

I was responding slowly, like my brain had stopped working, a sign of hypothermia. Leif realized there was no going forward. He had to get me off of that mountain.

"I'll get your stuff together," he said calmly. "Put on these rain pants. When we start hiking back, your body will warm up. We'll find a ride to a lower camping spot, and you'll sleep in my tent."

I didn't want to sleep in his tent. He'd only gotten one hotel room. Why did I have to compromise my space?

"I don't want to camp out here tonight," I said. It was nearing 2:00 a.m. "I want to find a hotel. How long is the hike back to town?"

"Thirteen miles," he said.

I'm a half marathoner, I thought. *I can walk thirteen miles.*

"That's way too far to hike down the side of a highway in the middle of the night," Leif explained.

On the hike back down the mountain, I began to warm up. I remembered all the times my dad had made me feel like this. He'd done it unintentionally, but so many times with him, I'd felt I was in danger, because he was unprepared.

I had a recurring nightmare as a kid that my brother and I were alone in a big boat of a car on the highway near our house. As the car veered all over the road, I had to grab the steering wheel to right it. I was maybe eight years old. But I had to save us.

It was too much for a little girl to do.

I told Leif about this as we walked. Maybe this was just the Carney way, I said. We were irresponsible.

But Leif was owning what had happened and trying to save me. And in doing so, healing decades of damage.

"I'm not a Carney," he said. "I'm a Ward."

His mother's maiden name.

He'd been raised by his mother, not by his dad. It didn't matter what he was genetically prone to do. He made his own choices.

While we hiked back down the mountain, I empathized as he described the more difficult aspects of growing up with a single mom, being her protector.

"You were just a kid," I said, "you shouldn't have had to go through that."

I froze on the trail and cried.

"Nobody listens to me!" I wailed. "I know what I'm talking about, and I try to warn people, and they don't listen!"

All the years of feeling misunderstood, of feeling like my voice didn't matter, came flooding out of me at once.

Leif stepped toward me.

"Hey," he said. "It's OK. You're with family."

When he hugged me, it was like my dad had come back.

246

The list item Leif was helping me with was "have five songs recorded."

But he'd taught me how to sing my own song.

After a mile of hiking on the highway toward town, a man picked us up. He took us to the next campground, which was warmer. We slept in Leif's tent the rest of the night—well, I slept. He said the warmth of the sun kept him awake. But so did his fear that the man who picked us up might kill us.

We came up with a new plan in a sub shop the next day after hitching another ride. Leif would continue with the nine-day hike. I would stay in a hotel for four days, then fly home. It was a ghost town, all desert and no people. But I didn't care.

All I wanted was a shower and a warm bed.

I apologized for not being able to continue. But back in the hotel, as I learned about hypothermia, I found myself proud. I could have died. I'd saved myself.

The old me might not have made that choice.

I talked to my brother from the desert at sunset. He joked about my "Bates Motel." The innkeeper kept checking on me. "My nightmare!" Dave joked. But I was grateful for the companionship.

In September, I competed in my second half Ironman, in Atlantic City. The current in the bay was so rough that it threw me off course. When I climbed out, my watch said I'd swum 2.5 miles, not the intended 1.2. But I was so proud that I'd swum so far, and so fast, without giving up, that I wasn't bothered when the race director said I'd missed the cutoff by one minute. My friend Danielle didn't finish either. But she posted this online:

> *I'm not ready to share my "race" "experience" (absolute hellscape nightmare) that was supposed to be my first 70.3. Some because I have some conversations I need to have privately with Ironman staff (they openly admitted my situation was a huge fuck-up) and a lot because I*

have spent four years now being vulnerable and sharing this dream on social media.... And I feel like it's entirely shattered. "Heartbroken" is just the beginning of how I feel. But I wanted to hop back on Facebook to talk about Laura Carney, one of the greatest people I've had the pleasure of meeting and all because of a triathlon Facebook group. This post is not to dismiss anyone else who was a part of this race, this journey, or this sport, but to highlight someone incredibly special to me.

When I was healing from my concussion in 2019, Laura shared her story on the now defunct Women for Tri Facebook group. She talked about how her dad was killed by a distracted driver (as many of you know, my concussion was due to a texting driver) and her brother found her father's bucket list years later. Her triathlon journey has been to "own a $200 suit," which she ABSOLUTELY HAS.

On the bike course, I was silently begging the universe for Laura to come riding by as I dry-heaved on the side of the expressway. Little did I know, this woman unfortunately was cut at the swim exit.... After swimming 2.5 MILES (the course was 1.2) of BREASTSTROKE. Anyone who swims knows that's an incredible feat; if she had been in the full Ironman where the swim is that distance, she made it in half the time. My heart broke all over again when I was informed that Laura didn't make it either, but I'm in awe of how she took this with so much grace, patience, and optimism. I certainly didn't (and still haven't). Laura and her husband, Steven, even waited with me and my parents while the Ironman staff wasted hours of my time promising to get my change of clothes from the finish line (don't lecture me about Ironman protocol—they actively promised me my bag, the regional director was horrid to me, I was there so I'm going to stick with what I experienced). Their kindness and dedication to others is unmatched, and I'll never forget that.

Someone commented on Laura's post "DNF=dreams not finished." Laura already has her plan to build back up, and in everything she does, she builds connections and builds others up. If that's not an Ironman, a superhero really, I don't know what is. The fact I get to be a witness to it all is just a bonus. I know no matter what, I have this incredible friend in my corner and I'm so insanely proud she calls me one too.

As I'd trained to own a $200 suit, I'd wanted to prove I could be an athlete. Instead I'd demonstrated I was a good friend. I'd wanted to live by my beliefs.

I'd succeeded.

A week later, I sent a letter to Pope Francis. But His Holiness had to write back so I could check off my dad's list item. I planted my biggest apple tree in my running park, where I'd trained to "run ten miles straight." Where my mission to check off my father's list began.

It was Grace, the apple tree named after me. After I removed her from the pot with the other trees, she'd flourished. She was the tallest one.

In October, I nearly gave up on "drive a Corvette." By some twist of fate, the Corvette a new friend had found me was only twenty minutes away from the intersection where my dad died. I texted my cousin Steph, who's a licensed therapist, as Steven drove.

"My chest is tight," I told her. "I think I'm dissociating. Everything around me feels far away, like I'm not here."

"Yes, try to breathe," my cousin said.

"This is trauma, right?" I texted.

"You might be having the beginning of a panic attack," Steph wrote.

"What do I do?" I asked.

"Sit down if you can."

"I'm in the passenger seat of our car," I told her.

"OK, breathe. Slow belly breaths. In through the nose, out through the mouth. Close your eyes. This feeling will pass. It just is. You want to trigger your calm and rest, which breathing does."

"Steven is bewildered," I said.

"It's OK, it happens sometimes," Steph explained. "I had a panic attack yesterday."

"But I don't get these!" I said. "I'm sorry that happened to you."

"The reason doesn't matter as much as the coping," she explained.

"It's the symbolism of this car being near where my dad died and the list ending," I said. "I am overwhelmed."

"Yes, which is making you anxious and worried," Steph said. "This will pass, cuz. I promise you."

"I will think of you the whole time I am driving this Corvette, and about how I am also driving near family," I said.

"Yes, I am with you always. Always."

"Why do I have to be so damn brave?" I asked. "This is ridiculous."

"I know, but you are brave," she said.

"I want to be an example of how to free yourself from trauma," I said. "It's what my dad wants for me."

"Yes, and I'll remind you that it's a process you've been working on. So please give yourself credit."

When I arrived at the house of the Corvette owner, I asked to use the bathroom. On the sink sat a small trinket dish, engraved with the words "I pledge to lead by example, to be true and brave."

I drove the black 2022 model Corvette alongside Ryan, its generous owner, with the top down, and thought of my father and how much he'd love feeling the breeze on his face and the yellowing fall leaves. Fall was his favorite time of year. We were driving it on the roads to my aunt's house, the safest roads I knew. Ryan gave us a coffee table book about his Corvette model after explaining its safety technology. His wife, Joan, a dog trainer, let us play with her dogs. I never imagined that this fast car would be owned by such a kind and calming couple.

I realized my father's cars were more than just cars to us—they were our country. The songs we sang to on the radio, more than just songs. They were our language.

Each car was like a new chapter of our lives.

When Steven and I pulled out of the driveway, I couldn't help but notice what was written on the Corvette's license plate.

Mulligan.

The next day we drove to my cousin Leif's house to finally record five songs—they were the songs my father sang most, at least to me.

Back home, I told Steven I'd already "taught a class about wine," in San Diego, when we toured the missions. I'd taught it to him! And "own a wine cellar of fine wines"—despite not being able to drink on my medicine, I told Steven I thought I'd already done this, too.

When my dad was twenty-nine, the year I was born, the year he wrote the list, he took a business trip to California. He was a liquor distributor then. He visited the Robert Mondavi vineyards in Napa Valley and picked up a cabernet sauvignon.

The vintage was 1974. He brought it home to Delaware and wrote on its label, *The finest wine America has made.* Then, at the top of the label, *Open on Laura's wedding day.*

After he'd moved out, he sometimes joked that my mom and stepdad had drunk the wine. They hadn't. They dutifully kept the wine in a cold spot in the basement for thirty-eight years, in four different basements. It survived moving three times.

When we planned our wedding, Steven and I spent a weekend at my mom's house in Connecticut, and I said, crying, that without my dad, my wedding would feel like a compromise. My mom said, "I have an idea," and went down to the basement. She came back up with the wine. "Why don't we bring the bottle," she said, "and when it's time to make a toast, we can pour a little into each glass?" That way, even though my dad wasn't there, we could fulfill his wishes.

The idea sparked a running debate in my family over whether the wine was still drinkable after all those years. My mom said it might not be the kind that aged well, and I pictured all my wedding guests choking and writhing on the floor.

So I did some research. I looked up the Robert Mondavi vintages from the 1970s and learned that in 1976, a group of esteemed French wine judges blind taste-tested California wines along with the best wines from Bordeaux and Burgundy (which had long been considered the finest). The California wines won. Both winning wines were from 1973, and the next year's vintage was said to be even finer. The taste test changed the reputation of California vineyards overnight. It also made what my dad had claimed very likely true.

The 1974 Mondavi really was America's finest wine.

Since we married in New Mexico, transporting the wine wasn't easy. Two weeks out, we drove to my mom's house to gather our decorations but forgot it. Steven drove two hours back, then carted the wine to our apartment like a baby. I stored it in our bedroom closet, then wrapped it in bubble wrap when I packed. When I opened my luggage in New Mexico, the bottle's label was sticky and red—the plane's pressure had burst open the cork. All that time, all that gentle care, and I'd ruined it in one fell swoop. All weekend, I couldn't get my mind off that bottle.

After our vows, we gathered our guests inside the inn and told them the story of the wine. Steven removed the cork (what was left of it), took a sip, and pretended to keel over. Then I took a sip, too.

It was the best wine I'd ever tasted.

Our guests gathered around us saying, "I want some!" It was like the last scene in *It's a Wonderful Life*. Here, I'd worried everyone would be humoring me by drinking this stuff or it would turn their stomachs inside out, but they all actively wanted it, this beautiful bottle my dad, mom, and stepdad had so lovingly preserved.

And it had turned out to be stunning, even more stunning after all that time.

I found out later that thirty-eight years was the best time to wait to drink it.

* * *

THE SECOND-TO-LAST ITEM on my father's list was "sing at my daughter's wedding." This was heartbreaking to discover that day in my brother's kitchen. But as far as I'm concerned, we checked that off for him on May 29, 2016. Because though he wasn't there to sing in person, our bellies were all singing just the same.

The last item on my father's list was "dance at my grandchildren's weddings." So I put aside a bottle of 2018 Mondavi cabernet sauvignon—the second-finest wine America has made. I didn't know where we'd drink it, but I knew this much:

I had my own list to check off.

And I would be dancing.

Epilogue

"Vatican Apostolic," the envelope said. I'd just driven home from an annual 5K in Delaware with my stepbrother Scott. It was a visit Steven had missed, just as he'd missed the last two weekend trips I'd taken. Since my Corvette drive, my car phobia was gone.

"Holy shit! Holy shit! Holy shit!" I whispered.

I wasn't wrong. It had taken six weeks, but the pope had written me back.

From the Vatican, 28 October 2022:

Dear Ms. Carney,

His Holiness Pope Francis wishes me to thank you for your thoughtful letter. He has prayed for the eternal rest of your father, and he asks Almighty God to sustain you and your family with the hope brought by our faith in the Resurrection.

Invoking upon all of you consolation and peace in the Lord, His Holiness sends his blessing.

Yours sincerely,
Monsignor Roberto Campisi
Assessor

Campisi had started his job that week. My letter was likely one of the first he'd responded to. Pope Francis's assistants respond to most of his mail. This meant I now only had one list item left: "have five songs recorded."

As my cousin's work schedule got busier, I waited for an opening to visit again. The seventh time we drove down, I sensed my dad's spirit like a totem pole in the guitar-bedecked studio, proud of us. "What are you doing to my voice?" I asked Leif. "It sounds great!"

"Nothing!" Leif confirmed. "This is just you!"

When we got into the car eight hours later, Bonnie Raitt's "I Can't Make You Love Me" came on—the song my dad had called my best recording. I broke down.

By the first week of December, when we still hadn't finished the recordings, I grew nervous. The only day all month Leif had free was one when I'd be away—I'd committed to a weekend in St. Louis, Missouri, after copyediting an article for *People* about a man there whose sixteen-year-old son, Ethan, had died in a car crash. Ethan's principal had gifted a book to Ethan's father, Dan, about a man who'd had a baseball catch with 365 strangers in one year, and by some weird coincidence, the author had the same name as Dan's son—Ethan Bryan. Inspired, Dan Bryan set out to have a catch with a different person every day of 2022, to honor Ethan.

I'd copyedited the baseball catch story for the August 8th issue, the anniversary of my dad's death. Despite being my age, Dan looked a lot like my father.

Steven couldn't understand why I wanted to take yet another crazy and expensive trip, to have a baseball catch with a stranger. But something told me I had to do this.

The first Christmas after my father's death was a blur. The second year, my brother Dave and I sat down to record Christmas songs to honor our tradition of recording with my dad. We compiled them into a CD for our mom, *The Carney Kids' Christmas*. I thought of this as I watched *Meet Me in St. Louis* to research my trip. My brother's "Have Yourself A Merry Little Christmas" expressed what all of us were feeling that year—we would get together, if fate let us. Growing up, those lyrics seemed sentimental. Now I knew they were true.

My first day in St. Louis, the reporter who'd covered Dan Bryan's *People* story—and had a catch himself—took me out for brunch. Jeff Truesdell was drawn to Dan because his husband, Nelson, his love of thirty-four years, had just died of a heart attack. *Meet Me in St. Louis* was one of their favorites, he told me. They loved to travel, and he'd begun a project to visit every town called Nelson in America. He called it "The Road to Nelson," a tribute to his love.

After brunch, Jeff gave me the tour my dad would have loved, of the historic landmarks of America's fourth city—which was now a partly run-down town. I hadn't rented a car, but this was no hindrance, as Jeff drove me around all day in his blue pickup, sporting his Christmas garb: the red light-up Cardinals scarf Nelson gave him.

We toured the 1904 World's Fair landmarks, including the Thomas Jefferson Memorial, and Jeff told me about Nelson, who'd planned all of their travel. He'd reserved a trip to Lake Placid for their wedding anniversary, coming up on New Year's Eve. Jeff said he didn't have the heart to cancel it.

So I told Jeff a story I hadn't told anyone but Steven about my last night in Vienna.

It started with dinner in a gourmet vegan restaurant, the best in the city. My meal was one I'd decided was my dad's congratulatory dinner for having sold my book—an empty chair sat across from me. The carnations in the vase on the table were yellow and peach, like our ice cream cone ritual—always banana for him, always peach for me.

After dinner I stopped in St. Stephen's then took a ride on the giant Ferris wheel in Prater, made famous by *The Third Man*. But at 213 feet, it still wasn't as big as the original Ferris wheel, the one in the museum Jeff and I toured that day—a 265-footer, built for the World's Fair, that truly provided, as my father put it, a view you couldn't get from anywhere else. After my Prater ride, I bought blue cotton candy, the kind my dad teased me for consuming at baseball games. "You're only here for the snacks," he'd said. I strolled the amusement park, sending snaps of unintentionally funny European signs for rides to Steven back home. I laughed so hard that I peed my pants. I was all the way across the globe, but it felt like I was reliving Morey's Pier with my dad. Just in a different language.

"Jeff, I think you have to go to Lake Placid," I said. I explained that my father had been there with me that last night in Vienna. Just as he had for every list item.

Three days later, after I was safely home from my baseball catch, I received this text from Jeff:

> *After talking with you and one other, I have decided to stick with the plans Nelson and I made to spend our December 31 wedding anniversary in Lake Placid. As you made clear, I will not be there alone...it's important, and who knows what I might encounter. Thank you for urging it.*

For weeks people asked me what came next, after my dad's list. Sometimes I said, "I'll finish my own list!" Sometimes I said I'd take a month-long nap.

The week before Christmas, I grew tired of waiting for my cousin. I'd had a full meltdown in St. Louis. "I can't do this anymore," I'd told Steven on the phone from my hotel room. "I need the list to be done! I have nothing left to give."

"When you come home, just tell Leif that you will record your remaining vocals here, on our microphone, and you can email them," Steven said. "He already recorded his instrumental tracks. He doesn't need you there to pair them."

I texted Leif to ask what he thought. When he didn't respond, I wrote him telling him what I *would* do, not asking for his permission. The day after Christmas, I set up Steven's laptop and microphone in our bedroom's walk-in closet. He'd bought the microphone for podcast interviews, a purchase I'd protested as frivolous.

My dad's impressions were so good that as a kid I was convinced he was the voice of Mickey Mouse. When he sang "Rainbow Connection," he sang it as a frog. When I sang it, I had to record it twice, because I choked up too much the first time.

* * *

THE DAY AFTER STEVEN AND I married in 2016 in Santa Fe, we drove up to Mesa Verde. It was the first stop on our desert honeymoon. As day turned into night, I could still see the tall trees lining the dark sky.

Mesa Verde is the oldest known dwelling in the United States. Ancestral Pueblo made it their home from 600 to 1300 A.D. The 600 cave dwellings still there are the best preserved in the country. They look like little apartments. I figured if this place was good enough for the first honeymooners, it was good enough for us.

The next morning we were late meeting my family at the Grand Canyon—it was the part of our honeymoon when they were still there. They didn't seem to mind, but I was stressed and started crying in the 109-year-old El Tovar hotel. After my tears dried and my family went to their hotel, we left to explore. Steven held my hand as we walked along the South Rim, and I started to feel better. I'd joked throughout my wedding planning that once this day arrived, I might jump in. But as we looked out into the canyon's vast ravines, my mood lightened.

Steven was becoming a photographer then, so he crawled out onto the narrowest ledges to get a good shot. I climbed to the edge of each cliff with him, but he'd yell for me to get back.

"How come you can go out that far but I can't?" I said.

"Because I worry I wouldn't be able to save you."

He'd spotted thunderclouds in the distance to photograph, so I started walking back. It began to rain. Devil's rain. Something told me to turn around.

Just behind Steven spread a vast rainbow. "Look!" I yelled. As I inched closer, I realized there were actually two rainbows. One for each of us.

If we hadn't been late that day, we would have missed it.

Steven took a picture of me pointing two fingers at the rainbows, which mostly looked like I was saying, "Peace."

At the exit we saw a sign we hadn't remembered. "Congratulations!" it said.

We knew exactly who it was from.

* * *

I'VE OFTEN SAID my father missed my wedding, but of course I know that's not true. It was the most important hike I'd ever navigated. I felt his spirit as the sun enveloped my back. He was still behind me, watching as I found my way.

Steven was asleep on the couch in the living room when I sang the last note of the last song. I'd finished my globetrotting in the most secure place I knew: home.

"It's done," I said, collapsing into his arms. I heaved, crying from my heart. "The list is done."

That night, as I lay in bed, I knew what to do with the 2018 Mondavi cabernet, my version of my dad's 1974 wine. I'd save it for my niece Savannah's wedding.

"I don't want it to go to an idea, a metaphor for a grandchild," I told Steven on New Year's Eve. "And I don't want it to go to a wish either. I'd rather invest in a living, breathing person, someone special."

It was what my dad had done for me.

When I finally did meet Dan Bryan for that catch in St. Louis, it was at the Gateway Arch. The doorway to the West, the arch represents the beginning of Lewis and Clark's mission with Sacagawea. But it also represents their mission's end. They came back to St. Louis three years after they'd set out, full of stories about the wilderness they'd explored.

The arch, of course, is the biggest upside-down horseshoe in America, and it also looks like a rainbow. Dan and I were standing directly under it.

For a split-second, as this stranger, and yet a person I knew well, threw me his late son's baseball, I saw my father's body in front of me, pitching to me like he had so many times. He was happy. He was proud of me. Just as he'd always been.

And how could he not be? I'd done what he'd taught me to do.

I'd found my way into adventures.
And I'd found my way back out.
Somehow, every time, I'd found the sun.

Things I Would Like to Do in My Lifetime!

1. Live a long, healthy life at least to the year 2020. ✓
2. Provide a comfortable standard of living for my family. ✓
3. Write and have a few novels published. ✓
4. Have five songs recorded. ✓
5. Make more money than I need. ✓
6. Talk with the president. ✓
7. Make three good family or friends movies. ✓
8. Play the piano or guitar. ✓
9. Type forty words a minute correctly. ✓
10. Sell millions of dollars' worth of merchandise. ✓
11. Make my wife feel happy, healthy, pretty, and young all her life. ✓
12. Give my children the most love, the best education, and best example I can give. ✓
13. Visit New Orleans. ✓
14. Paris. ✓
15. London. ✓
16. Vienna. ✓
17. Dresden/Berlin. ✓
18. Los Angeles. ✓

19. San Diego. ✓
20. Las Vegas. ✓
21. Chicago. ✓
22. St. Thomas. ✓
23. Run ten miles straight. ✓
24. Swim the width of a river. ✓
25. Beat a number-one seeded tennis player in a tournament. ✓
26. Play golf in the 70s a few times. ✓
27. Correspond with the pope. ✓
28. Speak to a TV audience. ✓
29. Do a comedy monologue in a nightclub. (Dad: ✓)
30. Be interviewed on a radio program. (Dad: ✓) ✓
31. Get my picture in a national magazine. ✓
32. Make money on the stock market. ✓
33. Set up a charitable fund. ✓
34. Drive a Corvette. ✓
35. Teach a class about wine. ✓
36. Have a thirty-four-inch waist again. ✓
37. Own a $200 suit. ✓
38. Own a black tux. ✓
39. Send Joan on a $1,000 shopping spree. ✓
40. Help Laura win a scholarship. ✓
41. Own a large house with our own land. ✓
42. Have my own tennis court. ✓
43. See a World Series game live. (Dad: ✓) (Phillies 2, Toronto 0)
44. Go to a Super Bowl game. ✓
45. See the NCAA basketball finals. ✓
46. Go to the Rose Bowl. ✓

47. Surf in the Pacific Ocean. ✓

48. Grow a watermelon. ✓

49. Own a wine cellar of fine wines. ✓

50. Plant an apple tree. ✓

51. Skydive at least once. ✓

52. Go sailing by myself. ✓

53. Be invited to a political convention. ✓

54. Help my parents enjoy their retirement. (Dad: ✓) ✓

55. Pay back my dad $1,000 plus interest. (Dad: failed) ✓

56. Own a great record collection. (Dad: ✓) ✓

57. Develop an impressive library. ✓

58. Ride a horse fast. ✓

59. Sing at my daughter's wedding. ✓

60. Dance at my grandchildren's weddings. ✓

Write Your Own Bucket List!

_____

_____

_____

_____

_____

_____

_____

_____

_____

_____

_____

_____

_____

_____

_____

_____

_____

Acknowledgments

"Surely, in the light of history, it is more intelligent to hope rather than to fear, to try rather than not to try. For one thing we know beyond all doubt: Nothing has ever been achieved by the person who says, 'It can't be done.'"

—ELEANOR ROOSEVELT

This book was a work of love and faith, nurtured by the hopes of so many.

This is a short list of those names.

I'd like to thank my agent, Beth Davey, for her brilliance, compassion and persistence, not to mention her sensitivity around this story. She has championed this book from the day she signed me and her faith in its success has never wavered. I know how lucky I am to have you on my team, Beth. (And as my second mom! Though you're much too young.) I'd also like to thank my film agent, Chris George, for immediately recognizing this story's cinematic potential and for explaining the film industry both eloquently and gently. Thank you for being someone I can trust.

My gorgeous book cover was the brainchild of the highly talented Jordan Wannemacher, who's as cool and fun as she is smart.

This manuscript couldn't exist without the help of Ruth Mills, my book proposal editor who put up with fear and resistance from yours truly but helped turn my story into something beautiful anyway. Thank you for your diligence and humor, and for giving this book a backbone. And thank you to Susie Stangland, for discovering me in the pages of *Good Housekeeping* in 2015, finding me again in 2019, and for referring me to Beth.

A big thank-you to my editor, Debra Englander, for enthusiastically acquiring this book, running the editorial side so pragmatically, and giving me votes of confidence. Every phone conversation with you makes me believe things are going according to plan. And to Anthony Ziccardi for championing my story and switching gears when that was needed. The same sentiment applies to associate publisher Allison Griffith, managing editors Heather King and Caitlyn Limbaugh, production manager Alana Mills, production editors Rachel Hoge and Christina Chun, and publicists Sara Stickney, Olivia Brothers, and Melissa Smith—everyone's grace under fire is inspiring and I'm continually impressed by your team's professionalism. Thank you. A big thank-you also to copy editor Sara Ann Alexander and proofreader Keira Baron. As a copy editor, I respect your eagle eyes.

I'd like to thank my early readers, who waded through word soup to tell me what should stay and what should go (thus helping me check off **"write and have a few novels published"**): Gabrielle Danchick, Hayley Downs, and Anna Katsnelson (my writers' group), Melissa Blake, James Tate Hill, Matt Friedrichs, Mike Shoupe, Pamela Nichols, Rob Wherry, Joel Feldman, Leif Carney, Jesse Dorris, Jordan Wannemacher, Colleen Kelley, Marc Serra, Art Milnes, and Lee Glass. I'd also like to thank, either for their endorsements or general writing advice, Garret Keizer, Laura Munson, Brooke Siem, Melissa Febos, Kristin Meekhof, Katie Arnold, Ethel Rohan, Melissa Petro, Dawn Raffel, Steven Pressfield, Mitch Horowitz, Joel Fotinos, Karen Bischer, Siri Lindley, Jen Doll, Kiersten Parsons Hathcock, Janine Reid, Brandi Larsen, Mary Latham, Shaun Zetlin, Dan Wickett, Jennifer Chen, Matthew Thomas, Shannon Luders-Manuel, Heather McFalls, books by Courtney Maum and Melanie Brooks, and the Mark Twain House.

This book wouldn't be possible without finishing the list, which wouldn't have been possible without a lot of help. Thank you, for **press coverage**, to Lydia Warren and Leigh Scheps from *Inside Edition*, Jenna Portnoy, Freddie Kunkle and Sydney Page from the *Washington Post*,

Amy Guth, John Duffy, WGN Radio, Linda Schmidt, Ernie Anastos, Jim Freed, the *Daily Mail*, Donna M. Post, Chanelle Neilson, iHeart Radio, Chris Hardwick, Elizabeth Rago, Tyler Rosenberg, Mark Thigpen, Mark Effron, Rohan Mohanty, Paul Porowski, Skydive East Coast (this was also **"skydive at least once"** and **"talk to a TV audience"**), the University of Delaware, Eric Ruth, Artika Casini, Don Shenkle, Diccon Hyatt, *Baristanet*, Jonathan Flores, *Women Empowered Podcast*, Joey Fresco, Laura Cathcart Robbins, Kyle Sanders, Arman Taghizadeh, Erin Hosier, Tom Everson, Betsy Pake, Caroline Gardiner, Kathy Banegas, Fred Ferris, Mike Bellini, Dr. Marcia Sirota, Melissa Llarena, Tom Prather, Rafael Francisco Jose Alvarado, Katie Wudel, *Little Things*, RJ Kern, Kimberly Elkins, *Guideposts*, Ginny Graves, *Health* magazine, Maria Shriver, the *Sunday Paper*, Peg Rosen, Allison McCabe at *The Fix*, Eric Pfeiffer at *Upworthy*, *Run Tri Mag*, Nikki Battiste at CBS News, Barbara Goldberg at Reuters, Jess Downey at *Real Woman* magazine, Drew Barrymore, Ross Mathews, Gayle King, Tamron Hall, the *Times of London*, the *NJ Star Ledger*, NPR, BBC, *Daily Blast Live*, *Voice of America*, *Breakfast with Isabel and Eamonn*, WGN News, NBC News NOW, NBC *Nightly News with Lester Holt*, and Jeff Pearlman; for **"swim the width of a river,"** to Brian and Sydney Wilson, the NYC and Montclair YMCAs, French Broad Outfitters, Best Western Hotels & Resorts, and the Omni Grove Park Inn; for **"ride a horse fast,"** to Emily and Lee Glass, Inn of the Turquoise Bear, Ghost Ranch, and Mount Atalaya; for **"talk with the president,"** to Mike Hicks of Alabama, President Jimmy Carter, First Lady Rosalynn Carter, the Carter Center, Jimmy Carter NHS, Stone Mountain, Maranatha Baptist Church, Art Milnes, the Windsor Hotel, and the Quality Inn Plains; for **"surf in the Pacific Ocean,"** to Drew and Kate Wilson, April Blair, 7th Street Surf Shop, the Avalon Hotel, Chuck and Priscilla at Venice Beach Surf, and Keanu Reeves; for **"go to the Rose Bowl,"** to the Solises, the Gamble House and the Pasadena Rose Bowl; for **"go to the NCAA basketball finals,"** to Scott Wilson, Karen Snyder Duke, Bill Walton, Clyde Drexler, NCAA March Madness, the Alamo, Susannah Brothers, Toron Wooldridge, aloft Austin, the Driskill, the Menger, and the Emily Morgan

Hotel; for **"beat a number-one seed in a tennis tournament,"** to Craig Hildebrand, the US Open, Serena Williams, Delaine Mast, and Orange Lawn Tennis; for **"visit London,"** to my family of origin, Broome Park Hotel, The Dean Hotel, Kiltimagh, Te Teolai Inis Oirr, and Fionnan and Becca at Bláth na Gréine; for **"visit New Orleans,"** to the French Quarter New Orleans, the New Orleans Jazz and Heritage Festival, New Orleans Jazz NHP, Maison Dupuy, the Roosevelt New Orleans, and the Bourbon Orleans; for **"golf in the 70s a few times," "visit San Diego,"** and **"go sailing by myself,"** to my mom, my stepdad, Joni Bilderback, Robert Jones, Willowbrook Golf Center, Fenwick Golf, Rancho Bernardo Golf, Sally Little, Hotel Coronado, and Mission Bay Aquatic Center; for **"go to the Super Bowl,"** to Hard Rock Stadium, Nick Nicastro, and Michael Mooney; for **"own a black tux,"** to Coco Boutique Montclair, Ecru, Pat Cross, Lori Farling, the NJ Cross-dressers' Support Group, Lyndsey Ariel Caudilla, Joey Fresco, and Adrian Bacolo; for **"be invited to a political convention,"** to Mary Beth Quirk, Ryan Cormier, Jesse Chadderdon, Jennifer Ley, Natalie Heard, Cathy Turiano Patullo, Adrienne Lewin, and Annemarie Conte; for **"grow a watermelon"** and **"plant an apple tree,"** to Home Depot, Jennifer Myers, Jessi Wilson, Kelly Burns Osvold, Lisanne Renner, Scott Kevelson, John Park, and Anderson Park; for **"make three good family/friends movies,"** to Laura Heberton, Chuck Hayward, Gerik Gooch, David James Kelly, Amy Guth, Oliver Hudson, and Meredith and Jay Lavender; for **"teach a class about wine," "own a cellar of fine wines," "sing at my daughter's wedding,"** and **"dance at my grandchildren's weddings,"** to Pat Myers, Pierce Conway, Brian McGinty, the Grape Collective in Montclair, the California Missions, and Robert Mondavi Winery; for **"visit Berlin/Dresden"** and **"visit Vienna,"** to my mom, David Way, the Vienna Boys' Choir, the Almodovar hotel and Hotel Harmonie; for **"correspond with the Pope,"** to Tom Everson, Father James Martin, SJ, Pope Francis, and Assessor for General Affairs for the Secretariat of State Roberto Campisi; for **"run 10 miles straight"** and **"own a $200 suit,"** to Kelly Solis, the Thanksgiving Day MS Run, the Harvest Hustle, the Philadelphia Rock n' Roll Half Marathon, the New York City Marathon, the L.A. Marathon, El Tour de Tucson, the Farm Fresh 5K, the Pasadena Triathlon, the Atlantic City Vegan Food Festival 5K, the Los Muertos 5K, Lenny and Joe's Turkey Trot, the Big Surreal, Litchfield Hills Triathlon, Atlantic City Triathlon, the Emily Schindler Memorial Scholarship Triathlon, Ironman 70.3 Florida, the New York City Triathlon, Courthouse Motel, the John Muir Trail, the High Sierras Trail, Giovanna De Matas, Ironman 70.3 Atlantic City, Danielle Moore, Women for Tri, and Girls on the Run; for **"drive a Corvette,"** to Steph Reed, Jennifer Hawkins, Greg Robertson, Johnny Duncan, Melissa Sears, and Ryan and Joan Forry; for **"have five songs recorded,"** to Leif Carney, the Vienna Boys' Choir, the thick walls at the Inn at Montchanin Village, Dipen Nayak, Dan Bryan, Ethan Bryan, and Jeff Truesdell; for **"visit St. Thomas,"** to Mary Latham and Olga's Fancy; and to all the special places we visited that I haven't mentioned here, such as Appalachian NST, Beach Haven, Big Bear, the Blue Ridge Parkway, the Catskills, the Grand Canyon, the Great Smoky Mountains, Joshua Tree, Mesa Verde, Palm Springs, Mount Rushmore, Red Rock State Park, the Rocky Mountains, Saguaro National Park, the Santa Monica Mountains, Shenandoah, the Torrey Reserve, Virgin Islands National Park, White Sands, and last but not least, Morey's Pier in Wildwood, New Jersey.

I'd like to show my appreciation for the friendly baristas at Eagle Rock Café in Montclair, New Jersey where I wrote and edited this book when I wasn't on my couch at home: Mondo, Milan, Mario, Michael, Kelsie, and Jason, to name a few. Thank you to my former landlord Kevin Anderson, and also to the Quality Inn and Best Western Plus in Fairfield, New Jersey where I escaped to write when I needed space to think.

A big thank you to my supervisors and coworkers through the years—who've helped shape my writing and editing and, in some cases, this very book (and through their gainful employment, I was able to check off **"make more money than I need," "provide a comfortable standard of living for my family," "help Laura win a scholarship,"** and **"send [my spouse] on a $1,000 shopping spree")**:

273

(at *Conde Nast*) Corey Sabourin, Michael Casey, Greg Robertson, and Robin Aigner; (at *People*) Joanann Scali; (at *The Knot* and *The Bump*) Beth Roehrig and Kate Traverson; (at *Real Woman*) Jess Downey and Meghan Rabbitt; (at *Guideposts*) Tanya Richardson, Colleen Hughes, Celeste McCauley, Amy Wong, Edward Grinnan, Rick Hamlin, Alexandra Chipkin, and Kimberly Elkins; (at *Bumble*) Kathy Green; (at *Audubon*): Jess Leber; (at *Diversity in Action*) Adrienne Lewin; (at *Document Journal*) Meg Hullander and Meg Thomann; (at Minnesota State College) Kate Nelson; (at *Good Housekeeping* where I checked off **"get my picture in a national magazine"**) Carla Rohlfing Levy, Meaghan B. Murphy, Jane Seymour Francisco, Carrie Carlson, Stacy Cousino, Benay Bubar, Dana A. Vivinetto, Miguel Rivera, Clare Ellis, Janie Mathews, Karen Snyder Duke, Gabriella Vigoreaux, Rachel Bowie, Arne Bostrom, Birnur Aral Nehozoglu, Emily Tiberio, Lexie Sachs, Lori Bergamotto, Stephanie Kilburn, Laurie Jennings, Lindsey O'Connell, Trent Johnson, Tula Karras, April Rueb McKenzie, Stephanie Dolgoff, and Devin Tomb, to name a few; (at *OK!* magazine) Karen Bischer, Rana Meyer, Helen Cooper, Ben Cake, Laura Sassano, Aimee Linehan, Amy Connell, Richard Jerome, Lynda Nardelli, Calvin Ki, Mary Beth Quirk, Brittany Tallarico, Carolyn LiRosi, Louise Barile, Loni Venti, Eloise Parker, and Christopher Rudzik; (at *Ladies' Home Journal*) Tom Claire; (at *New York Spaces*) Marjorie Gage; (at *More*) Jen Milne; (at *Greetings, etc.*) Noreen Walsh and Kathy Krassner; (and at *The Review*) Christopher Yasiejko, Carla Correa, Andrea Boyle Tippett, Sue Serna, Eric Townsend, Jonathan Rifkin, Dan Strumpf, Maria Dal Pan, April Capochino Myers, Jonathan Tracy, Erica Finamore, Noel Dietrich, Brian Callaway, Betsy Lowther, Ted Spiker, Brooke Forry, and more.

I'd like to give a special shout-out to two groups dear to me, the founders of the Enclave, a reading series in New York—Jim Freed, Jason Napoli Brooks, Scott Geiger, Julie Lockman and Ryan Penny—and the Maddicts, who encouraged my TV recapping: Nick Curcumelli-Rodostamo, Chauncey Phillips, Snorky Calvet, Hazel Laven, Pauline Francis, Liz Geier, Mambo Deb, Tokys Maddict, Cleo Clio, Jeffe

Maddict, Elizabeth Draper, Carol Herndon, Eva Dell Tashiro, George Antrobus, Tom TheBomb, Fiona Jorgenson, Margaret Woodford, Guy BigGuy Thompson, Donald Draper, Audrey Aster, Suzie Ryde, Lynell Garrett Smith, Jill Cardinal Pratt-Williams, Brian Duffy, and more. A special thanks to Deborah Lipp for posting my recaps of *True Detective* and to Fawn Neun for publishing my first essay.

I have to thank my favorite teachers, one of whom endorsed this book: Professors Ben Yagoda, McKay Jenkins, M. Dennis Jackson, Charles E. Robinson, and Michael Cotsell (whose classes I loved so much that I took three); Mrs. Walton, Mr. Smith, Mrs. Harasika, Mrs. Bigelow, Mrs. Morton, Mrs. Wiggins, Mrs. Twing, and Mrs. Camack. Thank you for making me feel seen.

An important thank-you also goes to my creative heroes: Ken Burns, Dave Eggers, Elizabeth Wurtzel, Malcolm Gladwell, Cheryl Strayed, Anne Lamott, Elizabeth Gilbert, Michael J. Fox, Steven Pressfield, Oprah Winfrey, Gloria Steinem, Alison Bechdel, Caroline Myss, Dr. Gabor Maté, Naomi Wolf, Ryan Holiday, Jon Krakauer, Jimmy Fallon, Jeff Jensen, Sylvia Plath, Kurt Vonnegut, Mary Shelley, Virginia Woolf, Jim Henson, Katherine Anne Porter, Ernest Hemingway, F. Scott Fitzgerald, Carol Ann Duffy, Carl Jung, A.A. Milne, Sam Shepard, Dorothy Parker, and Joseph Campbell.

I've made a number of friends in safe driving advocacy, people I've met due to a shared challenge: coping with a loved one's sudden death. Joel Feldman is someone I view as an uncle or a second father. He and his wife, Dianne Anderson, are family. A big thank-you also goes to Emily Stein, Jacy Good, Courtney Merriman, Brendan Lyons, Toron Wooldridge, Russell Hurd, Kim Burke-Hurd, Dan Dry, Mandi Williams Sorohan, Melissa Wandall, Colleen Kelley, John Myung and his wife, Doug Ralls, Patricia Stone Ralls, Jacob Smith, Jon Alex, Michael Savage, Mike Drury, Jeri Dye Lynch, Jeff Larason, Essence Owens Threlkeld, Michele Paden, Giana Mucci, Maria Esteves, Eileen Woelkers Miller, Paul Miller, Nina Todd, Tom Everson, Deb Trombley, and Laurie Hevier.

"Think where man's glory most begins and ends,
and say my glory was I had such friends."

—W.B. YEATS

Never has this quote held more true than while writing this book. I would be nowhere without my friends...and my husband's friends, my brother's friends, my mom's friends, and my dad's friends...OK, I'm a friend poacher.

To my college roommate Kelly Solis: Thank you for sticking by me through thick and thin, for being the peanut butter to my jelly—or is it the reverse? I can never remember. That's a first! I love you. To the whole Solis family—John, Dominic, Kevin, Ava, Papa John, Maria, Darlene Olivarez-Hee, Felicidad, Mark, Adam, Rosa, Mariana, and Tennielle Guitterez—thank you for embracing us like your own.

To Gabrielle Danchick: We have the kind of friendship that makes me feel I've known you forever, even though we only met five years ago. Knowing you has changed me. Thank you for giving me the confidence I needed to not only hear my voice, but trust it. I love you.

To Michael Bialaszewski: We have the kind of friendship where I actually HAVE known you forever.... I feel twenty-five again when I talk to you, a gift in this fast-moving world. Thank you for believing in my writing and in me and for befriending my husband (though I can't fathom how either of you watches that many films).

To Art Milnes: You have become my mentor, and it's because you are the real deal—unpretentious and in love with your craft. Thank you for your generosity and wisdom and for helping me find my way as a journeywoman writer.

To Shaun Zetlin: What an amazing gift that our paths should cross again, nearly thirty years later. You have a good heart and are a gift to this world: a strong man with a soft soul. Keep shining on others; you help them shine, too.

To Adrian Bacolo: I've always been more comfortable befriending men, particularly creative men, and I'm always fascinated when being male doesn't mean acting superior. You are a gentleman. Thank you for teaching me humility and that most of my troubles are created by me. There but for the grace of God go I.

To Danielle Moore: You are a superwoman; it's such a gift to watch you figure that out. Everyone who gets to call you "friend" benefits from your investment in their lives. I'm glad I get to be one of them.

To Kristin Meekhof: Thank you for teaching me to go with the flow, that matter is always changing form, change is not something to be feared, and nothing means more than finding your miracle. You are a role model.

To Melissa Blake: I'd like to vote for you as president because I think that's where you're headed. I've never known anyone who can facilitate change as rapidly as you and at such a large scale. You are a poet and superstar at the same time. Hey, look at us! We did it!

To Amy Guth: Thank you for reminding me to be a badass and embrace my why in life, ignoring the supposed-tos. You're a real-life feminist icon. I want to be you when I grow up (even though you're a week younger than me).

To Mary Latham: I can't wait for your book(s) to come out. I've never known anyone as brave or open as you, and I feel blessed in your presence. Thank you for making me feel less alone.

To Kiersten Parsons Hathcock: Thank you for teaching me to trust my intuitive gifts. My life changed when I met you. Thank you for your loyalty and wisdom, too. You are an inspiration.

To Faruq Alam, Joni Bilderback, Marc Serra, Ram Yogendra, Heather McFalls, Christina Giaquinto, Jennifer Hawkins, Henry Pierre, Aimee La Fountain, and Heather Packer: Thank you for the heart-to-hearts and opening my eyes to new ways of living. I have learned so much from each of you.

To Dr. Mermini: Thanks for taking care of my brain and heart.

To Liz Schneider: Thanks for taking care of Pinky.

To the high school friends I've reconnected with thanks to the list—Jen Leahy, Kristy Avino, Michelle Lazarus, Betsy Burke, Debbie Widenour, Kristen Stead Kelly, Drew Keim, Brett Levy, Julie Volkman, Alyson Holob, and Nicole Young—thanks for believing in me.

To my father's friends—Chris Jadach, Dan Skedzielewski, Rudy Antonini Jr., Marianne Antonini, Debbie Freeman Hoermann, Michael Miscoski—I hope you enjoyed this book and feel his presence when you read it. Thank you for sharing memories.

To Steven's friends—Craig Hildebrand, Shya Scanlon, Grace Kang, James Tate Hill, Lori Jackson Hill, Kevin Albers, Christine Diaz, Sofran McBride, Anna Gorovoy, Eddie Allen, Emily Walters, Laura Apperson-Pink, Jeremy Pink, Meg Healey, and Michele Wit Dee—thanks for let me be friends with you, too, for cheering me on, and for making sure my husband didn't go crazy while I did this.

To my brother Dave's friends—Diego Prieto, Alex Nemiroski, Micah Greene, and Rachel Bertone—thank you for your support, encouragement, and advice throughout this project. You each made me feel confident.

To my mom's friends—Rena Winters, Jo Moore, Lynn Woerner, and Sheila Wycinowski—thank you for rooting for me through my mom, who always shares your words of support.

"And now, the end is near, and so we reach, the final curtain."

—FRANK SINATRA

It's impossible to fully thank my brother, Dave, as much as I'd like to, but I'll try. Thank you for being my mirror, even if it's dirty sometimes. I could not live a life of integrity without you by my side, and it would also be a lot less fun! You are the wind beneath my wings. My magic feather. Thank you for giving me Dad's list, for giving me the space I needed to finish it and write this book, and for helping me edit it. And thanks for helping me take myself less seriously.

To Jaime: Thank you for being patient with me as I've completed this project and found a new voice, one that is more confident and so inspired by yours. You have taught me more than most people I've ever known about what it means to be strong, and I am so grateful you are my sister. Thank you for being Dave's best friend.

To Sha: I'm so happy you're my brother's mother-in-law! Thank you for bringing levity to our family gatherings!

I'm blessed to have so many cousins, who are like siblings but without the rivalry. Thank you to Jimmy Freed; Emily, Lee, Anna, and Elijah Glass; Steph, Shane, Jack and Jo Reed; Jennifer, Pat, Tali, and Darlene Myers; Mike, Tara, and Scarlett Buck; Leif Carney and his mom, Geralyn; Ashley, Sloane, and Caden Carney and Ashley's partner, Alexis; Kristen Harrison Downey; Michele Dorsey Walfred; Mary Ann Dawson Warner; Jim Dorsey; and David James and Evangeline Williams Kelly. You have each helped with my project in some way and helped bring this book into the world. Where would I be without you?

I get to walk this life with not just one brother but four, thanks to my mom's remarriage. A big thank-you to Brian, Sydney, Andrew, and Savannah Wilson: Our travels with you were so much fun, and your enthusiasm for my project kept me going. Thank you for believing in me and for reading my writing. To Scott, Jessi, and Ben Wilson: Thank you for supporting me as I've done this. To Drew, Kate, Chase, and Finley Wilson: Thank you for surfing with me, by far one of the most challenging list items, and thanks for always offering encouragement. A big thank-you to Sarah Detweiler Farugia, Kate's twin sister—you are my artistic role model. And to Marcia and Charlie, thank you for filling me up with love and support whenever I see you.

A heartfelt thank-you to my in-laws, Verna, Bob, Jeff, Tanner, and Talia Seighman and Ivy Gilbert. Thank you for loving me like one of your own. You have supported this project in so many ways, and I am so grateful to have you in my life.

I don't know what I'd do without my amazing aunts and uncles. Thank you to Jim, Rob, and Joan Carney for cheering me on with this project and supporting me from afar. I hope you find my dad's presence heightened while reading this book. To Nancy Carney: I cherished my conversations with you as a child and still do. Thank you for being an important part of my life and always validating what my father meant to me. To Patricia and Barry Buck, thank you for your kind words—I can always count on an amazing card from Aunt Patty to lift me up. And to David Way and Sarah and James Freed: You are the triptych I turn to when I need words of wisdom, outside of Jim and Mom. Thank you for loving my father and reminding me who he was in your own memories of him. Thank you for always making me feel special.

I am grateful for my stepfather's humility and trust—it takes a big man to support a project and book about his wife's late ex-husband. I appreciate that you've endeavored to learn more about my dad and understand my connection with him. I appreciate that you've become my friend. Thank you for teaching me the value of discipline, self-belief, and consistency—traits that are stronger in me solely because of you.

I don't really know how to thank my mom in words; I'd have to thank her for so many things, mostly my very survival. Mom, I know all you've ever wanted was the best for me and watching me go on this risky, uncertain journey was a challenge for you. But you did it anyway, and you stood on the outskirts of my path every step of the way, waiting in case I needed help. Thank you for always believing in me, even if you don't understand where I'm going next—half the time, I don't either! I love you, I am grateful for you, and I know I am the luckiest person when it comes to moms. Thank you for sharing your love for Dad with me as I tried to get the parts about our family right.

To my muse: Thank you to my cat, Pinky. You have been my little sidekick during every part of this mission and my nurse when I was tired, sick, injured...or sometimes just sad. You're really good at sad. I love you.

And finally, Steven. There aren't enough words in the English language to express my love and gratitude for you. You are more than my best friend. You are my hero. I want to be more like you. Thank you for helping me be more like me and for believing this path was the right direction for us, even when you knew more than anyone how challenging it could be. You have helped me peel off the layers and emerge from this cocoon I've been hiding in for twenty years. When I step off the branch and fly, it will be because of your love and faith in me, and you will be flying with me.

* * *

To my father:

I hope I've made you proud. I know you don't give a hoot whether I finished this list or not—or even whether I started it. You left it where you did so I would remember who you were and who I am; I'd forgotten. Thank you for creating opportunities in my life, and not just this one: to grow, to discover, and to learn. To get better. You taught me the value of selfishness though I didn't understand it then. I do now. You taught me how to write and that writing matters. Like Mark Twain said, "I am seriously scribbling to excite the laughter of God's creatures," though I always felt this book was just for me. And for you. I hope you know how much I loved you in life. I know you know it in death.

Thank you for guiding me still. Thank you for pulling these strings. I'm so glad I finally trusted you.

* * *

And a big thanks to all of you for buying this book. I am investing half of my author's royalties into the Michael J. Carney Foundation (**"start a charitable fund"**), an organization that will donate to the pet causes of everyone who helped me with the list. What's your pet cause? By buying this book, you're now a list helper, too!

About the Author

A writer and magazine copy editor in New York, Laura Carney has been published by the *Washington Post*, the Associated Press, *The Hill*, *Runner's World*, *Good Housekeeping*, *The Fix*, *Upworthy*, Maria Shriver's *The Sunday Paper*, and other places. She has worked as a copy editor in national magazines—primarily women's—for twenty years, including *Vanity Fair*, *GQ*, *People*, and *Good Housekeeping*. This is her first book.